RECONSIDERING THE
SOULS OF BLACK FOLK

Reconsidering the Souls *of* Black Folk

by Stanley Crouch
and
Playthell Benjamin

RUNNING PRESS
PHILADELPHIA · LONDON

9   8   7   6   5   4   3   2   1
Digit on the right indicates the number of this printing

Library of Congress Cataloging-in-Publication Number 2002107733

ISBN 0-7624-1349-2

Cover photograph © Bettmann/Corbis
Cover design by Bill Jones
Interior design by Alicia Freile
Edited by Michael Washburn
Typography: Adobe Garamond

Correspondence between Martin Delany and Frederick Douglass
reproduced from *Uncle Tom's Cabin & American Culture: A Multi-Media
Archive*, at http://jefferson.village.virginia.edu/utc

This book may be ordered by mail from the publisher.
Please include $2.50 for postage and handling.
But try your bookstore first!

Running Press Book Publishers
125 South Twenty-second Street
Philadelphia, Pennsylvania 19103-4399

Visit us on the web!
www.runningpress.com

Table of Contents

PLAYTHELL BENJAMIN:

—⚬—

I: *The Souls of Black Folk:* Poetry, Prophecy, Pioneering Social Science

In his 1903 book *The Souls of Black Folk,* W.E.B. DuBois, then an obscure young black scholar with contempt for conventional wisdom on issues of race and class, produced a text combining poetic mysticism, scholarly rigor, and passionate advocacy, rendered in a powerful style reminiscent of Shakespeare and the King James Bible. The book set the standard for engaged intellectuals in twentieth-century America. Its influence extended beyond America's shores, as verified by the remembrances of South African novelist Peter Abrams, the Trinidadian polymath C.L.R. James, and the British classical composer Samuel Coleridge Taylor. Francophone intellectuals such as the Haitian Scholar Jean Price-Mars, the poet Leon Damas of Cayenne, and the poet/statesman Leopold Sedar Senghor—who along with Damas is a founder of the "Negritude" literary movement and became the first president of the West African nation of Senegal—also testified to having been moved by the book. Hence the fourteen essays that comprise *The Souls of Black Folk* must be seen as the most influential of the literary texts that forged the racial consciousness of what the Afro-British sociologist Paul Gilroy has called the "Black Atlantic" world.

Yet it was in the U.S. that *Souls* had its greatest impact. It allowed white Americans a glimpse into the inner life and hopes of their black countrymen, and black Americans found an advocate with the courage, eloquence, and intellect to voice their "spiritual strivings" without the cautious apologia of Booker T. Washington—the most famous and powerful black man in America—who got his comeuppance in the essay "Of Mr. Booker T. Washington and Others." The ideas in that essay, particularly the idea of the "Talented Tenth," are still debated as I write. And yet a century has passed! And Gilroy argues, "Its power is still felt in the special resonance which the term 'soul' continues to enjoy in modern black political discourse and culture axiology."

Although the DuBois Institute at Harvard may be the best-known academic department named for Dr. DuBois—due partly to its devotion to research and publishing and partly because of Professor Henry Louis Gates's grasp of the techniques of public relations, which led him to recruit high-profile faculty—it was not the first; nor can it claim ownership of the vast and invaluable *DuBois Papers.* These distinctions belong to the University of Massachusetts at Amherst, a campus nestled in the western part of the state nearer DuBois's hometown of Great Barrington in the Berkshires. The plan to launch the first full-fledged Department of Black Studies on an American campus began on a balmy autumn day in October 1969. The New England landscape was ablaze in orange, green, and gold foliage as a group of white and black scholars and activist intellectuals met at Mills House, on the campus of U/Mass, to draw up plans for this historic department.

Among the questions on the agenda was what the department would be called. That turned out to be the easiest part of our task, as the committee—which included William J. Wilson, Bernard Bell, Sydney Kaplan, Jules Chemetsky, Esther Terry, Mike Thelwell, Eugene Terry, Cherif Guelal, Ivanhoe Donaldson, and the present writer, several of whom have gone on to become leaders in their academic fields as well as in politics and diplomacy—quickly decided that the department should bear the name of William Edward Burghardt DuBois. The reasons for this choice were so compelling that no other name was even considered. Aside from the fact that he was born and raised about an hour's drive from the campus, Dr. DuBois was a lifelong activist in the struggle against white supremacy, and the pioneer scholar in the field that we call "Black Studies." Since *The Souls of Black Folk* is the most widely read of Dr. DuBois's many texts—a work that argued, and laid out the rationale, for the development of a black intellectual class able to lead the masses and contributing to high culture—a reconsideration of the context, text, and legacy of this American classic on the centennial of its publication is, for those who are interested in setting the record straight on the history of race relations in America, akin to doing the Lord's work.

II: THE HISTORICAL CONTEXT IN WHICH *SOULS* WAS BORN

The first Afro-American to take a Ph.D. from Harvard University, DuBois's "Suppression of the African Slave Trade," was the first modern historical treatment of an Afro-American subject. It was written as a doctoral dissertation and published as the first volume of the Harvard "New World Historical Studies" in 1896—the same year the U.S. Supreme Court ruled in the infamous *Plessy vs. Ferguson* decision that the equal protection clause amended to the Constitution during the Reconstruction period did not bar the legal separation of the races. To be sure, there had been earlier attempts at writing Afro-American history by autodidacts like George Washington Williams, Edward Wilmont Blyden, et al. These were admirable efforts but they lacked the scholarly tools that DuBois would later have at his command.

Although DuBois was also a product of 19th-century ideas, having received all of his formal higher education between 1885 and 1896, he was lucky to have studied at Harvard when Albert Bushnell Hart was working out the techniques of modern documentary history that favored a "scientific" method over the popular literary approach to historical writing. This approach was exemplified by "Patrician School" history writers, like James Ford Rhodes, whose eight-volume *History of the United States* became a model of how not to write history in the eyes of the new "scientific" professional historians.

DuBois was also lucky enough to be at the University of Berlin working on a doctorate in economics when Max Weber was laying down the theoretical foundations for the discipline of sociology. Yet DuBois's luck did not hold out, as he was denied the prestigious Berlin Ph.D. after completing all academic requirements—including dissertation—only because the all-white, male, Christian trustees of the John F. Slater Fund for the Education of Negroes refused to support him for the additional semester needed to meet the residency requirement the university asked of all doctoral students. Endowed with a million dollars—a vast sum in 1882—by the Norwich, Connecticut, businessman after whom it was named, the Slater fund was established to help the former slaves and their descendents get a foothold in American society. Some believed John Slater was driven by guilt because he had made his fortune in the cotton business, thus profiting from slavery. Yet, whatever guilt or responsibility Slater might have felt about past injustices to his black countrymen didn't necessarily extend to the trustees, who decided to withhold the pittance of $350 that DuBois needed to meet his residency requirement at Berlin. It was a decision that baffled and angered DuBois, then a young idealist who still believed in the power of scientific argument to persuade reasonable men and women of the folly of racism.

Internal documents have since revealed that the trustees of the Slater Fund, which was headed by former U.S. President Rutherford B. Hayes, thought it a dangerous example to other blacks to have one of their number achieve such commanding intellectual heights. Ironically, when the rejection came, it was written by Daniel Coit Gilman, a fund Trustee and President of John Hopkins, one of America's elite universities, who had originally backed DuBois's application for a grant to study in

Europe, observing at the time that "Negroes as a race need the directive intelligence of characterful leaders." But DuBois wrote Gilman on March 28, 1894, informing him: "I must with great regret announce that the faculty of the University, in spite of the kind efforts of Professors Wagner and Schmoller and others, have found it impracticable to make so great an exception in my case as to admit me to the doctor's degree with but 3 German semesters . . . yet, my Professors thought it possible, and indeed, as they assure me, the petition would have been granted, had not at the last moment the Professor of Chemistry threatened that if so great an exception was made in my case, he must bring forth ten similar cases from his laboratory. This naturally settled the question." Gilman made no effort to provide the meager funds.

To help his case by showing that he had not overstated his own progress, DuBois had Dr. Adolph Wagner, his political economy professor, write to the Slater Fund trustees. In a letter of March 28, 1894, Dr. Wagner wrote, "Mr. E.B. DuBois has laid before me this work upon 'The Large and Small System of Farming in the (Southern) United states of America'; this careful as well as comprehensive work, resting on a wide basis of study, has impressed me very favorably. . . . The work proves that the author possesses talent and diligence, and that he has made good use of the time spent in study in Germany. It is much to be desired that it should be made possible for him to remain still a short time here and gain the outward completion of his studies through promotion to the Doctor degree. For this the rules of German Universities require that he shall have attended an university here somewhat longer than he has. The before-mentioned thesis would, without doubt, be received as a Doctor's thesis." Herr Doctor Professor Schmoller also wrote: "Mr. William Edward Burghardt DuBois . . . wished in course of the winter semester, 93-94 to pass the doctor's examination; for this purpose he prepared a scientific thesis . . . this work would have been sufficient; but the faculty refused to admit him to the oral examination, because according to their rules only those persons can be admitted to examination who have studied 6 semesters in German universities."

As these letters make plain, DuBois was right on track to take the coveted Doctor of Economics degree from the University of Berlin in record time, but, as he would discover over and over again in his dealings with white Americans, Gilman made a different response from what any reasonable person would have hoped from a man supposedly committed to the advancement of knowledge. In a letter of April 13, 1894 Gilman advised DuBois: "It seems to me you would do well to return to Harvard and offer yourself as a candidate there . . . I think the Harvard degree would be, in all respects, as advantageous to you as that of Berlin." Then Gilman expressed the main concern—anxieties would probably be more accurate—of the august white men who controlled the Fund. "The Slater Trustees inquired particularly in respect to your course of study, and some of them expressed, with great earnestness, the hope that, on returning to this country, you will devote your talent and your learning to the good of the colored race."

Historian David Levering Lewis, who won the Pulitzer Prize two years in a row—an unprecedented event—for volumes I and II of his biographies of DuBois, tells us: "When Gilman's turndown came toward the end of April, its tone suggested that the 'recent meeting' of Slater Fund trustees had been another of those pivotal gatherings at which leading white men, north and south, threshed out racial misgivings on African American backs. . . . The distinguished Johns Hopkins president seemed to be imparting the view—favored by grey colonels and portly divines—that DuBois's case, by its superlative success abroad, merely proved the original unwisdom of Hayes's experiment in the higher education for Negroes. How useful to the education of a people one generation removed from slavery could a University of Berlin minted teacher be, after all? . . . Black Ph.D.'s from Germany were not a priority in Booker T. Washington's America."

Thus was the attitude of the white cultural establishment when this intellectually gifted young black man who would recall in the autumn of his life that during his tenure as "a student in Germany," he had "built great castles in Spain and lived therein." And had "dreamed and wandered and sang; then after two long years . . . dropped suddenly back into "nigger-hating America!" By his own estimation DuBois was "educated within an inch of my life," when he returned to begin his professional career as a scholar in his native land. After a brief and unfulfilling stint teaching at a small Afro-American college in the Midwest, he would soon find himself in the position to conduct the first systematic study of black life in a major American city. The result was a classic, *The Philadelphia Negro,* a pioneering work of sociology whose insights into urban life remain useful today.

This unique scholarly opportunity came about by virtue of the efforts of a Miss Susan P. Wharton, a member of the wealthy and powerful Quaker family for whom the University of Pennsylvania's Wharton School of Business is named. She approached the university's provost, Dr. Charles C. Harrison, about "the cooperation of the University in a plan for a better understanding of the colored people, especially of their position in this city." And she was specific in what she wanted such a study to accomplish: "We are interested in a plan to obtain a body of reliable information as to the obstacles to be encountered by the colored people to be self supporting." As a member of the executive committee of the Philadelphia College Settlement Association since its inception in 1890, Ms. Wharton was deeply engaged in the kind of "social uplift" work that was au courant for conscientious women of substance and means, and she had long been involved with philanthropic work on behalf of Afro-American causes.

However, as Dr. DuBois would later write in *Dusk of Dawn,* the second of three autobiographies authored in the course of a long and eventful life (he lived to be 95 years old), the real purpose of the study as far as Provost Harrison (a former businessman who had made a fortune in the sugar trade) and sociology professor Samuel McCune Lindsay were concerned, was to demonstrate "under the imprimatur of the University" that black voters in the impoverished and crime-ridden Seventh Ward in south Philadelphia were largely responsible for the long tenure of the corrupt Republican administration that governed the city. Their suspicions were based on the tendency of Afro-Americans to vote Republican in the dawning years of the twentieth century, a legacy of the Civil War and the era of "Radical Reconstruction," which had come to an end only thirteen years earlier. Afro-Americans retained vivid memories of the time when old Abe Lincoln and the Republicans had overthrown the southern slavocracy, freed the slaves, and passed civil rights laws that extended the voting franchise to black folks in the first real attempt at democracy in America.

DuBois felt that the university's attitude toward him, his people, and his task was devoid of good will or enthusiasm. He later recalled, "There must have been some opposition, for the invitation was not particularly cordial," in spite of the provost's claim that he sought a "quiet, earnest effort to improve the Negro's condition." As evidence of a lack of enthusiasm for his project, DuBois noted that the university provided him no office space on campus, allowed no contact with students—except when he was once called on "to pilot a pack of idiots through the Negro slums"—failed to list him in the university catalogue, and paid him the miserly sum of $600 for a year's research and writing, in spite of the fact that he had earned two doctorates—one from the leading American University and the other from what many thought the leading university in the world. "The fact was that the city of Philadelphia at that time had a theory," he writes, "and that theory was that this great, rich, and famous municipality was going to the dogs because of the crime and venality of its Negro citizens. . . . Of this theory back of the plan, I neither knew nor cared. I saw only here a chance to study an historic group of black folk and to show exactly what their place was in the community."

The Philadelphia Negro, which was recognized at the outset as a pathbreaking study, relied on first-hand observation of its subjects and thousands of interviews conducted by Dr. DuBois himself, a practice virtually unheard of at the time. Convinced that the policies keeping his people under the heel of white society were based on prejudices with no basis in fact, DuBois was sure that the solution to the crisis lay in the scientific refutation of the assumptions that white society held. In his blind faith in the ability of science to solve all problems, and his belief in progress by education, DuBois was a quintessential child of the Enlightenment who embodied the zeitgeist of the modern age—which had barely arrived in American academia. He had been personally tutored by the top scholars of his time—Historian Albert Hart, and the philosophers George Santayana, Josiah Royce, and William James at Harvard; sociologist Max Weber, political scientist Heinrich von Treitschke, historian Leopold von Ranke, political economists Adolph Wagner and Gustav von Schmoller, et al. at Berlin—and thus felt himself the best-qualified man for the job at hand.

Morevoer, DuBois believed this project was of such *gravitas* that he was more than willing to put up with the humiliating treatment accorded him by people whose academic training was inferior to his own. Nevertheless, DuBois well knew that if it were not for his advanced academic training, he would not have been in position to serve his people in such an important task; that's why one of the themes in *The Souls of Black Folk* is the urgent need for Afro-American youths to receive a liberal education.

III: THE STRUGGLE FOR A FIRST-RATE LIBERAL EDUCATION

Having been born and raised as a black in a racist white society, DuBois was no stranger to adversity and struggle. Growing up in humble circumstances—what some would call genteel poverty—he had to endure daily the quiet assumption of superiority of his white fellow citizens of Great Barrington, while witnessing the privileges that accrued to members of the "superior race." Although he was not menaced by the threat of deadly violence nor subjected to *de jure* segregation as were his "colored" brethren in the South, he was, still, acutely aware that the positions awaiting a white high school graduate in business and in government were off limits to him.

In *The Autobiography of W.E.B. DuBois,* which came out posthumously, he explains why he chose to go into the Deep South, over the protests of family and friends, to attend Fisk University, a private black college in Nashville, Tennessee, that offered a rigorous New England-type academic curriculum taught by enlightened white New Englanders. "My family and colored friends rather resented the idea. Their Northern free Negro prejudice naturally revolted at the idea of sending me to the former land of slavery. . . . But I wanted to go to Fisk, not simply because it was at least a beginning of my dream of college, but also, I suspect, because I was beginning to feel lonely in New England . . . now that I had finished the public school, the close cordial intermingling with my white fellows would grow more restricted. . . . The educated young white folk of Great Barrington became clerks in stores, bookkeepers and teachers, and a few went into professions. . . . Great Barrington was not able to conceive of me in such local positions. It was not so much that they were opposed to it, but it did not occur to them as a possibility."

But life being the riddle that it is, this challenge proved a blessing in disguise, for had he been fully integrated into the economic and social life of the community, he might well have gone on to the same mundane life as his white schoolmates. Yet it was not simply a wish to escape the subtle racism—which almost got him sentenced to reform school for "stealing" a bunch of grapes from the yard of a wealthy white resident—and lack of opportunity for a young black man whose academic performance in high school had shown promise, that sparked his desire to go to a black college. The teenage DuBois had developed an insatiable curiosity about the cultural heritage of his people. Much of this curiosity was aroused when he attended a concert performed by singers from a black college. "I heard in these days for the first time the Negro folk songs. A Hampton quartet had sung them in the Congregational church. I was thrilled and moved to tears and seemed to recognize something inherently and deeply my own."

The quest to find the cultural essence of southern Afro-American sensibility is what drove him. Thus he tells us, "I was glad to go to Fisk." This choice turned out to be one of the key decisions of DuBois's life because he discovered the southern Afro-American community, where the great majority of African Americans lived, and met a fabulous group of young black folk who excited, delighted, and enlightened him about the trials, tribulations, and moral paradoxes that marked black life in the world's greatest democracy. "I was thrilled to be for the first time among so many people of my own color or rather of such various and extraordinary colors, which I had only glimpsed before, but who it seemed were bound to me by new and exciting and eternal ties. Never before had I seen young men so self-assured," he rhapsodizes, "and colored men at that; and above all for the first time I saw beautiful girls."

DuBois admits that among the white classmates he had grown up with in Massachusetts, "there were a few pretty girls," but notes that "they were not entrancing." He says of the white girls of Great Barrington: "I did not notice them." But it was quite a different story with the black, brown, and beige beauties who promenaded about Fisk's campus—the same species of rainbow beauties who would later inspire Duke Ellington's marvelous "Black, Brown and Beige Suite." He recalled over seventy years later the wonder he felt on his arrival at Fisk when "the never to be forgotten marvel of that first supper came with me opposite two of the most beautiful beings God ever revealed to the eyes of 17. I promptly lost my appetite, but I was deliriously happy! Of one of these girls I have often said, no human being could possibly have been as beautiful as she seemed to my young eyes in that far off September night of 1885." Then DuBois offers this comment: "She was the great-aunt of Lena Horne and fair as Lena is, Lena Calhoun was far more beautiful."

But the campus beauties were hardly the only thing that intrigued him about his new classmates; he was also fascinated by the lives they had led in a region of the nation that had abolished chattel slavery just twenty years before—and then only after the bloodiest carnage ever seen in the world, the first modern war in history. He explains that though Fisk was located in Tennessee, "which was never a typical slave state," the student body came from "Georgia, Alabama, Mississippi, Louisiana," states that formed the heart of the Confederacy. And unlike himself, a naive teenager who had been nowhere and done nothing, his classmates were "mature men and women, who could paint from their own experience a wide and vivid picture of the postwar south and its black millions. There were men and women who had faced mobs and seen lynchings; who knew every phase of insult and repression; and too there were sons, daughters and clients of every class of white southern-er. A relative of a future president of the nation had his dark son driven to school each day." This practice of powerful white southern males enrolling their illegitimate progeny in segregated black colleges contin-ued right up until the 1960s, when students attending such schools in South Carolina recall a famous southern Senator coming on campus to meet with his daughters in private rooms set aside for that purpose. But even this, as depraved as it is, does not compare to the behavior of Thomas Jefferson, who held seven of his own children as slaves.

Thanks to his New England high school education, DuBois was prepared for the Fisk curriculum, which was designed by New England educators; hence he entered the sophomore class at 17 years old. The fact that DuBois was a Northerner, and many of his classmates were much older than the normal college-age student due to their myriad struggles to acquire an education in a vanquished South where the white majority was opposed to educating their former slaves, made DuBois quite an anomaly: "I was a campus curiosity even for the teachers." And after coming down with an attack of typhoid fever that threatened to finish him off a month after he arrived, an event monitored by his fellow students, he emerged a campus hero. "When I at last crept out, thin and pale," he recalls, "I was the school favorite."

DuBois's reaction to coming in second to a girl on an annual test reveals that he was very much a man of his times on the gender question—although that would change in the years to come, when he would emerge as one of the most progressive male thinkers regarding women's rights since Fredrick Douglass. "I stood second with only Mary Bennett, the white German teacher teacher's daughter, outranking me. I could not quite forgive her as a girl and a white one at that." However, even then, at the very beginning of his college career, he saw how the experience of racist oppression stunted the growth of African Americans and placed them at a competitive disadvantage long after slavery was over and raised a question that is still being debated around the issue of standardized tests today. "I also knew that the test was unfair to most of the students who had never had decent elementary school training in the colored public schools of the south." An observation that is equally true in the North today.

Among the most interesting of DuBois's memories from his days at Fisk are the portraits he paints of some of his classmates—like big C.O. Hunter, who cuffed him one day and warned him about his smart mouth; or "rail-like" Procter, his main competition in debates, who would go on to become a progressive preacher in Atlanta where twenty years later they would work together around community problems, and Procter had "swollen physically to huge proportions"; or "tall and dark" L.B. Moore with the "scintillating mind," or G.D. Field "a little black man, serious, who knew and hated the white South. He always carried a pistol." These portraits, along with his observations about Afro-American culture and community only twenty years after the demise of slavery, show a people who are far from demoralized, a people who show an optimism that attests to the tenacity of the human spirit and leaves one wondering at its source.

One antidote to the depressing conditions under which African Americans had to build a life was song and dance, especially the blues. Albert Murray analyzes this phenomenon in his text *Stomping the Blues,* in which he argues—convincingly, I might add—that there is a misunderstanding about the meaning and function of the blues among most folks, including pundits, who have not lived in a blues milieu. This misunderstanding results in the belief that blues music is sad. However, Murray shows that while the "blues as such" are indeed sad and painful, the blues as music are optimistic, joyous, and an invitation to dance. In fact, he argues, "The blues are just the opposite of sack cloth and ashes"; its function on the psycho/spiritual level is to chase the blues away. This is the meaning of the folk term "Stomping the Blues"—which is widely used by blues musicians, and whence Murray took his book's title. For many people, "blues idiom dancing" is a cathartic experience, which offers the same kind of relief from pain, or boredom that others find in alcohol, cocaine, or religious ecstasy. In other words, blues music and dance is a counterstatement to the blues as such. However, the use of music as catharsis did not begin with the advent of the blues in Afro-American culture. Indeed, Frederick Douglass recalled that, "Slaves sing more to make themselves happy, than to express their happiness."

According to DuBois, black folks danced everywhere he saw them, north or south—though we know that the South is the cradle of African American culture, and that blues and Jazz were born there. Although W.C. Handy would not publish his first Blues composition until 1907, it is significant that he titled it "The Memphis Blues." While he became popularly known as "The Father of the Blues," after publishing "The Saint Louis Blues," a ballad to the trials, tribulations, joy, and hedonism of the emerging black city, he tells us in his autobiography that he did not invent the blues but simply notated the music he heard the working people of the Mississippi delta singing on the wharves. And while they may have danced to various kinds of music in Great Barrington, they were almost certainly dancing to some kind of blues in Nashville. And it was almost certainly played on pianos, banjos, mandolins, and other string or percussion instruments.

DuBois tells us of an ordeal brought on by the recriminations of a fundamentalist protestant student, "Pop" Miller (called "Pop" because he was so much older than the rest of the students and probably awkward on the dance floor to boot). "He soon had me and others accused before the church for dancing. I was astonished. I had danced all my life as naturally as I sang and ran. In Great Barrington there was little chance to dance on the part of anyone but in the small group of colored folk there was always some dancing along with playing games at homes. When I came south and was among my own young folk who not only danced but danced beautifully and with effortless joy, I joined and learned eagerly. I never attended public dance halls, but at the homes of colored friends in the city, we nearly always danced and a more innocent pastime I could not imagine. But Miller was outraged." Here we see the dichotomy between the sacred and the profane in Afro-American music as defined by the norms of a culture in which protestant fundamentalism was a major force; hence although musically blues and gospel are different sides of the same coin—or maybe because of it—there was a rigid separation between "God's music" and the seductive blues songs of "the Devil." But as we will see, this would not be the last time DuBois would find himself in conflict with the religionists.

However, it should be pointed out that complex and artful social dancing is an integral part of every neo-African culture, whether on the continent or the Diaspora, except where Islam reigns, with its grim and austere view of life, and its hyper-puritanical attitude toward any expression of female sexuality. The polyrhythmic character of all African-derived music—especially the marvelous Son Muntono and Rumba music of Cuba, which the whole world now dances to in a slightly mutated form called "Salsa," the Brazilian Samba, the Trinidadian Calypso, etc.—these infectious rhythms inspire dance movement because they are the product of a dance-oriented culture, a reflection, as Murray has observed, "of the African tendency to refine all movement into dance like elegance." This may account for the incredible grace of Michael Jordan and Muhammad Ali, as well as the Soultrane Dancers, Bill Bojangles, Janet Jackson, and James Brown. So in spite of the protests of uptight black pseudo-intellectuals like Shelby Steele, who complains about being ridiculed by his fellow black students in his integrated high school because he couldn't dance, Euro-Americans are close to the truth when they say "All Negroes have rhythm." The problem is that the racists, or the merely ignorant, think it is genetic when in fact it is in the culture. But it is nonetheless true, and woe be unto the African American who is awkward on the dance floor!

Hence there was no better way for the young DuBois to immerse himself in the soul of black America than to take to the dance floor with grace; black men as diverse and Martin Luther King, Malcolm X, Ralph Ellison, and Colin Powell could all dance gracefully. Even in Germany a few years hence, he would recall a party where "my dance card was always filled" with pretty and eager young frauleins. Hence it is puzzling that so many commentators on DuBois's life would try to paint him as an uptight prude. Even a scholar as learned and perceptive as Wilson Jeremiah Moses would greet with a barely concealed sarcasm DuBois's declaration that "I was not a prig, I was a lusty man with all normal appetites. I loved wine, women and song." Perhaps Professor Moses finds it impossible to conceive of DuBois as a swinger because, from all appearances, he is such a nerdy academic stiff.

However, along with DuBois's fancy dancing, he embraced other core cultural values treasured by African Americans that Professor Gwatley, a black cultural anthropologist, identified in his path breaking study "Drylongso." Chief among these are a reverence for education and the call to serve and elevate the black community. DuBois would go to teach black peasants in the backwoods of Tennessee, living and working closely with people who had emerged right out of chattel slavery, and still graduate from Fisk with top honors in three years. Lewis argues that DuBois became unambiguously "a Negro" at Fisk. Although he is responding to DuBois's earlier reference to himself as mixed blood or Mulatto—something he would do again after he left Fisk, and which is in any case an accurate description of many Afro-Americans—I think Lewis is grossly overstating the case. After all, DuBois chose to go to Fisk in the first place because he wanted to be among other black youths.

This is a curious argument, because Lewis supervised the research on Kenneth Janken's Ph.D. thesis on the life of Rayford Logan, the Harvard-trained historian who grew up in the mulatto middle class of Washington D.C. in the early twentieth century. Janken is candid about the color consciousness of Logan, his family and class. In Logan one finds the classic "tragic mulatto" syndrome. Rejected by the white society which he admires and whose privileged place in the American pigmentocracy he feels is his birthright, he has to live among blacks, in spite of the fact that he considers himself "forty-sixty fourths or ten sixteenths white, eighty-sixty-fourths or two sixteenths Indian, and sixteen-sixty-fourths or four sixteenths Negro." Of course, DuBois on occasion gave a rough analysis of his various racial/ethnic mixtures, but after giving us a precise account of his bloodlines, Logan remarks: "Legal legerdemain classifies me as a Negro, but I have occasionally had difficulty in convincing some persons that I am." I have read no such expression of racial ambiguity in the voluminous writings of DuBois, who could not possibly pass for white, nor does Lewis offer us an example.

Yet Lewis raises this question on several occasions, telling us at one point that he is surprised that other students of DuBois have not made more of DuBois's "racial ambivalence." I would argue that Rayford Logan is the personification of racial ambivalence—a "race man" and Pan-Africanist who was in the forefront of the black struggle as an activist/intellectual and historian, but also drew the color line against his darker brethren at various points in his life and hated the term "black" Americans. In his definitive study of Logan's life and thought, *Rayford W. Logan and the Dilemma of the African American Intellectual,* Janken tells us that Logan believed the term "black" homogenized the Negro race, "masking color differences . . . so insistent was he that he would terminate a conversation, break an engagement, even resign from an organization he had spent decades building if, in his presence the term 'black' was used to describe anything other than formal evening wear." The obvious difference between this attitude and that of DuBois is that in 1903, in the depths of the "Nadir," he titled his eloquent and learned text *The Souls of Black Folk!*

IV: THE STRUGGLE TO STUDY ABROAD

Having to scrape his way through Fisk on a tight budget, DuBois literally sang for his supper during the summer after finishing his senior year at Fisk University. Without financial resources, he had to go on the road as a troubadour, traveling through the Midwest with a vocal quartet in an effort to raise money to enter Harvard—after a failed stint as a busboy at a Minnesota resort, and before he managed to secure a Price Greenleaf fellowship. A great part of DuBois's problem with securing the financial resources to pursue an advanced education at Harvard, in spite of his excellent academic record and sterling promise, was the fact that he was applying for aid from organizations which were engaged in heated debates about whether it was good for the country's future to encourage Afro-Americans to seek a liberal academic education at all. And the leaders of these funding institutions were encouraged in this view by the fact that the general status of Afro-Americans in civil society was fast deteriorating.

In 1891, when DuBois first applied to the Slater Fund for financial aid to support his aspirations to study in Europe, he was given the runaround by its president, Rutherford B. Hayes, a man who had defended fugitive slaves while practicing law in Cincinnati, Ohio, in the 1850's, but is distinguished in history as the man who presided over the deconstruction of Radical Reconstruction after the Civil War. In a too-close-to-call election in 1876, the Republicans had entered into a compromise with the Democratic candidate Samuel J.Tilden. The basic issue in this Faustian bargain was that in return for the Democratic Party's support for a Hayes presidency, the Republicans would remove the last units of federal troops from the South. This of course spelled the end of Radical Reconstruction, because the absence of federal forces allowed the leading men of the white South to revert to "home rule" and use terrorist tactics to bar Afro-Americans from taking part in politics and eliminate them as economic competitors. Ironically, Hayes had declared in a letter to a friend before he was certain that he had won the Presidency, "I don't care for myself . . . but I do care for the poor colored men of the south . . . the colored man's fate would be worse than when he was in slavery." Yet his actions in the Oval Office made this dire prediction a self-fulfilling prophecy. Although he denounced the "oligarchy of race" which insured white supremacy in the South, such were the racist horrors visited upon African Americans in this post-Reconstruction period—from 1876 to 1915—that the younger Harvard-trained Howard University historian Rayford Logan, called it the "Nadir," i.e. lowest point, of their history in his study of the era, *The Betrayal of the Negro.*

But beyond the obvious political and economic motives for the genocidal white terror, there was another motive, which, in its psychological nature, may have been even more compelling. In the twisted minds of white southern males who had sexually exploited black women for two and a half centuries, the removal of black males as political and economic rivals also eliminated them as competitors for the sexual favors of white women. The hysterical fear of black men and white women interacting drove white men to slaughter thousands of black men in public rituals that Harvard sociologist Orlando Patterson argues were actually blood sacrifices and cannibalism in his insightful book, *Rituals of Blood*. It was in this atmosphere of escalating lynchings and political betrayal that the twenty-two year-old DuBois wrote to Rutherford B. Hayes requesting a stipend that would allow him to study in Europe in order to prepare himself for the work that lay ahead. Even at this early stage of his development, it was clear that DuBois was preparing himself for service to his oppressed race, telling Hayes in a letter of April 3, 1892, that he saw earning a Berlin Doctorate as not "a question of merely personal interest," but as proof of the abilities of the entire black race.

Although he was a moving force in the Mohonk conferences—a series of national meetings comprised of mostly white Anglo Saxon protestant males representing powerful church, business, educational, and political elites who gathered yearly between 1882 and 1891 to discuss how they could best assist in the future development of Indians and Africans in a rapidly industrializing American society—Hayes was ambivalent about encouraging advanced education among African-Americans. He had made this clear in an 1890 speech at Johns Hopkins University, where he committed the Slater Fund to pay for a European education for any black student who demonstrated "a talent for art or literature," but quickly added that he did not expect to find any such black person because "their chief and almost only gift has been that of oratory"—a point on which the impetuous young DuBois would soon challenge him.

The first seven Mohonk conferences had debated the Indian question, and the last two (in 1890-91) considered the status of African Americans in a post-slavery United States. And while there was division as to the role education should play in assimilating the former slaves into society as free men—some, like those who had taught ex-slaves in the South right after slavery, thought Afro-Americans should get the same basic education as whites—the dominant opinion favored approaches that would preserve white supremacy, even among well-meaning "friends" of black folks. Typical of this view was the opinion put forth at the 1890 conference by Samuel Armstrong, who had founded Hampton Normal and Agricultural Institute in Virginia, in 1868, only three years after the end of the Civil War. Working with former slaves, Armstrong believed that his first task was to help the freed men to overcome their anathema towards hard work, an attitude bred by the super-exploitative conditions of slavery, by providing them with "an idea of the dignity of labor." At the opening session, he told the conferees that "Labor is a great moral and educational force," and that "the Negroes are a laboring people." Thus Armstrong, like the majority of the conferees, thought it best to educate the "hearts and hands" of black Americans.

As early as 1875, two years before the collapse of Reconstruction, one conferee, Thomas Muldrop, a former general in the Confederate army and a leading figure in the transformation of the South from an agrarian to an industrial economy, expressed the view held by most business leaders of the "New South" as to the purpose of black education. He told a gathering of fellow industrialists in Virginia that when blacks were educated to play "their part in the social economy, the caste allotment of social duties might prove advantageous to southern society as a whole, on the principle of a division of labor applied to races." Since few Euro-Americans of any class were in favor of full equality for African-Americans, the education proposals offered up by the delegates, as well as the actions of the nation's highest political officials, reflected white society's desire to maintain a racial caste system in America, with whites on top and blacks and Native Americans on the bottom.

It was this widespread view that Afro-Americans were destined to form an inferior class in America, the drawers of waters and hewers of wood for their white countrymen—many of whom had owned them as slaves—that led Rutherford Hayes to renege on the Slater Fund's commitment to fund a European education for a qualified Afro-American student. Twice he had ignored DuBois, but DuBois's third letter of May 25, 1891, proved too much for the nearly seventy-year-old ex-President to ignore. In that letter, DuBois all but called Hayes's offer a hoax and virtually accused him of fraud—which was like *deja vu,* because after the back room horse-trading that put Hayes in the White House in 1877, he was widely referred to as "Rutherfraud" by political foes. "The outcome of the matter is as I expected it would be. The announcement that any agency of the American people was willing to give a Negro a thoroughly liberal education and that it had been looking in vain for men to educate was to say the least rather startling. When the newspaper clipping was handed me in a company of friends, my first my first impulse was to make in some public way a categorical statement denying that such an offer had ever been made known to colored students. I saw this would be injudicious and fruitless, and I therefore determined on the plan of applying myself. I did so and have been refused along with a number of cases besides mine."

Showing the independence of spirit and rugged self-reliance that would come to mark his life and career, the budding scholar made it clear that he would pursue his dreams of an advanced education with or without the aid of the Slater Fund. "As to my case I personally care little." He continued in the May 25 letter: "I am perfectly capable of fighting alone for an education if the trustees do not see fit to help me. On the other hand the injury you have—unwittingly I trust—done the race I represent, and am not ashamed of, is almost irreparable. You went before a number of keenly observant men who looked upon you as an authority in the matter, and told them in substance that the Negroes of the United States either couldn't or wouldn't embrace a more liberal opportunity for advancement. That statement went all over the country. When now finally you receive three or four applications for the fulfillment of that offer, the offer is suddenly withdrawn, while the impression still remains. If the offer was an experiment, you ought to have had at least one case before withdrawing it; if you have given aid before (and I mean here toward liberal education—not toward training plowmen) then your statement at Johns Hopkins was partial." Then, casting caution to the wind, the poor and powerless black student told the rich and powerful head of the Slater Fund, a man who could make or break his career with a stroke of his pen, "From the above facts I think you owe an apology to the Negro people." DuBois then issued this challenge to the former chief executive of the U.S. "We are ready to furnish competent men for every European scholarship furnished us off paper. But we can't educate ourselves on nothing."

As if he had decided not to leave any secret feeling unexpressed, DuBois observed with more than a hint of sarcasm: "I find men willing to help me thro' cheap theological schools, I find men willing to help me use my hands before I got my brains in working order, I have an abundance of good wishes on hand, but I have never found a man willing to help me get a Harvard Ph.D." The attitudes voiced by DuBois in this letter—a strong sense of the right, the courage to speak truth to power, and the peculiarly American belief, rooted in the Old Testament, that justice will triumph in the end—are indicative of traits which would drive his work, plunging him into a thousand struggles through a life that lasted almost a hundred years and straddled two eventful centuries when America went from a semi-slave, largely agrarian nation, to the most modern industrialized society in the world.

While Hayes's reply to DuBois's scathing letter is missing from both of their papers, we know that he encouraged DuBois to apply again the next year. And, heeding the old axiom that "the squeaky wheel gets the oil," he did. In a letter of April 3, 1892, DuBois wrote Hayes, "Sir: I venture with some diffidence to address you again on the subject of a European scholarship from the Slater Fund. You expressed the hope, if I remember rightly, that this year the board might see its way more clearly than last year. I wish, therefore, to bring the question to your mind again, and to state my present situation." DuBois goes on to describe a career as a graduate student at Harvard, which included the presentation of an original research paper before the annual meeting of the American Historical Association—the professional organization of American historians, then in its infancy—which was soon to be published, and the announcement that the first draft of his Ph.D. thesis was done. And based on the entries in Hayes's diary—which was published in 1926—DuBois's letters were having the desired effect on him. For instance, on April 12, 1892, Hayes wrote, "DuBois is to be recommended," and on the 15th he wrote, "At breakfast received a card from DuBois, the colored scholar from Harvard. Pres. Gilman and I arranged to give him seven hundred and fifty dollars—one half-cash donation, one-half on his note—to support him one year in Germany at some university. Very glad to find that he is sensible, sufficiently religious, able, and a fair speaker." (See *The Correspondence of W.E.B. DuBois 1877-1894*, edited by Herbert Aptheker.)

In spite of the fact that the Slater Fund trustees decided to back DuBois in his quest for a European education, meeting with him in New York a year later in April of 1892 to seal the deal, the basic belief of Euro-Americans that Afro-Americans should be confined to a subservient caste remained intact. It was, alas, enshrined in a plethora of laws and government policies. The final defeat of the Blair Bill of 1890, which had twice passed the Senate before dying there, clearly exposed the hostility of most Euro-American leaders of politics and opinion in regard to the quest for serious education by black Americans. This legislation, placed on the floor of Congress by the eloquent and thoughtful Republican Senator from New Hampshire, H.W. Blair, the reigning Senate expert on educational matters, along with Boston Congressman Henry Cabot Lodge, sought to redress the gap in educational opportunities between the rich and poor, black and white.

Among the provisions and requirements of the Blair Education Bill were: eight years of federal subsidies to states with high illiteracy rates in comparison to the national norm; that the funds for such subsidies be generated through high import tariffs; that the governors of states getting educational subsidies be required to certify to the Secretary of the Interior that the funding of public education took place on a basis of racial equity. Clearly the Blair Bill would have been a boon to a region struggling to industrialize, where a fifth of the white children were illiterate and the black illiteracy rate was several times higher. And even though there was nothing in this legislation that tried to interfere with the racial apartheid that had already become a fact of life in the public schools of the former Confederacy, it still met wide opposition in the South, as southern politicians and business leaders—who opposed the high tariffs as well as equal education for blacks—proved willing to sacrifice the education of white youths rather than meet the conditions for federal funding required by the Blair Bill.

This was the socio/political reality that existed in the American South—and reflected to varying degrees in every section of the country due to the national consensus on white supremacy—at the end of the nineteenth century. It was this atmosphere of repression (accompanied by the ritualistic murder of a black male every two and a half days, a reign of terror that would go on unabated for another decade and beyond) that bred the conditions under which the "Great Accommodator," Booker T. Washington, would rise to prominence as a racial conciliator, and "Black Willie" DuBois—as he was known in his home town—would grow into a uniquely American radical activist/intellectual who strode through twentieth century history like a colossus, a pioneering Pan-Africanist defending Africans and Afro-Americans against the current of white racism using word and deed.

V: THE ENGAGED SCHOLAR TAKES THE FIELD

DuBois returned from Europe a cosmopolite with a grasp of European culture and political economies. In "Dusk of Dawn," he tells us: "Europe modified profoundly my outlook on life . . . even though I was there but a few short years with my contacts limited and my friends few.

But something of the beauty of life permeated my soul . . . I came to know Beethoven's symphonies and Wagner's Ring. I looked long at the colors of Rembrandt and Titian. I saw in arch and stone and steeple the history and striving of men and also their taste and expression. Form, color, and words took new combinations and meanings." Having traveled widely on the continent, attending concerts and theatrical performances, hanging out at art museums, systematically interrogating the natives about their lives, and attending political rallies, he was far more knowledgeable about European history and culture—the music, literature, art, and politics—than the vast majority of formally educated Euro-Americans who considered themselves the heirs of the European tradition, a belief that, incidentally, retarded the development of a uniquely American art—a point we will return to later. By virtue of having enjoyed the society of some of the brightest young minds in Europe—including the affections of several beautiful and highly cultivated young ladies—DuBois had assimilated the style and manner of the German university student. This was most readily apparent in the gloves, cane and Vandyke beard—which he actually copied from the German Kaiser, Wilhelm II—that he now sported.

He had also embraced the reverence for science and the secularism that pervaded the German academic environment. Hence he was destined to find disappointment teaching at Wilberforce—a small religious college in Ohio founded and supported by the African Methodist Episcopal church, and named for the great British abolitionist William Wilberforce—the first institution of higher learning established to serve black students in America. DuBois entered this small private academy with high hopes for his educational mission on behalf of Afro-Americans, but found an impossible situation. Aside from having to deal with a backward dictatorial administration directed by the Bishop of the African Methodist Episcopal church—who ruled the college with an iron fist—he found that he was not only expected to teach the courses in Latin and Greek—which he had signed up for—but German, English, and history to boot!

But beyond the arbitrary exercise of power by the Bishops and the pedagogical burdens he had to bear, DuBois was shocked and offended by the realization that the princes and powers of the church who dictated policy were more devoted to cronyism than academic excellence. For example, the school's president, Bishop Benjamin Arnett, tried to appoint his semi-literate son to a professorship in literature while firing the distinguished black classical scholar William Scarborough, who had published two well-regarded texts in the field: *First Lessons in Greek* and a translation of Aristophanes's *Birds*. The first of these books came out while DuBois was entering high school, and the second while he was in his second year at Fisk. Interestingly enough, DuBois tells us in *The Autobiography* that he thought he was to serve as Scarborough's assistant until he arrived on campus and found that he was meant to replace the senior professor. In an uncharacteristic display of modesty, he humbly admits that "They were not my specialty and despite years spent in their study I really knew too little to teach them." He soon became aware that he could also meet Scarboro's fate, especially after he led the faculty's successful fight against the appointment of the Bishop's incompetent son: "Under my impetuous and uncurbed assault, the bishop had to bend, but I knew well that my days at Wilberforce were numbered."

"As I realized that none of my dreams would be fulfilled at Wilberforce," he writes in *The Autobiography,* "I knew all the sadness of a spent dream." Yet in spite of the fact that he decided to seek his fortune elsewhere he does not view Wilberforce and the AME church in a wholly negative light. With characteristic even-handedness, he recalls affectionately "The College was poor and neglected and yet the church which owned it and whose prized child it was, formed a marvelous human institution. Its leaders were of every sort: selfless saints like Payne, J.R. Lee, and William Mitchell; ruthless politicians like Arnett; scoundrels like W.B. Derrick; and charging bulls like Henry M. Turner. With high ideals and brute force, they rolled and jammed this mass of men and women forward and together until they became a force in the whole nation." Then DuBois asks this remarkable question: "Suppose I had had the cunning to help harness and guide this superhuman energy, what could I not have helped to turn it into?" And he answers: "Not into a university, certainly, such as I had dreamed, but perhaps into something greater."

Aside from questions of politics and pedagogy, DuBois was also affronted by the discovery that all professors, including himself, were expected to offer up prayers on demand from faculty or students, a situation that was especially offensive to his agnostic temperament. And he protested this unwritten rule—along with the young West Point-trained army officer Charles Young, whom the government had stationed at Wilberforce, probably to avoid giving him a command—by boycotting the revival meetings on campus. Hence the young and ambitious Dr. DuBois's eagerness to get away and engage in the kind of serious scholarly research which his next job as the principal investigator for a social study of black Philadelphians would offer. No doubt his religious skepticism, irreverence even, was nurtured by his matriculation at the University of Berlin.

He recalls in "Dusk of Dawn" that "In Germany I turned still further from religious dogma and began to grasp the idea of a world of human beings whose actions, like those of the physical world, were subject to law. The triumphs of the scientific world thrilled me: the X-ray and radium came during my teaching term, the airplane and the wireless." Indeed, Germany—which harbored theologians like J.G. Eichhorn, author of "Introduction to the Old Testament" and a leading exponent of what was then known as "Higher Criticism"—was an incubator of the growing secularization of intellectual life in leading European and American universities. Historian Arthur M. Schlesinger, Sr., speaks to this development in his essay "A Critical Period in American Religion, 1875-1900." "Like the doctrine of natural selection," he writes, "textural criticism of the Bible also called into question the infallibility of the scriptures. Imported from German university centers, the higher criticism, as it was known, subjected Holy Writ to rigorous historical analysis." However, this tendency toward secularization in the life and thought flowering in the elite universities was nonexistent at Wilberforce. The campus was often engulfed in waves of fundamentalist hysteria, where students and faculty broke out in fits of song and prayer.

Yet the reverence for science and secularism that DuBois had found in the German university had only recently made its way into the elite American universities, even the Ivy League. In fact, when DuBois entered Harvard in 1890, both secular thought and scientific knowledge had barely triumphed over the classical curriculum, with its obsession with Greek and Latin languages and literature, metaphysics and theology. Both Harvard and Yale had confined the teaching of science to special institutes: The Lawrence School at Harvard and the Sheffield School at Yale.

In his widely researched and thoughtful book *The Opening of the American Mind*—a worthy riposte to Allan Bloom's silly tome *The Closing of the American Mind*—historian Lawrence Levine tells us: "Thus for much of the nineteenth century students in science were not considered full-fledged members of the college communities. Yale, for example, did not permit Sheffield students to sit with regular academic students in chapel." To provide us a deeper understanding of the contempt with which scientific instruction was regarded at Yale, Levine quotes from an 1880 letter written by a student at the Sheffield Scientific School. "Shef had long since had well-established and successful elective group courses manned by distinguished scholars, but Shef did not count, at least not in the affirmative." And, Levine points out, at Harvard students of the Lawrence school were considered "shirks and stragglers." If this was the attitude toward the study of science at Yale and Harvard—the pinnacle of American academia—we can be certain that other colleges followed their example.

This denial in granting science a legitimate place in the academic life of the university reflected a deep-seated antipathy toward the innovations in curriculum that were essential to the kind of modern education demanded by a rapidly industrializing society. Hence one could say that the animus toward science represented a fear of modernity itself. As Levine tells us: "Subjects outside the golden circle of the classical curriculum—the biological sciences, modern languages, modern literature, modern history (and modern of course meant everything since the Greeks and Romans)—were either not available or available without credit and only at the student's initiative." Had DuBois entered Harvard before the reign of Charles William Eliot, who became President in 1869, he would have found an environment where the indifference toward teaching history was such that a lone professor, Henry W. Torrey, taught virtually all of the offerings in the field: ancient, medieval and modern history, plus American constitutional history. However, Eliot was committed to modernizing the Harvard curriculum, and this effort resulted in the hiring of historians Edward Channing, who would later distinguish himself with his six-volume *History of the United States,* and DuBois's great mentor Albert Bushnell Hart. Looking back on the course of his academic development, DuBois seems to have always been in the right place at the right time. And it paid off magnificently by placing him at the forefront of American social science at the turn of the twentieth century.

VI: *The Philadelphia Negro*

What excited DuBois most about the study of African-American communities, north or south, was that these communities were virtual living laboratories that could provide a unique opportunity for social scientists to observe the process by which an illiterate, poor, peasant community made the jump from a rural folk society to a modern urban people capable of surviving and advancing in an industrial milieu. And, most of all, he wanted to dispel the racist myths about African Americans that served as rationales for discriminatory public policies. "The Negro problem was in my mind a matter of systematic investigation and intelligent understanding. The world was thinking wrong about race," writes DuBois in "Dusk of Dawn," because "it did not know. The ultimate evil was stupidity. The cure for it was knowledge based on scientific investigation."

For several reasons, Philadelphia was an ideal site for sociological investigation of a developing black urbanity. Given the right socio/economic ingredients, plus the skill and labor of this self-assured young black scholar, it should surprise no one that the result was *The Philadelphia Negro,* a study in urban sociology whose findings continue to be valuable a century later. Reflecting on his work four decades later, DuBois observed: "I made a study of the Philadelphia Negro so thorough that it has withstood the criticism of forty years." Indeed, it has stood as a paragon of scholarship in the field for over a century. So influential was *The Philadelphia Negro* that no serious study of the history or sociology of black Philadelphians can escape referencing it, whether we are speaking of the massive Philadelphia Social History Project, directed by professor Ted Hershberg at the University of Pennsylvania, or monographs like Roger Lane's *Roots of Violence in Black Philadelphia,* and professor Elijah Anderson's studies of urban life and politics today.

The black Philadelphia community DuBois entered in 1896 had long been the leading Afro-American urban community in the nation. One consequence of the fact that the city had the largest and most developed black urban population is that it was the birthplace and headquarters of the powerful African Methodist Episcopal church, which was established there in 1792, by Richard Allen and Absolom Jones, just five years after the drafting of the Constitution of the United States in the city. Here the black community was mature enough to have a class structure, and some black men, like James M. Forten, had accumulated vast wealth long before DuBois made his way to Philadelphia with his notepads and interview schedules. Forten was one of thousands of Afro-Americans who fought in the Revolutionary War, as historian Benjamin Quarles documents in his book *The Negro in the American Revolution*, and, like Forten, many of them served in the navy.

They fought to defend the American coast from the British invaders in northern and southern waters, sailing on ships like the *Diligence, Aurora, Tempest, Liberty, Dragon, Patriot*, et al. Forten, however, served as a powder boy on the Royal Louis, commanded by Stephen Decatur. When captured at fourteen and offered a haven in Britain by English officers who mistook him for a slave, he refused, telling them that he was a free man willingly fighting for his country. I suspect that there were not many more acts of valor and patriotism to compare to Forten's heroic stand, especially as he belonged to a race of people who were enslaved in colonial America.

But this heroic stand would later pay off handsomely. As Forten hung around on the deck of the British warship where he was held as a prisoner of war, he studied the riggings, and he would later design a sail that made him a very rich man. While Forten made his fortune as a businessman/sail maker early in the 19th century, the younger Robert Purvis, another prominent black Philadelphian, came by his fortune as a result of an endowment from his white slave-owning father.

Yet both had participated in the fight for full citizenship for Philadelphia's black community and were leading figures in the anti-slavery movement. In fact, as historian Benjamin Quarles points out in his pioneering book *Black Abolitionists*, Forten was an original financial backer of William Lloyd Garrison's American Anti-Slavery Society in 1812, putting up the money to start *The Liberator*, which was the literary organ of the organization, and for a while the most influential literary voice of the abolitionist movement. While Forten was of an earlier generation, Purvis, born in 1810, was the reigning elder statesman of the Afro-American community by the time DuBois arrived. In fact, just two years after DuBois did his study, Purvis passed away. But his activist's days were behind him, the high point of which was before the Civil War.

Ironically, the unique role Purvis had played in recruiting white allies to the black struggle was made possible by the fact that he looked white and was independently wealthy, both of which were due to his white slaveholding father in Charleston, South Carolina. Like other famous "white Negroes"—such as Walter White and Adam Clayton Powell, who became key figures in the struggles for civil rights and political empowerment in the twentieth century—Purvis chose to be black. The behavior of these men shows the arbitrary nature of race in America, and the absurdity of "white" America's obsession with the idea. These men defied the racial classifications of the time.

With his money and Amherst education, Purvis could have moved to Europe, Canada, South America, Asia, or the Caribbean, and lived the life of a wealthy white man, since in any of these locales one is white if one looks white. He could also have stayed in the U.S. and "passed" across the color line, as millions of mixed-blood Americans who were classified as "Negroes" chose to do, although as long as he stayed in his native land he would risk exposure as a "nigger" and thence a return into America's untouchable caste. Thus it is a measure of the character of this remarkable man—like Powell and White—that he chose to cast his lot with Afro-Americans and risk all in the fight for their liberation. Indeed, Roger Lane shows us that Purvis not only used his position to recruit powerful white allies to the black freedom struggle, but also personally faced down racist white mobs and armed himself to defend his life and property. Among Purvis' closest comrades in the struggle was William Still; a self-made man ten years his junior.

Whereas Purvis had arrived in Philadelphia well-fixed, Still had started at the bottom and gained wealth through hard work and business acumen, making a financial killing when he was awarded a government contract to supply black troops who were training for service in the Union army at Camp William Penn on the outskirts of Philadelphia. Both of these men—along with many comrades, black and white—were involved in smuggling runaway slaves on the "Underground Railroad," an illegal activity that became a federal offense after the passage of the Fugitive Slave Act in 1850. Still, however, continued to make money after the war was over by going into the coal, ice, and real estate businesses. And much of his money went to philanthropic causes like the black branch of the YMCA that he had incorporated, or a home for indigent black senior citizens, or his support of the aging and sickly Sojourner Truth, a former slave in New York who was perhaps the most famous of the female abolitionists, and many other causes locally and nationally that sought to liberate and uplift his fellow Afro-Americans who were everywhere suffering horrors in a society bent on racial tyranny.

Yet there would come a time when Purvis and Still would fall from favor with more militant blacks of a younger generation, such as saloon keeper and political functionary Gil Ball, and a dynamic fellow with the unlikely name of Octavos V. Catto, a name that suggests a *dramatis personae*. A spiffy dresser who ran up a hefty bill with his haberdasher, Catto was a pragmatist who, unlike Purvis and Still, was willing to dive into the mud of municipal politics and fight for a share of the pie. Riding on a wave of growing black militancy inspired by a series of events brought on by the struggles over the attempts of bounty hunters to recapture runaway slaves and return them to southern slaveholders, Catto began to rise to prominence as a leader in the Afro-American community. The attempts to capture ex-slaves led to many dramatic clashes between blacks and the white authorities. This is not to imply that no whites took part in these struggles, for there were many white abolitionists willing to risk all in the defense of liberty, which meant fighting to end the massive crime against humanity personified by the system of chattel slavery—which was by now located solely in the southern states. Yet it was the black community who felt most strongly on the anti-slavery issue, since many of them had friends and relatives who were still under the yoke of southern planters.

When the Civil War came in 1860, events heated up as black folk grew bolder and refused to accept many things that had once been taken for granted by both sides in relations with white Philadelphians. One flashpoint for conflict was the fact that black citizens were barred from riding the streetcars on the same basis as other citizens of the city. For most of their history in the city, Afro-Americans were barred from riding on the streetcars at all, fostering scenes of inhuman callousness like pregnant women trying to get to the hospital and being thrown off the trolley by conductors with the support of white passengers. But persistent agitation had led to a modification of policy, which allowed blacks to ride on the outside platforms of the trolleys. The attempts to enforce these policies led to increased resistance from black citizens, resulting in clashes with white mobs that grew more intense as the Union went to war and Afro-American citizens of Philadelphia grew enraged at the sight of black soldiers—men about to go off to combat against white southern traitors in defense of the Union—being denied seats on the trolley. While this kind of racist exclusion and public humiliation is generally thought of as unique to the "Jim Crow" societies that arose in the post-reconstruction South, as Leon Litwak has shown in "North of Slavery," these racist practices were common fare in the north well before the Civil War. Indeed, practices against blacks were something that all whites could agree on regardless of political affiliation or region.

Thus it was in this period of national crisis that ambitious men like O.V. Catto rose to positions of power and influence. The government began to call up black troops in 1863, and by October 1864, Afro-Americans had set up the National Equal Rights League, with black Philadelphians hosting its largest chapter. The league soon became the leader in the fight against segregated streetcars, and its popularity grew, providing a platform for activist members like Catto. However, it was in the struggle to win the right to vote that Catto rose to prominence. A man of many talents, he was a founder of one of the first baseball teams in Philadelphia, the Pythians, on which he played shortstop, the most athletically demanding position on the field, and also served as captain. Roger Lane tells us that the Pythians were not only the best team in the city athletically, but counted the most powerful black men in Philadelphia among them.

It was a position from which to gain friends and influence among the cream of black Philadelphia. Thus he soon became influential in the Union League, then the principal of the Institute of Colored Youth, and a major in the Pennsylvania militia. He was indeed a man for all seasons, and in a non-racist society, there's no telling how far he could rise. But his experience in Philadelphia was a metaphor for the experience of black people in America. As the Pythians showed their superior skills on the baseball diamond, the white teams conspired to kick them out of the otherwise lily-white baseball league. And after the successful agitation over the right to vote, an event celebrated by a mass rally in which the Afro-American elders in the struggle, like Purvis and Still, were joined by the great Frederick Douglass in addressing the audience, Catto was murdered outside his home by a drunken white guy during a riot on election day in 1871, only a year after the ratification of the 15th Amendment extended the vote to Afro-Americans. Catto's funeral was one of the most impressive spectacles the city had seen—attended by members of all races—but the fact remained that one of Philadelphia's most able leaders, black or white, was cut down in the prime of life by a racist drunk.

Catto's life reflected the dilemma of the tragic hero of DuBois's short story "The Coming of John," the sole fictive piece in *The Souls of Black Folk,* whose intelligence and ambition brought him not the rewards that America showers on white boys who possess these virtues, but death at the hands of a racist mob. It was a thrice-told tale that symbolized the predicament of all black males in America throughout most of the nation's history.

Black Philadelphians would continue to exercise their right to vote, although that right was compromised by the nullification of the third "Force Bill" in 1894—a measure that provided federal protection for black folks seeking to cast their ballot. While the bill was designed to protect the voting rights of the newly emancipated Freedmen in the former Confederate states of the South, its protections extended to Afro-Americans in every part of the nation. When Pennsylvania, which had a clause in its state constitution barring blacks from voting, ratified the 15th Amendment, it was one of the last states to do so. However, led by men like Gil Ball, a small-time racketeer and bar owner who was the opposite of the cultured Purvis and the frugal Still, the Republican Party would manipulate the black vote by hook or crook. Working through shady characters like Ball and his band of ruffians, the Republican Party in Philadelphia regularly committed what amounted to election fraud by having groups of blacks vote for their candidate repeatedly by using bogus names.

Of course the Irish ward leaders in the Democratic Party did likewise with the working-class white ethnic vote, many of whom were immigrants who were rewarded with jobs and other patronage. As a result of the various backroom deals that were cut with different supporters of the political parties, vice and other forms of criminal economic activity was protected by the party in power—especially in the mostly black Seventh Ward. And since the dominant party in post-Civil War Philadelphia was the Republicans, it is no wonder that the members of Philadelphia's white elite—some of whom still kept stately mansions and townhouses in proximity to the poverty-stricken blacks—was convinced that the escalating crime rate in the city was a result of collusion between black deviants and corrupt white Republicans. This is the conviction that they fully expected Dr. DuBois's study to prove when completed.

This was the Philadelphia that DuBois entered in 1896 to begin his investigation. It was rife with racism and corruption, plus the Afro-American community which was to be the subject of his study was divided—by color, class, neighborhood, regional origins, north vs. south, West Indian vs. American-born, political affiliations, by virtue of their attachment to various political clubs, and law abiding citizens vs. the sporting crowd who lived flamboyantly from illegal enterprises. At the start of this unique project, DuBois sets forth his objectives clearly. "This study seeks to present the results of an inquiry . . . into the condition of the forty thousand or more people of Negro blood now living in the city of Philadelphia. This inquiry extended over a period of fifteen months and sought to ascertain something of the geographical distribution of this race, their occupations and daily life, their homes, their organizations, and above all, their relation to their million white fellow-citizens. The final design of this work is to lay before the public such a body of information as may be a safe guide for all efforts toward the solution of the many Negro problems of a great American city."

What DuBois intended was to paint a detailed portrait of an urban Afro-American community which had already existed for over a century when he arrived, yet was still in the process of formation. While his methodology would use the techniques of science—careful observation, sifting and evaluating evidence, statistical analysis, comparative analysis with what was known of similar social formations, etc.—his sensibility is that of a literary artist, and his prose style avoids the polysyllabic Latinate jargon that has since come to mark sociological discourse in favor of the poetic phrase. Indeed, the challenge posed by most scholarly texts is to find a quotable phrase, but in DuBois's works we meet with an embarrassment of riches. The reader of this text will soon wonder if there has ever been an observer of social phenomena who identifies himself as a "scientist," rather than an "artist," and who has written so well. The study—carried out between August 1896, and December 1897—began with a house-to-house investigation conducted by DuBois himself—a feat that is unthinkable among contemporary social scientist with their generous foundation grants and legions of researchers. Explaining his decision to study the Seventh Ward, he tells

us: "This long narrow ward . . . is an historic center of the Negro population, and contains today a fifth of all the Negroes in this city. It was
therefore thought best to make an intensive study of conditions in this
district, and afterward to supplement and correct this information by
general observation and inquiry in other parts of the city."

To accomplish this task, DuBois designed six "schedules," or ques-
tionnaires, that inquired into a wide range of conditions that defined the
lifestyles of black Philadelphians. These included family schedules that
surveyed all aspects of familial relations; an individual schedule to try
and ascertain the quality of life for single persons with a special version
for live-in domestic workers; a home schedule which sought to define
the nature of the various lodgings of the populace—home ownership,
rental, number of rooms, etc.; a street schedule that sought to define life
in the streets and back alleys of the Seventh Ward, anticipating Elliot
Liebow's sociological classic, *Talley's Corner,* several decades later; and a
schedule designed to define the institutional and organizational life of the
community. Added to this firsthand observation, "such official statistics
and historical matter as seemed reliable were used, and experienced persons, both white and colored, were freely consulted."

After such careful firsthand fact-finding backed by documentary evidence, the young social scientist insisted upon testing the validity of his
analysis by checking it against similar social facts in other districts of the
city. He tells us: "This study of the central district of Negro settlement
furnishes a key to the situation in the city; in the other wards therefore
a general survey was taken to note any striking differences of condition,
to ascertain the general distribution of these people, and to collect information and statistics. . . . This general inquiry, while it lacked precise
methods and measurements in most cases, served nevertheless to correct
the errors and illustrate the meaning of the statistical material in the
house-to-house canvass." It is clear from the rigor of his research that
DuBois was as devoted to scientific method as a route to arriving at the
truth, as he was to the uplifting of his race.

In spite of a sincere commitment to rigor and impartiality, DuBois warns the reader that "The best available methods of sociological research are at present so liable to inaccuracies that the careful student discloses the results of individual research with diffidence; he knows that they are liable to error from the seemingly ineradicable faults of the statistical method, to even greater error from the methods of general observation, and, above all, he must ever tremble lest some personal bias, some moral conviction or some unconscious trend of thought due to previous training, has to a degree distorted the picture in his view." However, while prizing the objectivity necessary to a valid interpretation of the social facts he was uncovering, DuBois does not find it necessary to pretend to a stance of neutrality on issues of moral *gravitas*. Instead, he reminds us that "Convictions on all great matters of human interest one must have to a greater or lesser degree, and they will enter to some extent into the most cold-blooded scientific research as a disturbing factor." Finally he leaves no doubt of his conviction that there is a virtue in having the data collected and analyzed by the same researcher. "Again," he tells us, "whatever personal equation is to be allowed for in the whole study is one of unvarying quantity, since the work was done by one investigator, and the varying judgments of a score of census takers was thus avoided."

The result of this effort to use science in the service of truth—in the hope that it would advance the cause of black progress by helping to find solutions to their most pressing social problems. He also hoped to shape a favorable opinion among the powerful literate classes of whites who would then become sympathetic to the interest of this powerless and much–wronged class of their fellow Americans—was a study from which sociologists of urban life are still taking their cues. Indeed, Elijah Anderson, the Charles and William L. Day Professor of Social Science and Professor of Sociology at the University of Pennsylvania, the reigning authority on the contemporary Philadelphia Negro, tells us a century after DuBois's study was published that "many of his observations can be made—in fact are made—by investigators today." Divided into eighteen chapters, with maps, statistical tables, and graphs supporting the elegantly written text, *The Philadelphia Negro* presents the kind of full and accurate picture of black life in the big city—from marital practices, family formations, and church life, to secular organizations and institutions, business ventures, work and living arrangements, race relations, recreations and amusements, to vice and violent crime—that can serve as a yardstick to measure how far Afro-Americans have progressed in the last century. And when DuBois's conclusions about the problems and prospects of black Philadelphians—and by inference black urbanites in general—are compared with the contemporary prognosis of Professor Anderson, the result is troubling.

For instance, of the charges of rampant criminal activity in the Afro-American community that prompted the study in the first place, DuBois tells us: "In the city of Philadelphia the increasing number of bold and daring crimes committed by Negroes in the last ten years has focused the attention of the city on this subject. There is a widespread feeling that something is wrong with a race that is responsible for so much crime, and that strong remedies are called for. One has but to visit the corridors of the public buildings, when the courts are in session, to realize the part played in law-breaking by the Negro population." But DuBois thought that this pattern of criminal behavior was related to a mix of circumstances that conspired to seduce, or force, some black Philadelphians to resort to a life of crime. And he also noticed that criminals were differentiated: "The loafers who line the curb in these places are not fools, but sharp, wiley men who often outwit both the police department and the department of charities. Their nucleus consists of a class of professional criminals, who do not work, figure in the rogue's galleries of a half-dozen cities, and migrate here and there. About these are a set of gamblers and sharpers who seldom are caught in serious crime, but who themselves live from its proceeds and aid and abet. The headquarters of all these are usually the political clubs and poolrooms;

they stand ready to trap the unwary and tempt the weak. Their organization, tacit or recognized, is very effective and no one can long watch their actions without seeing that they keep in close touch with the authorities in some way."

In contrast to the master players DuBois describes above, there were "a large crowd of satellites and feeders: young idlers attracted by excitement, shiftless and lazy neer-do-wells, who have sunk from better things, and a rough crowd of pleasure seekers and libertines. These are the fellows who figure in the police courts for larceny and fighting, and drift thus into graver crime or shrewder dissoluteness." However, the criminal behavior described by DuBois—involving prostitutes, purse-snatchers, and muggers—was occurring in the context of a rapidly expanding economy. America was completing her industrial revolution. Hence there was reason to believe that with training and expanded opportunity, Afro-Americans would find their place in the evolving socio/economic order, and with time the racism of the moment would subside.

This proved to be true for the best-educated Afro-Americans, which reflects a process of class differentiation ably described by DuBois—who was as much an economist as a sociologist and historian—in *The Philadelphia Negro.* "There is always a strong tendency on the part of the community to consider the Negroes as composing one practically homogeneous mass . . . the people of Negro descent in this land have had a common history, suffer to-day common disabilities, and contribute to one general set of social problems. And yet if the foregoing statistics have emphasized any one fact it is that wide variation of antecedents, wealth, intelligence and general efficiency have already been differentiated within this group. These differences are not, to be sure, so great or so patent as those among the whites of today, and yet they equal the difference among the masses of the people in certain sections of the land of one hundred years ago; and there is no surer way of misunderstanding the Negro or being misunderstood by him than by ignoring manifest differences of condition and power in the 40,000 black people of Philadelphia." And I can report, without fear of contradiction, that this would also be the response of the black Ivy League intellectuals who rail about DuBois's "elitism" as if it were sin, should they be mistaken for a faculty member at a state university.

Thus, it was his experience of the achievements of this able and striving class, in Philadelphia and the emerging black colleges, that confirmed for DuBois their role in uplifting the untutored masses—a matter we shall soon return to—and validated his call for Afro-Americans to seek a liberal academic education. But the current situation of the black lower classes, who continue to dwell in the inner cities, is fast deteriorating; the industrial revolution has come and gone and the great American cities have undergone a transformation from manufacturing centers to post-industrial wastelands often devoid of legitimate prospects; a place where hope struggles to stay alive and even the popular music of the youths is rife with nihilism.

Indeed, surveying the sociological landscape a century later, Prof. Elijah Anderson sums up the chances of the proletariat and lumpenproletariat among the Philadelphia Negroes today. "Presently," he wrote in 1995, "the very social programs that once aided so many and gave them hope for the future have been slashed. The Philadelphia public schools that serve so many of the black poor and working classes have been allowed to deteriorate. With widespread joblessness, families cannot form, and social breakdown prevails in many inner-city black neighborhoods, leading to a class of street-oriented 'desperate poor' who have little hope for the future and whose moral sense is sometimes lost to mere survival." An underground economy of drugs and vice and other crime steps in to employ many of the young men wandering the streets. "Moreover, rampant street crime and violence attends [the undreground] economy, becoming ever more prevalent and at times purely random. . . . As neighborhood resources decline, as residents become even poorer, the social breakdown spreads."

Clearly, this is a different phenomenon from that described by DuBois, who paints a portrait of the urban hustler as an enterprising part of a dispossessed group whose socio/economic fate is predetermined by membership in a despised and oppressed class. These are men and women who have embraced the old street players haiku: "A man can't fool/ with the golden rule/ in a crowd that don't play fair." The universality of the outlaw view of life held by this class, as well as the illegal enterprises in which they are forced to engage in the Darwinian struggle for bread and treasure, is reflected in the tales of Jewish life in the ghettoes of Eastern Europe told by writers such as Isaac Babel and Isaac Beshevitz Singer. As well as Irving Howe, the New York cultural critic of Eastern European Jewish descent, who paints a compelling portrait of this class among the Jewish immigrants who populated the teeming ghettoes of the Lower East side of Manhattan at the turn of the century—the same era treated in *The Philadelphia Negro*—in his masterful social history *World of Our Fathers*. We encounter such characters once again in Bertolt Brecht's "Three Penny Opera," a musical drama about life in the decadent underbelly of Weimar Germany, as well as the work of many twentieth century Afro-American novelists covering a wide range of abilities—from a great writer like Chester Himes, to lesser lights such as Iceberg Slim and Donald Goines.

However, there is a recent novel by a young black Philadelphian who came of age in the bleak socio/economic milieu of post-industrial Philadelphia described by Professor Anderson. *True to the Game, An Urban Fable*, written by Terry Woods, is a realistic story unadorned by literary pretensions and unencumbered by academic theories about the underclass. In fact the author, a solid member of the hip/hop generation, tries her best to "keep it real" and as a result manages to place a human face on the social debris so aptly described in the sociological treatises of Elijah Anderson. The decision to include these characters in his study of Philadelphia is further testimony to the depth and insight that characterizes DuBois's analysis of the various elements that make up black city life.

VII: *THE PHILADELPHIA NEGRO:* A FINAL WORD

In a last chapter titled "A Final Word," a wide-ranging philosophical musing written with a power and eloquence that foreshadowed *Souls* six years hence, DuBois ends his 1897 study with the observation that "Two sorts of answers are usually returned to the bewildered American who asks seriously: What is the Negro problem? The one is straight forward and clear: it is simply this, or simply that, and one simple remedy long enough will in time cause it to disappear. The other answer is apt to be hopelessly involved and complex—to indicate no panacea, and to end in a somewhat hopeless 'there it is; what can we do?' Nevertheless the Negro problems are not more hopelessly complex than many others have been. Their elements despite their bewildering complication can be kept clearly in view: they are after all the same difficulties over which the world has grown grey: the question as to how far human intelligence can be trusted and trained; as to whether it is possible for the mass of men to attain righteousness on earth; and then to this is added the question of questions: after all who are men?"

This question is a prelude to a discussion of the racial caste system that formed in the crucible of chattel slavery, and that was retrenching itself in post-bellum America through a series of legislative acts, Supreme Court decisions, public policies that privileged Euro-Americans, an endless barrage of racist propaganda in the press, academia, and popular entertainment, capped off by a wave of white terror exemplified by the public torture and crucifixion of African-American males by Euro-American mobs.

To this "question of questions," DuBois replies with panache. "Is every featherless biped to be counted a man and brother? Are all races and types to be joint heirs of the new earth that men have striven to raise in thirty centuries and more? Shall we not swamp civilization in barbarism and drown genius in indulgence if we seek a mythical humanity which shall shadow all men? The answer of the early centuries to this puzzle was clear: those of any nation who can be called men and endowed with rights are few: they are the privileged classes—the well-born and the rest who are accidents of low birth called up by the king. The rest, the mass of the nation, the pobel, the mob, are fit to follow, to obey, to dig and delve, but not to think or rule or play the gentleman."

DuBois then calls the attention of white Americans to their professed creed, "all men are created equal," ridicules their pretensions to superiority by reminding them how bad things had been in their old world homelands, and signifies on their hypocrisy in race matters. "We who are born to another philosophy hardly realize how deep-seated and plausible this view of human capabilities and powers once was; how utterly incomprehensible this republic would have been to Charlemagne or Charles V or Charles I. We rather hasten to forget that once the courtiers of English Kings looked upon the ancestors of most Americans with far greater contempt than these Americans look upon Negroes—and, perhaps, indeed, had more cause. We forget that once French peasants were the 'Niggers' of France, and that German princelings once discussed with doubt the brains and humanity of the Bauer. . . . Much of this—or at least some of it—has passed and the world has glided by blood and iron into a wider humanity, a wider respect for simple manhood unadorned by ancestors or privilege. . . . Not that we have discovered, as some hoped and some feared, that all men were created free and equal, but rather the differences in men are not so vast as we had assumed."

Yet, in spite of this flash of optimism, DuBois returns to the realities of a racist society: "in America a census which gives a slight indication of the utter disappearance of the American Negro from the earth is greeted with ill-conceived delight."

VIII: SOME ANTECEDENTS OF *SOULS*

In the introduction to the 1899 edition of *The Philadelphia Negro*, James McCune Lindsay, Professor of Social Science at the University of

Pennsylvania, who had recommended DuBois to do the study, touched on some of the intellectual and ethical assets that would come to mark DuBois's *oeuvre*. "Many readers of this report will look most eagerly for what is said on the subject of race-prejudice and the so-called 'color line,'" said Lindsay. "I feel sure that no one can read Chapter XVI without being impressed with the impartiality and self-control of the writer. Dr. DuBois has treated the facts he obtained with the delicacy of an artist." This assessment of DuBois's work could also have been said of "The Suppression of the African Slave Trade," and the seeds from which these virtues blossomed can be found in his Harvard baccalaureate address, "Jefferson Davis as a Representative of Civilization." It is in "Suppression" that we first see his skills as a researcher, his even-handedness in weighing the evidence, and his poetic approach to language that reached a summit in *The Souls of Black Folk*. We also witness his insightfulness and ability to relate a specific set of facts to a panoply of ideas and situations from different times and places, in order to make a larger point.

In "Suppression," DuBois adds rigorous research into British Parliamentary debates, colonial records, debates and proceedings of the U.S. Constitutional Convention, bills of lading from U.S. and British ships, newspapers, personal papers, etc., to penetrating philosophical observations about the cynicism of white Americans who were willing to betray their grand moral principles in a Faustian bargain for black gold. He wrote: "There is always a certain glamour about the idea of a nation rising up to crush an evil simply because it is wrong. Unfortunately, this can seldom be realized in real life; for the very existence of the evil usually argues a moral weakness in the very place where extraordinary moral strength is called for. This was the case in the early history of the colonies; and experiences proved that an appeal to moral rectitude was unheard in Carolina when rice had become a great crop, and in Massachusetts when the rum traffic was paying a profit of 100%."

This analysis of the triumph of commerce and the acquisition of wealth over morality and religion is also interesting because it gives an answer to those who argue that DuBois was uncritical of the evils of capitalism until he grew fond of Marxist theory. Yet this was written at a time when he had dismissed Marxist philosophy. Having first encountered Marx as a figure ridiculed by his German economics professors, DuBois had rejected Marx before he had ever met him in print. "I was overwhelmed with rebuttals of Marxism before I understood the original doctrine." He tells us. But having read the public professions in defense of personal liberty mouthed by the slaveholding "Founding Fathers" of the nation, however, he hardly needed Marx to lead him to the conclusion that the love of money had led the likes of George Washington and Thomas Jefferson to corrupt their own creed.

In more than one instance, DuBois spoke directly to this question in the text. His comments show a grasp of how few white Americans have ever believed in the universal humanism voiced in the Declaration of Independence—a fact that many contemporary Euro-American intellectuals, and a few Afro-Americans, downplay or deny. Speaking of the handful of intellectuals who were the philosophical architects of the American Revolution, he argues: "The clique of political philosophers to which Jefferson belonged never imagined the continued existence of the country with slavery. It is well known that the first draft of the Declaration contained a severe arraignment of Great Britain as the real promoter of slavery and the slave trade in America." However, DuBois points out that this section was excised from the Declaration, as was any negative reference to African slavery, at the insistence of the slave-holding plantation colonies. And he would note that this hypocrisy, this acquiescence in a crime against humanity, would eventually drive the nation to the most destructive war in the history of the world up until that time.

Furthermore, unlike his white counterparts in the historical profession, DuBois also explored the role of Toussaint L'Overture, leader of the Haitian revolution, in the decision of several states to bar the importation of African slaves. In his explanation of the genesis of the 1794 act that gave Congress the power to regulate the slave trade, he tells us that in spite of petitions from Quakers and other abolitionists for Congressional action to restrain the trade, "Congress was, however, determined to avoid as long as possible so unpleasant a matter, and, save an angry attempt to censure a Quaker petitioner, nothing was heard of the slave trade until the third Congress." It was the triumph of the Haitian revolution that got their attention and shocked Congress into finally taking steps to end the African slave trade.

"Meantime," writes DuBois, "news came from the seas southeast of Georgia which influenced Congress more powerfully than humanitarian arguments had done. The wild revolt of despised slaves, the rise of a noble black leader, and the birth of a new nation of Negro freeman frightened the pro-slavery advocates and armed the anti-slavery agitation. As a result, a Quaker petition for a law against the transport traffic in slaves was received without a murmur in 1794, and on March 22 the first national act against the slave-trade became a law." When DuBois published this work in 1896, it came as a surprise to most Americans who had no idea that their government's policy was so influenced by a black revolution in the Caribbean. But white Americans would soon learn many unpleasant truths about themselves from the writings of Dr. DuBois.

Both DuBois's talent for analysis and his commitment to balanced judgment are on display in his 1890 Harvard baccalaureate speech, in which he examines the President of the slave-holding Confederacy, Jefferson Davis, as a symbol of civilization. It was a complex assignment for such a young man, but he tackled it with intelligence and objectivity. Since this speech was presented only twenty-five years after the country had cannibalized itself in a civil war that was the most destructive military conflict in history, and all that southern blood and treasure was spent in defense of the system of African-American slavery, the consequences of which DuBois had seen first-hand just a couple of years before in rural

Tennessee, it was reasonable to expect a tirade from the young black scholar, a fiery polemic denouncing Davis and the civilization that bred him in a hail of invective.

But DuBois stunned the audience with a broadly learned treatise of uncommon fairness that sought to locate the impulse for Teutonic aggression in the cultural ethos that propelled their history. The oration, "Jefferson Davis as a Representative of Civilization," began with a simple declarative statement putting forth his central thesis: "Jefferson Davis was a typical Teutonic hero; the history of civilization during the last millennium has been the development of the idea of the Strong Man of which he was the embodiment. The Anglo-Saxon loves a soldier— Jefferson Davis was a soldier."

While this emphasis on race—which here seems to be merged with what we now think of as mere ethnicity—may sound strange to contemporary readers, such talk was common fare in the 19th century. And at the turn of the century there was a wave of Anglo-Saxon revivalism in America aimed at protecting their "racial" pedigree from inferior eastern and southern European immigrant stock. This point of view was epitomized in the pseudo-scientific tome, *The Passing of the Great Race*, by the WASP anthropologist Madison Grant. In this 1907 book, Grant argues that American Civilization was in danger of decline because the "great" Teutonic race, who were the true source of American ascendancy, was in danger of being diluted and overrun by these men from failed civilizations in the old world—with a special warning about Polish Jews. Indeed, such ideas were the *raison d'être* for the social Darwinist and eugenicist movements, whose ideology was then being promoted by a web of "research" organizations funded by the WASP elite.

Thus DuBois's discussion of race as a motive force in history was in keeping with the intellectual orthodoxy of the times. In fact, just seven years later he would clarify his views on the importance of race in a paper entitled "The Conservation of Races," read before the American Negro Academy, an organization of leading black intellectuals. On this occasion he argued that "In our calmer moments we must acknowledge that human beings are divided into races; that in this country the two most extreme types of the world's races have met, and the resulting problem as to the future relations of these types is not only of intense and living interest to us, but forms an epoch in the history of mankind."

But what is of real interest in the Harvard speech is its prophetic character—a feat DuBois would repeat on several occasions over the course of the twentieth century, beginning with several ideas introduced in *Souls*. For instance, in his characterization of Teutonic civilization, he describes what would become the Third Reich, which lay four decades into the future, and presaged the world-renowned psychiatrist Carl Jung's analysis of the German character—they who would claim to be the ultimate representatives of the virtues of Teutonic civilization. If we examine more of DuBois's speech and then compare it to Jung's analysis, the common themes are obvious. He says of Jefferson Davis: "I wish to consider not the man, but the type of civilization his life represented: its foundation is the idea of the strong man—individualism coupled with the rule of might—and it is this idea that has made the logic of even modern history, the cool logic of the club."

DuBois goes on to tell us what happens when these ideas become the philosophical basis for a national state. "The Strong Man and his mighty Right Arm has become the Strong Nation with its armies. Under whatever guise, however, a Jefferson Davis may appear, as man, as race, or as nation, his life can only logically mean this: the advance of part of the world at the expense of the whole: the overweening sense of the I and the consequent forgetting of the Thou . . . a system of human culture whose principle is the rise of one race on the ruins of another is a farce and a lie. Yet this is the type of civilization which Jefferson Davis represented; it represents a field for stalwart manhood and heroic character, and at the same time for moral obtuseness and refined brutality." Then he tells us that the Teutonic conqueror's "brutality buried aught else besides Rome when it descended golden haired from the blue north."

Some twenty-eight years after DuBois gave his warning about the danger of the Teutonic Strong Man as the ideal for a national state, Carl Jung published *The Role of the Unconscious,* in Germany. The book, which celebrated the German/Prussian martial spirit, was a salve to a crushed German manhood. Hence it came at a propitious time in German history, when the nation had suffered a humiliating defeat at the hands of the British, French, and American allies, and this defeat would soon be codified in the humiliating Treaty of Versailles. Lord John Maynard Keynes, the brilliant British economist whose ideas would later rescue the western world from the collapse of the international capitalist system known as "the great depression," proved to be a prescient observer at the conference in Versailles Palace—where the treaty was crafted and signed in the great Hall of Mirrors—when he predicted in his book, *The Economic Consequences of the Peace,* that the treaty would fuel German nationalism and plunge Europe into war again within a generation. Ironically, as it turns out, it was precisely the provisions of this treaty that Hitler used to mobilize German nationalism, labeling its German signatories "The October Criminals."

Hence Jung's contention that in the German subconscious mind there was a "blond beast heard prowling in its underground prison," and that this blond beast represented "a still uncorrupted treasure, a sign of youthfulness" and "earnest rebirth"? This had the ring of divine providence to the German ultra-nationalists who would metamorphose into Nazis. Jung's conclusions about the true German psyche led him to attack his former mentor, Sigmund Freud, for promoting a view of the unconscious that the Nazis would later label "Jew Science." Jung was very clear on this issue, accusing Freud of promoting "specifically Jewish doctrines," which were "thoroughly unsatisfactory to the Germanic mentality; we still have a genuine barbarian in us."

These ideas made Jung the favored psychiatrist of the Nazi regime, which rewarded him with the directorship of the German Association for Psychotherapy, a position from which the German psychiatrist, Dr.

E. Kretchmer, had resigned rather than act as a tool for the Third Reich. During his tenure in office, he would share the editorship with Dr. M.H. Goering, a cousin of Hitler's right-hand man, Hermann Goering, the head of the German air force. And this new regime directing German psychiatry showed its true face in a December 1933 editorial advising all German psychotherapists to read Hitler's ramblings in *Mein Kampf*, and make his ideas the basis of their psychoanalysis.

But this glorification of the Teutonic strong man does not begin with Jung. As early as 1848, the great German Romantic composer, Richard Wagner, a Saxon from Leipzig, was also inspired by a view of the Germans as a barbaric warrior nation. This is what *The Ring of the Nibelugen* is all about, the attempt to recreate a vision of a once vital pre-Christian Teutonic culture in his "Theater, drama, festivals," a term the composer preferred to Opera. That's why Wagner was Hitler's favorite composer. A poseur esthete and failed artist, whose inability to make a career in painting or architecture eventually led him to become a charismatic racial redemptionist—just as Black Muslim minister Louis Farrakhan's failure to find a much deserved career as a violinist led him into a similar role among African Americans—Hitler was a generous patron of Bayreuth, home to the annual Wagner Festival, and a close friend of Wenifred Wagner.

In his memoir, *Inside the Third Reich,* Hitler's architect and confidante Albert Speer, recalls how important the festival was to *Der Führer,* as he boarded with the Wagner family, who had added "a spacious wing to Haus Wahnfried," the Wagner family home. "On these festival days Hitler seemed more relaxed than usual. He obviously felt at ease in the Wagner family and free of the compulsion to represent power. . . . He was gay, paternal with the children friendly and solicitous toward Winifred Wagner. Without Hitler's financial aid, the festival could hardly have been kept going. Every year Bormann produced hundreds of thousands of marks from his funds in order to make the festival productions the glory of the German Opera season. As patron of the festival and friend of the Wagner family, Hitler was no doubt realizing a dream which even in his youth he perhaps never quite dared to dream."

(Even as I write, a grandson of Richard Wagner, a musician and a scholar who holds a Ph.D., is touring the world giving talks on his great ancestor's anti-Semitism as an act of public contrition for the role his family played in fostering the aims of the Third Reich. He spoke at the 2002 summer session of the Chappaqua Symphony Orchestra, and he made it clear for those who still offer up ill-informed apologia for Wagner, that it is impossible to separate Wagner's art from his hatred of Jews and the Holocaust.)

In retrospect, the communion Hitler felt with Wagner seems preordained; the bombastic brass and tympani, framed with large choruses, make great background music for mass rallies of the sort favored by the Nazis. Not only can the sensitive listener hear this in the music, but Wagner's Teutonic chauvinism regarding the Jewish influence on German music was in perfect harmony with Jung's assessment of Freud's influence on German psychology. Speaking of the music of Robert Schumann—who along with Johannes Brahms was his great rival in the marvelous age of German Romanticism, when the piano, strings and the orchestra itself reached an apotheosis—Wagner said there was an early Shuman who was original and showed great promise, and a late Schumann "whose talent was trivialized and destroyed by the Jewish influences of Mendelssohn." In both instances the Jewish influence is seen as diluting the dynamic power of the "true" German spirit.

In his book, *The Mind of Germany,* intellectual historian Hans Kohn tells us that Wagner was clear in his purpose; he "was a Romantic artist who expected his total artwork—a never before conscious attempted unity of sound, word, image, and movement—to bring about the cultural and spiritual rebirth of the German people and, through its leadership, a new civilization. . . . All this bore a message of specific and Germanic values, an interpretation of history and society, based upon the incomparable pre-eminence of Wagner's art and of German folkdom.

Wagner saw himself not only as a musician of Genius but as a prophet and savior." Hence, Wagner saw his role as a great artist the same way that Adolph Hitler would later envision his role as a soldier and statesman. Kohn sums up Wagner's artistic project with this observation: "All his creative work was infused with, and served, this avocation. His music dramas thundered this message."

In order to appreciate the messianic strain in Wagner's character and its expression as art, we must take into account the fact that he was living in a revolutionary time in Germany, and that he was a part of the Romantic "New German" movement—popularly known as "Forty-Eighters"—that engaged in the failed revolution of 1848, when a movement led by a motley crew of radical intellectuals and artists tried to seize power, but were crushed by Prussian military might. This failure forced Wagner to flee Germany, along with his fellow Forty-Eighters, Karl Marx and Ottilie Assing. Marx would go into exile in England, where, living in poverty, he would spend the rest of his life writing his three-volume masterwork *Das Kapital,* which, along with the *Communist Manifesto,* would change the world by inspiring the communist revolutions of the twentieth century.

Ottilie Assing—musician, actress, writer/intellectual, and radical activist—who was also half Jewish and struggled against anti-Semitism in the revolutionary movement, would resettle in America and, as the German scholar Maria Diedrich has shown in her unique contribution to Afro-American studies, "Love Across Color Lines," began a thirty-year love affair with Frederick Douglass, working side by side with the great editor/orator in the abolitionist movement that defeated American slavery.

Richard Wagner, however, would eventually return to Germany after spending eleven years in exile. When he fled into exile, he was only the assistant conductor in Dresden's Royal Opera House, but he returned a hero and favorite of the Kaiser. However, still alienated from the conventional bourgeois values that dominated German society, Wagner would conduct his revolution on the musical stage with his "Theater-Festival-Drama," "The Ring of the Nibelugen," an operatic masterwork that became his magnum opus. In this work, pagan Nordic warrior Gods struggle with demons and man in a dream-like spectacle set to some of the most magnificent music ever composed.

Ironically, it was the creativity of Wagner's music that enabled the Nazis to put it to such destructive purposes. As Mao Tse-Tung noted in his lectures at the Yenan Forum on Literature and Art—presented under field conditions during the Chinese revolutionary war— "In order for art to succeed as propaganda, it must first succeed as art." Even though it was performed in 1876, Henri Malherbe, a French music critic, wrote after seeing the a performance that the work was "the most striking work of the 1848 revolution and the most outstanding work of that period of European history." But he also saw something deeply disturbing in the Opera, calling it "A savage gospel of anarchy, it is so deeply steeped in poetry and dreams that its dangerous significance may not be noticed."

However, Hans Khon, speaking with the added dimension of historical perspective, is certain what it all means: "Wagner found his inspiration not in the *Nibelungenlied* but in the older sagas of the Edda, the realm of the primitive, pre-Christian myth. Wagner's interpretation turns them into a denial of civilized life as such, into primordial forces hostile to good faith, to treaties, and to law. These Nordic-Wagnerian myths, rediscovered and adapted in the age of nationalism for nationalistic purposes, had nothing in common with the Greek myths which moved Goethe and Shiller, Holderlin and Heine. . . . Primitive Nordic mythology . . . remained isolated brilliant moments in the history of German art: outside the sphere of art, however, the Nibelugen, in Wagner's barbaric and weird interpretation, had their influence on the vagaries of German nationalism."

DuBois's Teutonic "Strong Man," who met civilization and crushed it, and created "a system of human culture whose principle is the rise of one race on the ruins of another," found political expression in "the policy and philosophy" of the Confederate government and the Third Reich. Alas, DuBois's idea of the Teutonic man as conquering warrior was synonymous with the way these Teutonic nationalist intellectuals and artists saw themselves, and the character of the Third Reich, whose armies rolled out of Germany four decades later and started a war that resulted in fifty million dead, showed that he was right about what such a warrior ideal would look like when expressed in the form of a national state. And the leader of that state, *Reichsführer* Adolf Hitler, was the epitome of the Teutonic martial spirit, by temperament and design.

No less brilliant is the other major theme in DuBois's treatise, his contention that in order to move beyond barbarism, the warrior culture of the "strong man" needs the input of the "submissive man" as a counter-statement and restraining influence—just as the Christian piety that suffuses the music of Brahms, and the *joi de vivre* in the music of Franz List, a musical *bon vivant* who appears to have been dedicated only to the celebration of ostentatious virtuosity, were counterpoints to Wagner—was a wholly original idea. "What then is the change in civilization, by adding to the idea of the Strong Man, that of the submissive man?" He asks. "It is this: the submission of the strength of the strong to the advance of all. . . . No matter how great or striking the Teutonic type of impetuous manhood may be, it must receive the cool purposeful 'Ich Dien' of the African for its round and full development." This anticipates by half a century the passive resistance philosophy of Gandhi and Martin Luther King, and calls to mind the Jewish philosopher Martin Buber's philosophical construct of "I and Thou," passionately embraced by Dr. King, and which is precisely the humane element that DuBois found missing from the civilizations based upon the Teutonic warrior ideal.

However, the lesson for Americans in all this—as John A. Williams demonstrates in his last novel, *Clifford's Blues*—is how much this discussion of German racial ideas reminds one of the fact that the traditionally racist ideas of white Americans about things such as racial character and hierarchy, were the same type of phenomena as that which bred the Third Reich. After all, it was ante-bellum American civilization, not Germany that DuBois was referencing in his critique of Jefferson Davis, and it was the post-bellum caste society established with *de jure* segregation that served as the blueprint for the anti-Jewish laws instituted by the Nazis.

In studying the worship of the strongman, as DuBois outlined it, and its place in the history of Germany, we see that it reflects deeply held cultural values, values that defied rational thinking. This worship of a Teutonic ideal sheds some light on why the most intellectually accomplished society in the world could sink into barbarism in a few short years; the humiliation of defeat in war, and the severe economic crisis resulting from the economic demands of the Versailles Treaty, was merely the catalyst that unleashed the "blond beast" roaming about the unconscious psyche of Germany. And this same doctrine of Teutonic superiority so perverted a civilization based on the ideal that "All men are created equal," that it could condone a crime against humanity, chattel slavery, for 250 years.

In the future, DuBois would point to the parallels between Nazi racial ideology and American racism. But oddly enough he never made the connection between his thesis of the Teutonic strongman and German nationalism when he was studying in Germany two years later, although the signs were everywhere. He recalls in the *Autobiography:* "The pageantry and patriotism of Germany in 1892 astonished me. In New England our patriotism was cool and intellectual." He wrote. And he distinguished that patriotism from German nationalism: "Ours was a great nation and it was our duty to preserve it. We 'loved' it but with reason not passion . . . When I heard my German companions sing *Deutschland, Deutschland, Über Alles* . . . I realized that they felt something I had never felt and perhaps never would. The march of soldiers, the saluting of magnificent uniforms, the martial music and rhythm of movement stirred my senses. Then there was that new, young emperor . . . blessed by God,

German Kaiser, King of Prussia, who led and pinpointed the pageantry. Ever and again he came riding ahead of his white and golden troops on prancing chargers through the great Brandenburg gate . . . I thrilled at the sight."

DuBois had heard and loved Wagner too: "I heard Wagner before Verdi: I listened to Tannhauser before Il Travatore." He also heard Wagner's Ring Cycle, but got no hint of its meaning for German nationalism. To him it was all just music: "Germany took up my music and art where Fisk had left me; to religious oratorio was now added opera and symphony, song and sonata." Not only did he fail to see the danger in these vulgar nationalists spectacles, he even took to wearing a Vandyke beard fashioned after the Emperor's! One might reasonably ask: How could he miss all the obvious signs of the celebration of the Teutonic strong man and soldier, the mighty arm that became mighty armies when projected through the medium of the militaristic and chauvinistic national state?

The most plausible answer to this riddle lies in the reception the German people gave DuBois, accepting him as a human being. His classmates treated him as a colleague, and even a member of the haughty German professorate invited him to dance with his daughter, showing not the slightest alarm as the girl developed a crush on the handsome young Afro-American. All of this was unthinkable in his native land, where he was largely ignored by his Harvard classmates. In the South, where he had lived, any sign of erotic attraction on the part of even the lowliest Euro-American girl would almost surely have led to a gruesome death! Hence, like Paul Robeson in revolutionary Russia a half century later, where racism was a crime and feelings of brotherhood were real, the young DuBois could see or hear no evil. Yet two years earlier, he had described with uncanny insight the martial psychology that informed the Teutonic nationalism which would drive the Germans to plunge the world into war in less than twenty years, and launch the Nazi holocaust in less than fifty.

Living amid the omnipresent symbols of German nationalism, DuBois reflects on his relationship to the land of his birth, a land where less than thirty years before the great Frederick Douglass was owned by a white man as if he were a horse or cow, and all black Americans were denied passports for foreign travel because, slave or "free," white Americans would not grant them citizenship. Hence we see in his thinking an alienation and ambivalence toward his mother country that presaged his famous and much debated "double consciousness" metaphor that he would introduce in *The Souls of Black Folk.*

Speaking of his positive response to these displays of German national pride, DuBois asks: "If I as a stranger was thus influenced, what about the youth of Germany? I began to feel that dichotomy which all my life has characterized my thought: how far can love for my oppressed race accord with love for the oppressing country? And when these loyalties diverge, where shall my soul find refuge?"

Many of the ideas developed by DuBois over these early years by virtue of his research and firsthand observations—through books and wide travel—and thinking deeply, would show up later in his writings and enrich his texts. This is readily apparent in *The Souls of Black Folk,* a twentieth-century masterpiece that could hardly have been written without the wide-ranging study and broad experience of the young Dr. DuBois, which will become evident as we examine this unique text. Most importantly, *Souls* represents a contribution to the mission he had set for his life's work on his twenty-fifth birthday in Berlin. DuBois recalls the celebration in his *Autobiography:* "The night before I had heard Schubert's beautiful "Unfinished Symphony," planned my celebration and written to Grandma and Mabel and had a curious little ceremony with candles, Greek wine, oil, and song and prayer."

With his characteristically poetic sensibility, race pride, intelligence, and self-confidence, he wrote:

Night—grand and wonderful. I am glad I am living. I rejoice as a strong man to win a race, and I am strong—is it egotism—is it assurance—or is it the silent call of the world spirit that makes me feel that I am and that beneath my scepter a world of kings shall bow. The hot dark blood of a black forefather is beating at my heart, and I know that I am either a genius or a fool. O I wonder what I am—I wonder what the world is—I wonder if life is worth the Sturm. I do not know—perhaps I shall never know: But this I do know: be the truth what it may I will seek it on the pure assumption that it is worth seeking—and Heaven nor hell, God nor Devil shall turn me from my purpose til I die . . . I therefore take the world that the unknown lay in my hands and work for the rise of the Negro people, taking for granted that their best development means the best development of the world.

Here it is important to take notice of the fact that it is Schubert's Eighth, the great symphony in C minor popularly known as the "Unfinished Symphony" because the master musician died before its completion—though anyone who has listened to it must agree that it does not sound at all incomplete—as he strove to match the incomparable achievement of Beethoven's nine symphonies, that DuBois chose to hear. After all, this was the prelude to writing his commitment to life, the general outline of the hopes and aspirations that would guide his actions for the next 71 years as his life moved toward its centennial. Hence it is significant he that sought inspiration in the delicately beautiful, life affirming, spirit nurturing music of Franz Schubert, rather than the dark and brooding *Sturm* and *Drang,* or messianic bombast of Wagner.

In our age of musical illiteracy—the logical consequence of trashing musical education in the public schools—this may not mean much. But for the great 19th-century German composers, all intelligent and thoughtful men, music was a medium through which one could convey a philosophy of life. Robert Schumann, who resurrected Schubert's symphony from the vast graveyard of forgotten German musical scores, began his professional life as a writer, but came to believe the symphony was far a more effective medium to communicate grand ideas and evoke a deeper understanding of history. Whether that is actually the case is a matter for debate; what is important here is that that is what Schumann, and probably most of the great composers, believed. Wagner, as we have seen, believed it so deeply that he devoted himself to the operatic form so that his message could be conveyed not just through the power of his technically brilliant musical compositions, but with the punch of a written text, singers, visual art expressed as set designs, and even dance.

Hence the fact that DuBois listened to Schubert on this auspicious occasion, even if the choice was not consciously made because, after all, music is an art that speaks first to the heart and soul, then the brain, means that he was inspired by music that expressed the earthy power of the folk—since, unlike Wagner, Schubert mined the German folk song for his orchestral compositions. The upshot of all this is that perhaps we have been afforded a glimpse of the soul of DuBois, a man of the people whose love and admiration for the gifts of the common folk is revealed again and again, but nowhere more poignantly than in his essay "Of the Sorrow Songs," his panegyric to the body of sacred music forged by Afro-American slaves that became world famous as the "Negro spirituals."

It is more than a little instructive that so many of these latter-day bourgeois savants, who prattle on *ad nauseum* about DuBois's elitism, have neglected this jewel which peers into the souls of the black folk and reveals their beauty to the world. It also celebrates the saga of the artist—all budding members of the "Talented Tenth"—who concretized their message of boundless faith and miraculous fortitude to the world.

The keen observer, with a little knowledge of German history, might also conclude from all this that in the perpetual German struggle over who represented the German Ideal: the soldier and statesman, or Poet and philosopher, DuBois chose the spirit of "Great Goethe" over the "Iron Chancellor," Otto von Bismarck.

The fact that Goethe was both a poet and a scientist, who spent many years delving in politics and editing journals, plus lived nearly a century, proves that he and DuBois were men cut from the same cloth—though they differed on the purposes of literature, Goethe being a foe of "committed literature," a divergence for which historical time and circumstance can account. And in the fourteen essays that comprise *The Souls of Black Folk,* we see the poet, the scientist, and the politician at his best.

—⟨⟩—

A Two-Part Invention on the Black Willie Blues

I: Blues To Be There

An American can read almost anything about the past and feel as if he or she has already been there, especially if the topic is the strife provoked by relationships based on race, which are so complex and cross so much territory that they are basic to any accurately epic sense of the history of this nation. These conflicted relationships also reflect a certain body of argued ideas about ancestry, blood, scientifically proven distinction, culture, intellectual capacity, and civilization. With these arguments in place and the events that resulted from them, it should be far easier now to clearly see how the Negro fits into the history of this nation, and how the part of West Africa—from which that ancestral side comes—fits in as well. Yet, that is far from true even now, and when we find ourselves contemplating W.E.B. DuBois and his life as well as his times, it is obvious that there is a vast tradition that precedes him in the realms of reason and irrationality, the former sometimes so connected to the latter that we must call into question almost everything we have ever thought was stable and everything that we thought had any one answer, any single victim, any one-sided way of looking at things.

We cannot deny that, for a few hundred years, American men in power who were white, and also those who were not powerful but had the cache of skin privilege, did terrible things to those who were sold into America as slaves or who were free men and women but of African descent. We should also note that some American men and women who were white did far more in opposition to the enslavement of Negroes than anyone in Africa did, or even considered doing. Though we can brag about the democratic ideas that came from the Founding Fathers, we can also point at how even men of genius, such as Thomas Jefferson, were mightily flawed when it came to matters of color and bondage. At the same time that we can self-righteously talk of the hypocrisy of white Americans, we must also acknowledge that had the most enlightened of them not been willing to push an abolitionist's agenda for so long—and had thousands upon thousands of others not been willing to lay down their lives to hasten the destruction of the slave system—our history would be very, very different.

So it is all a mixed bag of fact, passion, rhetoric, superstition, junk science, technology, economics, and religious belief that makes the story of the Negro in America so complex. The life and thought of DuBois are at the center of the best to the worst aspects of that story. It the tale of an intellectual who championed some of the best and the worst of the ideas proposed to make the world better for Negroes. That bag of troubles formed the kind of mess that DuBois found himself facing throughout his lifetime and the same kind of mess—part brilliant, part ridiculous—that one finds in his own thinking when it comes to defining the meaning of race, of heritage, and group potential that he tries to order in his *The Souls of Black Folk*. What made DuBois important, however, was the fact that he had a high level of intelligence joined with a bracing and charismatic arrogance that caused him to assume before he was twenty-five, while he was still a student in Germany, that he would make an impression on the world. Oh, yeah: the young brown-skinned man from Barrington, Massachusetts, had a messianic sense of his fate, which is to say that on some level he assumed that his role would be to teach people the profound things that they desperately needed to know if they were ever to save themselves from the narrows of misinformation, superstition, and manipulative lies. The ordinary messiah often has a religious message that rocks the wall and turns the present order into Humpty Dumpty. In the case of Black Willie from New England, the message was political and cultural primarily because the question of color was so twisted up in the nation's politics and in the assumptions underlying the "correct way of living" that abided a racist hierarchy.

As a man who can be called nothing other than an intellectual, DuBois inherited not so much the "zeitgeist of the age," as Mr. Benjamin puts it, but the ideas that purified a body of thought made extraordinarily complex due to the intricacy of the human situations out of which they arrived. They were ideas that came forward during the Age of Reason and were pushed toward a purity through great struggle within the United States, where the African slave trade, Afro-American bondage, the Enlightenment, the American Revolution, and the epoch-making Industrial Revolution, that mechanical enforcer of the idea of progress, All these concepts wove themselves together and inspired a new thing, a fresh perspective. That new thing came to define the possibilities of democracy through the demanding means of representative government, public argument, bloody constraints, and political positions that evolved—by way of the checks and balances process inspired by Montaigne—into the specific dictates of policy determined by the rule of law. In terms of social rights, those unprecedented aspects of democratic identity arrived within a context of ongoing reconsideration that led to an innovatively broad reassessment of human equality that eventually moved across the lines of color and sex.

While the completion of the process did not arrive in his lifetime, DuBois knew that shifts in society, the motion of rights and privileges across lines that finally did come to fruition due to the quality of ongoing reconsideration were not what the Founding Fathers had in mind when they drew up and ratified the Constitution. That, finally, means nothing of significance in terms of the ideas themselves. After all, since our democracy posits the idea that greatness can arrive from under the very filthiest soles of the society, or from the humblest of beginnings, we should not be so sentimentally shocked or disappointed or outraged or grow too, too self-righteous when that rule spins around and we see that those at the top turn out to be low–down and rotten—even given to stinking up their private lives with the fumes of avarice, opportunism, and greed—but remain, however comfortable within their shells of bigotry, capable of producing unprecedented pearls of social vision. That is how it actually was.

That is not all of how it was, however. What has to be said clearly and with no drop in volume is that, just as unintentionally as the Founding Fathers, the bush league kings of West Africa—lovers of umbrellas, rum, and rifles—made their greatest contribution to the world in the last five hundred years by selling other Africans into the Western Hemisphere, especially those who arrived in America. The consequences were huge, and those primitive kings have to be given, with a sense of tragic irony, the same kind of slack as the Founding Fathers, but for very different reasons.

Let us get very clear, since the subjects are individual liberty and democracy, they are issues of such great significance that once in America, Alexis de Tocqueville realized that the democratic form of government the Founding Fathers created to bring order to the United States was relevant to the future of the world at large, not just a former set of British colonies. The democratic ideals written into the Declaration of Independence and the Constitution were so profoundly important—when taken seriously by the people of the United States—that the South had to be beaten within an inch of its life once enough people realized that a country could not exist half-slave and half-free. As far as those ideals and the questions that they raised went, the kings of West Africa provided no ideas—or ideals—of any democratic importance because there was nothing inside the "pure" African vision of life itself that would have ever led to the end of the slave trade, primarily because tribalism—which is the father of racism, by the way—was in full and bloody swing. That ethnic enmity was so strong that all was possible. But from beneath the tribal dress that identified these bigots, and even when accompanied by majestic and intricate poly-rhythms produced with hands attuned to the nuances of drums, no inspiring pearls of social philosophy ascended. None. Absolutely.

Further, the slave trade in Africa met resistance here and there, mounted by such as the Christian King Alfonso I of the Congo and the Angolan Queen Nzinga, Alfonso following the dictates of the Bible, Nzinga aiming to free her country from the rule of the Portuguese. But these examples are not really germane to the point, because, as George Steiner points out in *In Bluebeard's Castle,* our Western culture is one in which the fall of a convention almost always comes from within, not from without. As is more than slightly evident, the African regimes committed to slavery were devoid of the kinds of internal arguments and the movements to abolish slavery—in the interest of other ethnic groups—that had a considerable history, for instance, in a city like Philadelphia and its surroundings. These were the kinds of arguments that the young DuBois intended to sustain and to use in order to redress the arrogantly thick, bloody, and sticky residue of racism. His knowledge and his imagination were dedicated to things that were not of any importance within the traditional African context.

This cannot be set aside if we are to address the thinking of a man more than a few consider a major intellectual. While Mr. Benjamin exaggerates its actual value and more than generously celebrates the young DuBois's 1890 commencement talk on Jefferson Davis—given that it was an argument of the sort that had been made by certain critical Negroes more than forty years earlier—I think my point can be better made by quoting one aspect of his discussion of the tradition of the Strong Man, referring to the Goths and the Visogoths who sacked Rome, "The Teutonic met civilization and crushed it—the Negro met civilization and was crushed by it." Perhaps the Negro in Africa had already been crushed before "meeting" civilization. In Ghana is Salaga, which was a major port of slave sale back in those days when the area was known as the Gold Coast. On the BBC, the major king of Salaga recently said for the record:

> Salaga is in the southern part of the northern region. Salaga was an old slave market. Caravans used to come all the way from northern Nigeria and other places, Burkina Faso, Mali and so on. Salaga became important for its market in human beings.
>
> The slaves were brought in here. There were places to store them and most of the time they were actually tied around trees in the market. There were just one or two rooms that can even be seen up to this date. But most of the time they were tied around, big, big trees, guava trees, close to the markets.

The regent went on to say that with hindsight, he and his subjects feel remorse over what their ancestors did. But at the time, it was only normal. Just as in our day, it was a market, and people were buying.

Unlike the majority who showed a lack of concern in Africa by supporting slavery, or ignoring its existence, certain religious and successful men in the America of the late seventeenth century as well as the eighteenth and nineteenth centuries—Quakers, Methodists, and Presbyterians early on—made resolutions, organized societies, and worked against the dirty blues wrought by that so "peculiar institution." From such people descended early supporters of DuBois. These were special people. In the last quarter of the eighteenth century, Quakers expelled from their congregations any who refused to free their slaves.

Their official public expression of disagreement with the business of slavery in the environs of the City of Brotherly Love began in 1688 when four German Quakers raised their voices against the trade in Germantown, which was then just outside of Philadelphia.

True: There were surely limitations within the anti-slavery perspective that cannot be denied. They rhyme with the troubles DuBois had when his career ambitions were not seen as the kind that would do his ethnic group any good. In hard fact, not all were even up to being moral Cub Scouts and Campfire Girls. One strain of the abolitionists who sought to end slavery thought black people inferior and would, therefore, now have to be considered akin to members of a fervent society for the prevention of cruelty to animals. Even so, the ups and downs of the developing abolition movement in America had no parallels of any sort in Africa; this was a purely Western phenomena played out in a nation that was defining itself on the run, on the go, in motion, as it settled and fought and slaughtered its way into an ever larger land mass. Yet, however hard that might be to deal with in such self-flagellating times as these, wrap your mind around this: those sustaining the idea of freeing the slaves were Christians, who are so often addressed exclusively as hypocrites. Without a doubt many were, and some were quite willing to use the Bible to excuse the sale of human beings. There were also those who were not willing and did not choose to hold their silence over the matter either.

At the same time, in order to understand the world that DuBois inherited, we have to look at the arguments against slavery as another aspect of progression—when it actually progresses—in which an essential aspect of social evolution and democratic ideas rose up against monarchies. While Europeans were concerned with monarchies of religion and class, Negroes in America had first to struggle against monarchies based on color, which is what each plantation actually was. This was equally true but far, far less brutal in the ethnic pecking order beyond the plantations—in the North. (Though there were cases such as the one of Philadelphia in which Negroes remained at home after the Fourth of July celebration of 1805, when drunken white mobs attacked black people as if they had not the right to enjoy a national holiday, even though thousands of them had done plenty of what historian Ira Berlin calls "the dirty work of war" in his illuminating *Many Thousands Gone.)*

In this Northern world of slave and half-free and free blacks, the fight for recognition of the Negro's humanity should also be comprehended as part of the extraordinary battle against hierarchy, and DuBois can surely be seen as one who chose to join up. That very battle, in all of its breadth, could quite easily be the most monumental reinterpretation of social and natural rights in the history of the species, especially since it has expanded over the last one hundred and fifty years to include not only all colors and nationalities as well as both sexes, but labor issues and sexual issues such as harassment in the workplace as well. As a lover of the pastoral, I'm sure that DuBois would be glad to know that this battle against heirarchy has evolved to embrace lower forms of animal life and even the inanimate environment, primarily because all of its most high-minded aspects can be reduced to something as simple but as fundamental as the Golden Rule of doing unto others as . . . (Though, at its worst, such struggles with hierarchy have brought about a bullsh-t academic vision of leveling that pretends all things are "culturally determined," meaning that there is no such thing as a fact that is good or bad, high or low, great or insignificant—which is as insipid as the idea of innate superiority based in assumed value.)

The central value of democracy is the rejection of prestige and power based on ancestry (a tenet of what DuBois continued to lay before the United States). So in a profound sense, the struggle of the Negro within the context of the American experiment was the most important post-Enlightenment battle with hierarchy because it took on issues of individual liberty and argued against the clenched fist of superstition that is the idea of race, which was basic to hierarchy in the United

States. Yet part of what those black people had to argue against came from the Enlightenment in its initial form, which we usually think of as a body of ideas rooted in reason and a rejection of the power of the church in favor of science and philosophical deduction. So far so good‹but not good enough when an unsentimental pupil is cast upon the eighteenth century. Both the science and the nature of the deductions in the area of color were not only off, they were racist to the core and prove out why skepticism should be basic to the democratic mind and sensibility. In the face of so much external agreement by men of letters and respected adherents to what we now call the scientific method, those Negroes proved themselves farseeing marvels in their confrontations with science as it was thought of over the century preceding the birth of "Black Willie." They eloquently rejected the purported reason underlying the science of the time and championed an idea about universal humanity that would later—much, much later—be borne out by brain research, blood plasma, DNA, organ transplants, and all of the other things that can now be proven. The importance of this will be examined in the next part of this essay.

A good deal of what DuBois's predecessors had to face, when we step all the way down into the snake pit of racism, is located in the assumptions focused upon physiognomy because the Negro, of all of those people whom we do not associate with Europe, looks least like the white man and the white woman. The Negro is darker in skin tone, has thicker lips more often than not, does not possess as wide a range of eye color, and has, in kinky or nappy hair, a quality that is separate from that of the European, the American Indian, the Indians of India, and the Asians who have impressed the West since the expeditions into China that produced the imitative European trend of chinoiserie in the seventeenth century, when things Chinese took on status as both exotic and highly refined. Since Europeans and Americans who arrived after the Renaissance were given to imitating nothing from black Africa before the start of the twentieth century, they were left with what academics now call "the black body." Thomas Jefferson, for one, thought Negroes somehow less human because their skin tone did not give in to blushing and, therefore, made their emotions more mysterious and less obvious to the eye. So once that Negro was accepted as a human being, not a lower order, everybody else had a much easier ride. An idea about human equality began its most difficult journey—which is to move beyond physiognomy—and may well be said to have set the stage for the United Nations, which stands as a paean to universal humanity, however jive the nature of politics and alliances sometimes makes the organization seem. DuBois was a child of that version of the Enlightenment perspective, those ideas, the most important rejection of racism in the history of the modern world, a turning away from the high-toned rhetoric of tribalism that gave the provincial version of the Age of Reason, an intellectual stench which had to be washed away so that the fundamental union of humankind could be apprehended. That is the door through which he enters history. What we now know, in fact, due to Mia Bay's *The White Image in the Black Mind,* is that almost every idea and stance that we associate with DuBois at the time of *The Souls of Black Folk* had its precedents in the eloquent and brave refutations of racist ideology and the rejection of the "rightness" of the slave system by Negro Americans who had showered down the rebuttals and counter-accusations by 1835.

But in order to put all of these things in the right perspective, we have to take another kind of a look at the decades that preceded DuBois, understanding that what we will see is that Afro-American history basically breaks down into three parts—slavery from 1619 to 1865, Reconstruction from 1865 to 1877, and the struggle for local and national civil rights that did not finish until 1968, when the Civil Rights Movement ended shortly after half of Martin Luther King, Jr.'s face was blown off as he stood on the balcony of the Lorraine Motel in Memphis, Tennessee. DuBois had died only five years earlier at 95, having finished out his life in Ghana too soon to see how his shared fantasies of pan-

Africanism would confuse and mislead the young American Negroes who then thought themselves radicals and were beginning to pretend that they were Africans "lost" in America.

II: Blues in the Background

By the middle of the nineteenth century, things were getting, as Jelly Roll Morton once said, "awful hot." The Negro had always been more mysterious than true to the majority of white Americans—an image, a shade, a figment in flesh and blood. While there had surely been slavery in the North, there were also "free men of color" who lived in the North as laborers of one sort of another or who had their own businesses and read books and sent, as James M. McPherson's The Negro's Civil War *proves, letters to newspapers as eloquent as any we see in our better newspapers today. Even so, the Negro was a largely unknown element in terms of his and her humanity. But that unknown and mysteriously individuated human quantity, growing in numbers by the decade as the slave population grew, assured the nation, in almost a whisper arriving in a prophetic mist of blood, that the wrong things presently in place would not be wrong or in place forever. Things were boiling and had been boiling for a while. One could be sure of that: The soul of the nation's integrity, to get all the way down to it, was in a cauldron and the flame was rising, notch by notch. It seemed that the lid was about to blow and rise so high, a red-hot disk, that it would sear a hole in the roof of the land and burst into endless shrapnel when it hit the ground. The upshot was that the Negro, more than any other figure of that century, became the subject of a discussion in which the highest ideals of American democracy were not only put to the test but made more concrete. In order for those ideals to become more concrete, however, an arrogant order had to be brought down through the means of fire and steel. No other selection would avail itself. There were those in the South who had built a schizophrenic empire of genteel manners on the top and barbaric practices backed up by brute force on the bottom. The plantations were not at all enigmatic. They were testaments to why one of the Founding Fathers said that slavery was a serpent under the table. That serpent would have its head chopped off. O, yes, it would.*

In that time of rising controversy, formidable things stood in front of those Northerners on top, who were part of what has been called "the ruling race." As the nineteenth century moved beyond the halfway point, there was a sticky red whirlwind gathering momentum. People were dying in Kansas because some, like the mad and glorious John Brown, were determined to make sure that slavery did not spread, and then there were others who aimed to have more markets for the sale and purchasing of slaves. Whether or not a state allowed slavery also had political effects that were important, as William C. Davis observes in *Look Away! A History of the Confederate States of America:* "If slavery could not spread as new states were formed, then the existing slave states would be doomed to perpetual minority in the representation in Congress, guaranteeing that if the day came when Northern antipathy to slavery itself became hot enough, the majority could use the government to subvert the Constitution and abolish the institution where it already existed. In short, the South could not afford to lose any battle over slavery, nor even over issues on its periphery." This created a feeling of uneasiness among those outside of the slave states, especially when it came to thinking about the Negro people over whom blood was being shed and whose case was being argued with ever stronger hostility toward all who held them in bondage.

Yet some of it was just too abstract. One couldn't really get a grip on the matter. After all, what could those white Northerners who saw the country slouching on its slow thighs toward epic conflict know of Negroes if they had not often been in their presence, if they had not labored together, prayed together, attended marriages together, watched their children grow up together, argued politics together, gone to the burying ground together? They could know little, which did not make them good opponents of the Southerners who were sure that they were either doing the right thing or were doing something that was not all that bad, given that the Negro was not out of place as a slave, not at all.

It was not then as it is now, when every human type in our society has finally been represented beyond the stereotype, no matter how many of those stereotypes still periodically bedevil them and society at large. There was no radio and there was no television, which meant that most white people got their information from newspapers or hearsay, and most white Americans had seen more white men in minstrel shows wearing blackface than they had seen actual black Americans. If the Negro didn't exist solely for hard labor, you could be sure he was pretty darn good as an entertainment subject—catchy tunes, dancing, buffoonery. Who would want to get into even a light skirmish over that kind of person? So part of the battle against slavery was about, as they say today, "putting a human face" on the slave.

That must be understood because the little that was known of the Negro as a human being still determined so much of the history of the country and the society into which W.E.B. DuBois was born, three years after the Civil War had ended and five years after the Emancipation Proclamation had been signed into law. Slavery had been brought to an end, but freedom was not just around any corner. Though 600,000 people had lost their lives during a conflict in which modern warfare had been invented and modern surgery had gotten a beginning due to the enormous number of casualties, national sympathy for the Negro was short-lived because white people wanted to get back together with each other, wanted to walk a path not mushy with the memories of blood and slaughter, memories that resonated bitterness, resentment, and disregard—the Northerners bitter toward the Southerners for trying to split the Union, the Southerners bitter against the North for having had their world destroyed. That black soldiers had fought in nearly five hundred engagements and that twenty-three of them had been awarded the Congressional Medal of Honor was part of an uncelebrated aspect of that war which had not been missed by Abraham Lincoln. He wrote that had the 180,000 black people involved in the Union effort decided to back out of the battle, the South would have won the effort to defend the plantation system. Lincoln was largely alone in his understanding— or, what was true soon became less important than what was desired, which is so often the nature of history and color in the nineteenth century. As Mia Bay observes in *The White Image in the Black Mind: African American Ideas About White People, 1830-1925:* In the long run, white Americans did not see the military contributions of black soldiers as proof of black manhood. Indeed, the contributions black soldiers made to the war were soon discounted and obscured by Northern and Southern whites anxious to reinstate the status quo. Bent on recovering their former superiority, Southern whites terrorized former soldiers and claimed that blacks had "fought no battles; or if engaged at all in such, they were trifling affairs." At the same time, the contributions of black soldiers were soon forgotten by Northern whites focused on political struggles over the South's Reconstruction—struggles that finally used up their limited enthusiasm for black civil rights.

To that end—the reuniting of the souls of white folks—the Negro was hung on the meat rack of second-class citizenship, where there was to be neither whining nor crying nor bleeding nor complaining. If there was any such thing, especially below the Mason-Dixon line, violence was always an option in order to maintain a terrorist regime of injustice and bigoted conceit. So the ambition of W.E.B. DuBois, as he grew into adulthood, was to take the baton handed off by men like Frederick Douglass and run as close to the finish line of actual freedom as he could.

The epic American relay run of those from whom DuBois was descended, whether from Africa or from Europe, was determined by the degree of that aforementioned unfamiliarity with Negroes as human beings and how that lack of personal experience was incrementally obviated by a confluence of democratic ideas, Christian morality, and debates that brought what had been slave-owning colonies into confrontation with the truth of bigotry as the glue that sealed the founding documents of the United States. As Samuel Johnson had written in 1758 of those on the American continent who would eventually wage and win the Revolutionary War against what was then Great Britain, "Slavery is now no where more patiently endured, than in countries once inhabited by the zealots of liberty." Here was a nation founded on an idea of universal rights decreed from God that excluded Negroes, who were defined as three-fifths human in order to keep happy those slave-owning lovers of a newly born democratic republic. Moving beyond racism and getting those other two fifths solidly in place was the ongoing issue that had to be engaged if black Americans were ever to achieve their birthrights as United States citizens.

DuBois himself, the Negro at large, and America were part of the fundamental sweep of redefinition of what was then the fairly modern history of the Western world by the time that DuBois wrote *The Souls of Black Folk,* forty years after the Emancipation Proclamation. In essence, the New Testament idea of there being no chosen people, of all human beings having equal access to God, had been secularized during the Enlightenment. That aspect of that Age of Reason was the conception that human commonality transcended nationality, meaning that the essential quality of human existence should not be misunderstood due to the styles, cultures, forms of government, religions, and so on that were merely the varied ways in which men sought to cope with the burdens and mysteries of existence and nature as they fell upon them. A man was a man for all that.

The ideas of the Enlightenment were given more and more weight by the American and French Revolutions. The Enlightenment thinkers saw themselves as part of a community that transcended class and place—in Europe. None of them seriously thought about Africa, Asia, Australia, or the Western Hemisphere. In some sense, one could say that they were provincial thinkers, that their ideas were meant to express relationships among European nations and among individuals within European societies. Their countries were Christian and, seeing themselves as part of a line that stretched from Greece through Rome and through all that had taken place within Europe up to their Age of Reason, the men who graced this era with their ideas were less global-minded than what is expected of intellectuals today.

The opposition that was still in place by the 1890s was rough a hundred years earlier. In the work of George M. Frederickson and Mia Bay, we find that the ideas about polygenesis began to take hold by 1820 as imported junk science from Europe and worked well as a defense for slavery. But as Bay reports, by 1779, just three years after the writing of the Declaration of Independence, "a group of Connecticut slaves petitioned their state's general assembly with the protest 'that we are the Creatures of that God who made of one Blood and Kindred all the Nations of the Earth; we perceive in our own Reflection that we are endowed with the same Faculties as our masters, and there is nothing that leads us to a Belief, for Suspicion, that we are any more obliged to serve them, than they us.'" In essence, even at that point, the ideas of the Enlightenment—while tied to a religious source that those shapers of the Age of Reason would have rejected—were uttered with fire and grace by those slaves, toting forward Jefferson's document as if those "unalienable rights" included the men, women, and children who were presently chattel. This suggests that those Connecticut slaves had either heard of the Declaration of Independence, or had read it and had taken seriously the ideas that would, in one frame, lead to victory over Cornwallis at the hands of George Washington and, in another frame, mount Robert E. Lee on his horse Traveler and take him to the court building where he would find himself signing the terms of surrender at Appomattox, while red-eyed Ulysses S. Grant waited with grace, even though he had suffered from a migraine the evening before and had had to listen to his officers celebrating the night away, shouting and singing and banging on a piano in the same house where he, the leader of the Army of the Potomac, was quartered. While the great minds and military men among the American revolutionists were often slave owners, those who did so much of the thinking and writing to give voice to Negro concerns were either free men of color or runaway slaves who, as DuBois said late in his life of Booker T. Washington, had "tasted the lash."

These black men had different issues from those of Jefferson and his crew, who were not being held down due to their supposed inferiority, but merely because they were colonials. Those Negroes did not have the same privileges as the English whose march toward a parliamentarian government had begun with the Magna Carta and, say some, daggers at the neck of King John in order to encourage his best penmanship as he signed the document. That Magna Carta, which was originally drafted to settle a dispute between the king and the barons of England, was extended to provide rights for the free men of John's reign as well as all of those free Englishmen who came after he was long dead and gone. Jefferson and the fellows who signed the Declaration of Independence, as well as those who argued the Constitution into shape, had no idea that they had produced a body of ideas that inspired black people to work against slavery and against racist ideas. The Negro drew upon them just as the Magna Carta and English law were drawn upon by the Founding Fathers. There was the American continuity. The chords of unintended consequences were subjected to some extended blues choruses in which the tragic optimism of American democracy wafted through the atmosphere, setting loose enough building wind to blow the candles off of the table of slavery and burn down the house. (One also thinks of how DuBois, so confident and so given to study, walked through Europe with his head held high and his intentions limited by nothing he knew, taking in the art and culture of people who had built nothing for him but whose humanity spoke to a man unimpressed by those who thought that his heritage was anything less than whatever in the world inspired him, regardless of its source, regardless of the color of its makers.)

DuBois's predecessors didn't play. They were rough customers. These were not timid people, nor did they lie down in the darkness as if they were no more than receptacles for the waste matter of bigoted stereotypes. Like Melville's Ahab, they would slap the sun if it insulted them. On August 19, 1791, an Afro-American tinkerer of talent named Benjamin Banneker called out Thomas Jefferson himself, who had excised from the Declaration of Independence an attack on Britain for its support of the slave trade. Though, as Roger Wilkins reminds us in *Jefferson's Pillow: The Founding Fathers and the Dilemma of Black Patriotism,* John Adams pushed to have the document authored by Virginia Tom for his writing fluency and to make sure that the battle royal about to begin was not seen as just the agitation of some Northerners—the most impacting piece of the document didn't make the cut. Going after King George, old red-headed Jefferson—whose tune on slavery would change from a dirge in the minor to a reel in the major after he inherited a hundred chattel—originally wrote:

> He has waged cruel war against human nature itself, violating its most sacred rights of life & liberty in the persons of a distant people, who never offended him, captivating and carrying them into slavery in another hemisphere, or to incur miserable death in their transportation thither, this piratical warfare, the opprobrium of infidel powers, is the warfare of the Christian king of Great Britain. Determined to keep open a market where MEN should be bought & sold, he has prostituted his negative for suppressing every legislative attempt to prohibit or restrain this execrable commerce: and his assemblage of horrors might want no fact of distinguished die, he is now exciting those very people to rise in arms among us, and to purchase their liberty of which he has deprived them, by murdering the people

upon whom he has obtruded them; thus paying off former crimes committed against the liberties of one
people, with crimes which he urges them to commit
against the lives of another . . .

Banneker knew nothing of that. Had he, the man would probably
have had lava bursting out of his head since what was left out about the
injustice of slavery—its being a crime against the natural rights of life
and liberty, a terribly brutal business, and a monstrous thing for a
Christian leadership to impose—was in perfect alignment with the abolitionist argument. Banneker had other things going on in his head,
however. It was fifteen years after the Declaration of Independence had
given new thoughts to the world, and Banneker felt that he had to
upbraid Jefferson for having written of the inferiority of the Negro, just
as DuBois would later feel the need to pour some hot coals in the seat
of Rutherford B. Hayes's pants for playing possum with his money.
Banneker put this on Jefferson, showing how the legacy of the founding
documents would continue to be turned around until their principles
were opened up in policies intended to make true what had by then
become an international vision of idealism:

> Sir, how pitiable is it to reflect, that although you were so
> fully convinced of the benevolence of the Father of
> Mankind, and of his equal and impartial distribution of
> these rights and privileges, which he hath conferred upon
> them, that you should at the same time counteract his
> mercies, in detaining by fraud and violence so numerous
> a part of my brethren, under groaning captivity and cruel
> oppression, that you should at the same time be found
> guilty of that most criminal act, which you professedly
> detested in others, with respect to yourselves.

Jefferson, then Secretary of State and the owner of a few hundred slaves, while actually feeling contempt for Banneker, responded with the hollow geniality now as common to Los Angeles as it was then to the South:

SIR,

I THANK you, sincerely, for your letter of the 19th instant, and for the Almanac it contained. No body wishes more than I do, to see such proofs as you exhibit, that nature has given to our black brethren talents equal to those of the other colors of men; and that the appearance of the want of them, is owing merely to the degraded condition of their existence, both in Africa and America. I can add with truth, that no body wishes more ardently to see a good system commenced, for raising the condition, both of their body and mind, to what it ought to be, as far as the imbecility of their present existence, and other circumstances, which cannot be neglected, will admit.

Interestingly, four years before the exchange between Banneker and Jefferson, the Constitutional Convention held its first meeting in 1787 in the very same Philadelphia where there had been the previously mentioned tradition of argument against slavery that had begun in 1688 when those German Quakers stepped up and spoke out against slavery. It is unfortunate that Mr. Benjamin makes celebratory mention of Richard Allen and Absalom Jones of the A.M.E. church but does not clarify how much help they were given by the white abolitionists of Philadelphia, such as Anthony Benezet whose funeral in 1784 was attended by hundreds of black people because he was described as "the single most prolific antislavery writer and the most influential advocater of the Negro's rights on either side of the Atlantic."

It is doubtful that Jefferson had not heard of Benezet, but it was not in his interest or in that of any other slave-owner to consider that the kind of experiences that they had had with slaves did not reflect much about their chattel other than the intellectual confines imposed on them by the practices common to bondage. As *Jefferson's Pillow* makes clear, the detailing of the specifics of the troubles with slavery that were in that paragraph excised from the conclusion of the early draft of the Declaration of Independence leave no doubt that Virginia Tom was far from unaware of what the real deal was. (Jefferson was lying to himself and to the rest of the world, somewhat parallel to Malcolm X, who had been to Saudi Arabia in 1959 but claimed not to know that whites were allowed into Mecca until he broke with Elijah Muhammad in 1964 and found—on his second trip!—that Islam was not just "the black man's true religion," but was open to all. You bet.)

Anthony Benezet was another kind of a man. The things that he knew were consistent with what he said and what he did. Benezet was an educator and the man who called to order the first meeting of what became the Philadelphia Abolition Society. Benezet never accepted the idea that the Negro was inferior and used his teaching experience with both black and white pupils to back up his beliefs, saying that he knew personally the "African genius" and could attest to the fact that, given the same level of preparation, the Negro student would do, on average, as well as the whites. (Here, of course, lies the recognition of how important education would be to the future of the Negro, an awareness that DuBois, following the long black tradition that soon developed, would champion over and over, even in his argument against Booker T. Washington in *The Souls of Black Folk.)* Moreover, resulting from unprejudiced human contact, Benezet's position was the heart of the matter, the vision of equality necessary to purify the Enlightenment ideas, the Declaration of Independence, and the Constitution. In fact, black abolitionists Richard Allen and Absalom Jones echoed Benezet's ideas in a rejoinder written in 1793.

Benezet was so powerful a moral presence in Philadelphia that he had mystical influences even after his death. Benjamin Rush, one of the strongest supporters of Jones and Allen and a slaveowner himself, had been inspired to join more forcefully in the fight against slavery by a dream in which he saw himself on a beach listening to some Negroes who told him heart-piercing stories of slavery as the deceased Benezet, surely with the aura of a saint around him, came walking to meet the black people. The point here is that goodwill toward Negroes and the ability to either transcend the prejudices of the day or to learn from experiences with children and from the observation of how free black people conducted themselves in Philadelphia was what the best whites of their day brought to that aspect of the American story. They were the kinds of people all of DuBois's predecessors had to believe would eventually equal or outnumber those committed to the superstitions of bigotry. DuBois himself referred to such people in *The Souls of Black Folk* when he wrote, "while it is a great truth to say that the Negro must strive and strive mightily to help himself, it is equally true that unless his striving be not simply seconded, but rather aroused and encouraged, by the initiative of the richer and wiser environing group, he cannot hope for great success."

Yet we still have to keep our heads high and straight so that our brains don't run out of our ears. The one-sided, self-righteous among us who would, even now, dismiss the Enlightenment because of racist ideas held by men such as Voltaire, Hume, and Rousseau when it came to melanin and wooly hair, reveal themselves as less then completely serious when they repeatedly refuse to hurl the theories of Marx and Engels into the trough as well, despite the clear evidence of their equally racist ideas. (In their letters and private conversations, neither brother Marx nor brother Engles was shy about expressing contempt for Negroes and calling them "niggers," which is documented in *Karl Marx: Racist* by Nathaniel Weyl.)

Those who would sneer at the creators of the Age of Reason do not ever grasp that the profundity of those Enlightenment ideas is only the first part of the story. An idea is always only the first part; in fact, most of the story of life is about how long and in what manner an idea becomes an active fact or a fundamental belief that informs the literal ways in which societies conduct themselves. So once the idea of universal humanity was there, it had to be—as stated earlier—expanded and purified, freed of its reservations and its exclusions. So the next chapter of the story of the idea is that every excluded group—women and whomever else—has had to deal with its version of getting the two-fifths in place and arriving at recognition as human beings.

We sometimes think of that fight for recognition as something far simpler than it was because our modern science has finally liberated us from the idea of race. (As Paul Hoffman wrote in the November 1994 issue of *Discover*, "race accounts for only a miniscule .012 percent difference in our genetic material.") This is important to recall as we look at the world from 1800 forward that the liberating aspect of science had yet to arrive during the nineteenth century because the scientific study of "race," then known as ethnology, was far behind the brilliant mechanical engineering and building that gave so much of the nineteenth century its identity, with bold appropriation and manipulation of mineral ore, fire, architectural fact, and mechanical design that led to the railroads and to the marvel of the suspension bridge, which remains with us while we now laugh, or cringe, at the images of black people that were held by even the most sophisticated people in far too many cases. To build upon an earlier observation, let something be made clear: what passed for science in the nineteenth century tended to corroborate the superstitions of bigotry when it came around to the discussion of human beings and their natures, their capacities, their limitations, and their potential for growing into mature men and women. The idea of polygenesis—something that DuBois himself more than toyed with—was in vogue. It meant that ethnic groups developed independently of each other, some superior, some inferior. Those born superior were able to realize high levels of abstraction, while the inferior groups could only rise so far before, as they said in the minstrel shows, their heads started "swimming." In an essay entitled "Recognizing Academic Bias," Irving Hexham (www.ucalgary.ca/-hexham/ study/T-1.htm) reminds us that Voltaire himself was an advocate of this way of looking at the world, which he clearly expressed in an essay called "The Negro":

> The NEGRO race is a species of men as different from ours as the breed of spaniels is from that of grey-hounds . . . if their understanding is not of a different nature from ours, it is at least greatly inferior. They are not capable of any great application or association of ideas, and seem formed neither of the advantages nor abuses of our philosophy.

That is why Hexham also observes that certain figures such as Voltaire helped create the vision of modern racism. To perceive this embracing of what would become a fraudulent scientific assessment of race, we might look at a review of George L. Mosse's *Toward A Final Solution: The History of Modern Racism* (www.nationalismproj-ect.org/books/bookrevs/toward.htm). It contains a summary of Mosse's ideas about racism and science:

> The Enlightenment saw the development of early anthropology, which attempted to place man in nature by studying behavior, measurements, and making com-parisons of groups of men to animals. It did not prove hard for anthropology to quickly become tied with phrenology (reading the skull) and physiognomy (read-ing the face), pseudosciences which attempted to learn about mankind by aesthetic means alone. By judging men on their appearance and comparing groups living in

less modernized ways to animals, early racial thinking
was able to adopt a scientific validity. . . . Groups which
fell outside of this accepted range, especially blacks, were
seen as sub-human and morally undeveloped and wild.

In essence, that amounts to one of the most twisted jokes in all of
history. What began as a turn away from religious dogma toward reason
and toward the world of science went on to aid and abet racist dogma!
If monotheism was to be rejected in favor of the life of the mind and the
things that it could both discover and bring into existence, then mono-
genesis should also be rejected, since polygenesis was the best
explanation for why people the world over did not look like Europeans
or their white American descendents. Also, given that anthropology, as
noted, was still a primitive discipline, what passed for information about
people outside of Europe did not then benefit from independent cor-
roboration or from scholars living in the field with the subjects and
coming to grasp how their vision of life actually functioned, how it
formed a human perspective on the beginning of the species, the relationship of humanity to nature, and how the seen and the unseen were
thought to work together or in conflict.

Then there was the influence of folklore. The claims of experience
with non-Europeans that intellectually blotched the public record were
often the ingredients of one big mishmash, a hodge-podge, a gumbo of
hearsay, exaggerations, and lies meant to entertain the listener or the
reader (the kinds of tall stories that the middle-aged Othello told
Desdemona in order to so dazzle the Italian girl that she would become
his, smitten with that old ram of a Moor who saw things that nobody
else whom she knew had experienced).

In the Age of Reason, those tall tales got over very easily, and under-
standably so. The black Africans had, apparently, been where they were
for centuries. Clearly, there was no proof of intellectual sophistication
in their history and, therefore, such people in the brain trusts of

European societies felt that slavery wasn't so bad an institution for them. What other labor could these dark people do, after all? What, precisely, had they ever done? Had they built any great architectural wonders? Had they even risen to the level that the Greeks and the Romans functioned on a few thousand years before? Unless they had been conquered by the Arabs, they had no written language, which meant no literature of any kind that was not passed on orally. Had they produced the kinds of cultural improvisations that Marco Polo had seen in Asia, where those yellow people had a written language, skill at refining fabrics, architecture original to them, plates, cups, and saucers that were the envy of the West, as well as all else that defined a civilization, however exotic? Of course not. These Africans lived in huts, were cannibals, and had more than one wife. Some were reported to walk on all fours and reveal strange dental deformations, or so Voltaire had read. So the demon blacks were both barbaric and sexually degenerate. Certain of the males, it was said, died early deaths due to the year in, year out grind of excessive erotic engagement. Thusly, those given to discussions of philosophy and the varied kinds of perspectives on the essences and the meanings of life—such as Voltaire, Hume, Rousseau, and Hegel—did not think that black people even had the intellectual capacity for complex consciousness. So anyone who took those intellectuals seriously as men whose every word was like a flare going up in the night of ignorance could conclude of Negroes, or Africans, that the slave quarters would do. Let them serve as beasts of burden. Beasts already, they might as well carry something.

In the United States, what they came to carry forward, actually, was the great dream of the American nation, straightening out far more than they left bent and warped by prejudice and opportunism. Those black people were to become their own homemade, flesh-and-blood Enlightenment, which meant both refusing to accept the justifications for either their own conditions or for the conditions of those who were not free. That is why I say that those black people and their white supporters where the purifiers of the Enlightenment, which was more than a buck dance or a cakewalk and was often thought of as nothing beyond whistling in the dark. They provided the iconoclastic foundation for what DuBois would bring to the battle by the time that he wrote in his preface to *The Philadelphia Negro,* "that Negro problems are the problems of human beings; that they cannot be explained away by fantastic theories, ungrounded assumptions, or metaphysical subtleties." As Mia Bay observes "The world was thinking wrong about race: *The Philadelphia Negro* and Nineteenth Century Science," "Du Bois broke ranks with the white social scientists of the 1890s, who almost invariably assumed that deficiencies characteristic of the race made Negro problems quite different from other people's problems."

But that white goodwill was not always so good when others got into the story after the deaths of men like Benezet and Rush, those who saw things quite differently and began to feel that there was one big problem with slavery and all that: Negroes were in the United States. Wrong place for them. If they were sent back to the bush, all would be well. The shouting would be over, the violence against black people would end, and the trouble of reconciling two such different groups would be done with, given a few very strong moves.

This position was taken by the American Colonization Society, which wanted to send back the free black population first. They pre-figured the "back to Africa" movement that has fogged up the windows of the national house more than a few times, often ranted by black nationalists with such intensity that one would think that Negroes had thought first of the idea, especially when those West Indians deeply tainted by the autocratic manners they had picked up from their British colonizers attempted to lecture black Americans on how they should go about being authentic and why they should become obsessed with Africa.

There is nothing odd, however, about whites looking to repatriation as an easy way out of a serious problem. There is nothing odd about Negroes thinking of it deeply in times that were as harsh as those they faced during the years when the scent of Civil War battle had yet to come into the air. They had to counter the devilish ideas of religion twisted to justify slavery when they were not fighting the whites with their explanations that had satanic impact on the condition of black people. They also had to fight a southern kingdom of slavery that might well have fallen as abolitionist ideas grew in force and clarity, had not Eli Whitney's invention of the cotton gin made the processed cotton crop so lucrative that plantation owners who found themselves accumulating wealth becoming even more recalcitrant when the idea of freeing the slaves was volunteered or argued. This was another example of how technology had brought about so much trouble for colored people, starting with the improved European ships that could sail down to West Africa and from there to the West Indies and from the Caribbean to America, as J.M. Roberts points out in his *History of the World.* Those ships were essential to the trade that came in the wake of Whitney's invention.

Margaret Washington, Associate Professor of History at Cornell University, said for the PBS show *Africans in America,* "Officially, the Atlantic slave trade ends in 1808. From 1801 to 1808, in anticipation of the closing of the Atlantic trade, 39,000 Africans are brought into the United States, most of them through South Carolina, legally. After 1808, because the cotton gin has revolutionized cotton production, the illegal slave trade is still very much a factor. The domestic slave trade is creating a situation where Africans are being pushed into the frontier, and there are not enough. . . . Africans continue to come in. . . . And this continues all the way up to the Civil War."

The nature of the times and what those of goodwill, intelligence, and belief either in the environmental arguments made against racist claims for natural predispositions toward Negro social inferiority had to do battle with explains a good deal of what DuBois examined and theorized about in his work, and also explains the black nut line that has traveled its loony way from the age of slavery to the present. The disdain for intellectualism, the vulnerability to paranoid ideas about the tricks being played by those in high places, and the roller coaster inclinations to make far too much of African connections were all set in motion by the abuse of power and political authority, the ongoing impositions of bad science, and the willingness to sell out black people whenever there was money to be made or whenever much was demanded of a society that had become used to moving along with its double standards in place. This is not to say that the various black nuts and demagogues who have come to power should be excused or should be seen as less than crazy or less than demagogic; but it is to say, bluntly, that every strain of Negro American thought, good, half-good, bad, half-bad, arises from an American context in which fair play and reason took a long, long time to arrive and has yet to get all of their bags to the hotel.

African nationalism is easy to understand. In a world where slaves were still being brought into this country—men and women who were straight up Africans from illiterate and polytheistic countries and who would be transformed by the generation into Americans—the idea of Africa was not a fantasy, nor was going back or being sent back a less than real thought to Negroes during those long years before the Civil War. Africa was absolutely real. Those slaves who had forgotten all, or nearly all, of the ancestral details could see them in these amorphous Africans who came from wherever they had been captured by other Africans and brought to the market. These fresh captives did not speak English, and even the "breaking" in the Caribbean did not make them immediately attuned to anything American. They only knew that they were to go along, to learn the language, to work, and not to make trouble for fear of the kind of strong punishment that goes with "breaking." American slaves who were old or who were young, who were trying to buy their way off of the plantation or who would become runaways— risking the metal traps in the swamps, the teeth of the hounds, and the public tortures that followed capture—saw some version of their African ancestry right there in front of them, and would not forget it. What they saw as those Africans slowly became slaves (and with whom they had once shared a language with) was the arrival of the human being and the departure of the exotic. They could see these Africans laugh and cry, become swollen with children, heal from work injuries, catch colds, rear their offspring, become closer to some than others, and move through the nature of plantation life just as they did, as human beings, not talking work animals. So there was a bond, not so much to Africa itself, but to the common experience of bondage, which made it very obvious to those who ever had a chance to say anything at all that those who would try and pretend that black people came from some kind of subhuman stock, no matter how white and how mighty they might have been, such people were talking out of their backsides and stinking up the air of human discourse.

Given the ongoing tradition of speaking with forked tongues as well, I am less taken than Mr. Benjamin is by those who pretended to be interested in the education of DuBois but who actually believed that he had already stepped too far and that his academic success would mean nothing to Negroes. They are stock characters and part of a less-than-grand old tradition that Frederick Douglass discussed in his first autobiography when writing of a woman who was teaching her husband's slaves to read but was stopped by her spouse. He explained that education could make a slave unfit for his condition, bring on melancholy, anger, and resistance of one sort or another. In short, educating a slave could lead to a heap of hell and trouble. The master was Hugh Auld, to whom we will return. (One can wonder, however, if the experience had by DuBois and described in his writings could have inspired the "keep this nigger boy running" motive that recurs in Ralph Ellison's *Invisible Man*.)

What strikes me as most noteable, however, is that Rutherford B. Hayes finally submitted to DuBois's argument for academic support. After all, Hayes is the man who became president in 1877 and followed up on the example set by Andrew Johnson, at whom too much sputum can never be spat. His were the actions as president after Lincoln's assassination that set the precedent for letting the South have its way—despite being overrun with whites of whom the best that could be said was that they were traitors, lower than snakes in wagon tracks, and ready to destroy the Union if they could not have their way and keep their slaves in bondage. Johnson encouraged the Black Codes that foreshadowed the dictates of the segregated era and taught the South that it should look to keep its racist structures in forms as close to the good old days as possible—not through war, however, but through politics.

Yes, Lord: Johnson passed on an invaluable understanding of what was available. Southerners came to grasp something that they knew on one level but had not considered on another: War was fruitless, something proven by the stomping put on them by the Union Army; but politics was thick with possibilities. Losing the War of Rebellion did not mean that they had to lose their dominion over black people. No, no, no. This dominion included reestablishing the traditional recourse to intimidation and murder if, of course, left no other choice by insolent black creatures who had gotten drunk on the fact that the great Robert E. Lee had had to sit down and sign the surrender in the same courthouse room with a failed tanner and drunk, a perfect henchman for that long tall drink of polluted water from Illinois who had not been assassinated soon enough.

Though the radical Republicans of the day did Johnson and his policies in, the point had been made that what the South needed was friends in the command tower, people who had no interest in how much blood and slaughter the Union had waded through in order to maintain itself and bring down slavery. That was it: an intended shot straight through the heart of a democratic dream. No argument: Andrew Johnson was the arch bad guy. He was the actual father of the recalcitrant and unapologetically racist attitudes common to Southern politicians for more than a hundred years after the end of Reconstruction. Hawk whenever you hear his name.

Willing to sell out the rights of Southern black people by removing the protection that had made possible the imposition of democracy below the Mason-Dixon line, Hayes agreed, as Mr. Benjamin has reminded us, to recall the Federal troops and bring an end to Reconstruction, letting loose the redneck hellhounds waiting to get on the trail of Negro freedom and tear its body politic to pieces. Savage attacks occurred as soon as the soldiers were not around; home rule was established with murder.

No, his great sin was not erased by rubberstamping Black Willie for so loudly and indignantly wailing the blues at him with pen and paper, but Hayes perhaps provides a foreshadowing of what was to happen with Negroes at large when Lyndon Johnson, a former segregationist, became president and passed the most powerful package of civil rights legislation since Abraham Lincoln. Hayes also reveals—by finally unfisting the cash necessary for DuBois to finish his education—that the former president had chosen, even at what seemed the pace of an arthritic tortoise, to renege on his idea that such a well-educated Negro would mean nothing to his people at large. That he did not have to submit to the pressure put upon him by DuBois should be obvious.

There lies the great point. The young scholar had no power at all and there was no access to media, which then consisted only of newspapers and magazines, neither of which would have been interested in some self-important colored man haughtily complaining because he was denied a bit of money he thought he deserved from some white people who were obviously so generous that he felt encouraged to step out of his place. Silly Negro. I also doubt that the tone of DuBois's letters moved Hayes as much as the logic of what he had to say, and it may well have been his own submitting to that logic which prodded the old man to come through on the promise. That, after all, is what the Negro was striving for all along, a logical response to the conditions and the troubles engendered by the illogical worldviews and ways of white folks with and without power.

By the way, since he never makes mention of blues himself, however many bathtubs of them he soaked in, I sincerely doubt that DuBois and his fellow students danced to some form of early blues at Fisk. The far greater possibility is that they, like everybody else, were doing dances that grew out of the Southern Negro fiddle tradition and may well have included waltzes, which were hot stuff during those years because they put the man and woman quite close to each other, three beats to a bar.

See you at the end.

Playthell Benjamin:

—⁓—

IX: *The Souls of Black Folk:* Interpreting the Text

"Herein lie buried many things which if read with patience may show the strange meaning of being black here at the dawning of the Twentieth Century. This meaning is not without interest to you, Gentle Reader; for the problem of the Twentieth Century is the problem of the color line. I pray you, then, receive my little book in all charity, studying my words with me, forgiving mistake and foible for sake of the faith and passion that is in me, and seeking the grain of truth hidden there. . . . Before each chapter, as now printed, stands a bar of the Sorrow Songs,—some echo of haunting melody from the only American music which welled up from black souls in the dark past. And, finally, need I add that I who speak here am bone of bone and flesh of flesh of them that live within the Veil?"

Thus began "The Forethought" of *The Souls of Black Folk.*

By 1903, when *Souls* came out, DuBois had already published a first-rate study in history and a pioneering sociological study and had also published the results of sociological investigations carried out under the auspices of Atlanta University in of the South. For DuBois, who was still a professor at Atlanta University and director of the research when *Souls* hit the book stalls, these studies were the logical outgrowth of his Philadelphia study, and he was animated by the belief that African

Americans were a living laboratory in which the social scientist could study the development of an illiterate peasant people who had to adapt abruptly to one of the most complex modern civilizations in the world.

"I was going to study the facts," he tells us in the *Autobiography,* "any and all facts concerning the American Negro and his plight, and by measurement and comparison and research, work up to any valid generalizations which I could. I entered this primarily with the utilitarian object of reform and uplift; but nevertheless, I wanted to do the work with scientific accuracy. Thus in my own sociology, because of firm belief in a changing racial group, I easily grasped the idea of a changing developing society rather than a fixed social structure." However, once again the question of his religious beliefs almost became an obstacle to his professional career as a scholar, just as it had been at Wilberforce.

It was like Wilberforce all over again; everywhere there were forces trying to suffocate the free black thinker with religious dogma. It is no wonder that even today the black community is overrun with religious fanaticism; one need only watch any award ceremony honoring Afro-American achievers to see it. But DuBois would have none of that. Yet, even today Cornel West, a professor of religion who sounds like a wanna-be preacher, holds this against him, just like the church reactionaries who dominated black higher education in the 19th century, a point we will examine later when we discuss West's reply to a passage in the essay, "Of Our Spiritual Strivings."

Dr. Horace Bumstead, the white scholar who served as President of the all-black Atlanta University when they recruited DuBois in 1896, recalls that DuBois "seemed to be one of those persons who when asked about their religion, reply that they have 'none to speak of.'" But Bumstead refused to make an issue of the matter, because he had seen something in DuBois that he considered a far better indication of his character than simply professing to believe in God while acting like the devil. "I observed that at the time of my interview with him that he was living with his newly-wedded bride in the center of the Negro slums of

Philadelphia, doing the beneficent work to which Provost Harrison had called him, and I thought there were some indications of genuine religion in that fact." Here, at last, was a president of a black college who was more interested in deeds than words, and thus DuBois went down to Atlanta to build the first department of sociology dedicated to the study of Afro-American life.

Expanding on the work he had done in Philadelphia, DuBois published a series of sociological monographs that systematically investigated the status and condition of Afro-Americans in a range of activities. These studies were the product of the Atlanta University Conferences of Negro Problems, and included such titles as *Mortality among Negroes in Cities* and *Social and Physical Conditions of Negroes in Cities,* which were the first two studies in 1896-7. And David Levering Lewis lists an impressive variety of student research papers conducted under the exacting tutelage of the young scholar: "Poverty," "The Credit System," "Wages and Negroes," "The Negro as Consumer," "The Legal Position of the Negro," "The Negro Merchant in Atlanta," "The Well-to-Do in Atlanta," and "The Negro Labor in Atlanta." As can be seen from his prolific scholarship, this period of DuBois's career was happily consumed conducting social studies of black life. This is what he had trained all those years preparing to do. And he would continue publishing his own monographs based on the Atlanta conferences as well: *The Negro Artisan* (1902), *The Negro Church,* (1903), *The College Bred Negro, The Negro Landholder of Georgia* (1901), and *The Negro Farmer* (1906). Using a network of black college graduates, whom DuBois had taught his research methodology, he gathered first hand information from all over the South. DuBois carefully analyzed this data and the first reliable picture of the lives of the black freedmen in the American South began to emerge.

"From the fall of 1894 to the spring of 1910, for 16 years I was a teacher and a student of social science … and for 13 years at Atlanta University in Georgia. I sought in these years to know my world and to teach youth the meaning and way of the world. The main result of my schooling had been to emphasize science and the scientific attitude," writes DuBois. These studies, along with his two published books, would began to win DuBois a wide reputation among serious scholars and persons concerned with social policy. And just as the rich northern industrialists were streaming into Tuskegee Institute in Alabama to see "The Wizard," as its principal Booker T. Washington was known, scholars and intellectuals were finding their way to Atlanta University to visit the Doctor. Among this caravan of seekers of wisdom and truth was Columbia University sociologist Dr. Edwin Seligman, and the great German sociologist, a founder of the field, Dr. Max Weber.

The Atlanta conferences and the studies they produced not only deepened DuBois's knowledge of the problems facing blacks in the South as they tried to find their way as free men, but also brought him notoriety. Major Euro-American publications invited him to pen essays for their pages in an age when the printed word reigned supreme as a medium of mass communication. *Dial, The World's Work, The Atlantic Monthly, Harpers Weekly,* and *The Annals of the American Academy of Political and Social Sciences* were some of the publications that featured DuBois's work. In fact, some of the essays that appear in *Souls* came out first in these journals of opinion. Yet despite the grueling pace at which he produced original social studies, he also assembled and mounted an exhibit on the progress of Afro-Americans at the 1900 Paris Exposition Universelle, placing Afro-Americans before the scrutiny of the world at the dawning of the Twentieth Century—just as Frederick Douglass had done at the Chicago World's Fair in the 1890s. And after the judges rendered their judgment, Dr. DuBois had won a Gold Medal.

Following the Paris Exposition, DuBois would have an experience that would add another dimension to his life as a black man living in a world of triumphant European racism and imperialism. He attended the first Pan-African Conference. His developing interest in African affairs was a sign of intellectual growth, an indication that he was starting to see the global dimensions of African oppression. In 1885, when he began his freshman year in college, there is no mention that the Berlin Conference, where the nations of Europe carved up the African continent among themselves, was also taking place. The Pan-African Conference was a natural development given the state of the African "race" in that period of world history. Let me reiterate that I accept the current consensus that race is not a biological category but it would be silly, as well as dangerous, not to see it as a socio/political fact that continues to restrict the chances of black folks.

The idea of race as a biological fact that determined human worth was the common wisdom at the turn of the century. Indeed, the number of Afro-Americans who were being slaughtered was swelling based of this idea. DuBois says of his years at Atlanta University, "Lynching . . . was still a continuing horror in the United states at the time of my entrance upon a teaching career . . . in the 16 years of my teaching nearly 2000 persons were publicly killed by mobs, and not a single one of the murders punished." Hence DuBois, convinced that the idea of Europeans being naturally superior to the rest of humanity was murderous hokum, chose to fight the racists on the world stage.

In the *Autobiography,* he explains his gradual recognition of the ties between the American race problem and the global system of white supremacy. "I did not have any clear conception or grasp of the meaning of that colonial imperialism which was beginning to grip the world. My only approach to meanings and helpful study there again was through my interest in race contact. That interest began to clear my vision and interpret the whirl of events which swept the world. Japan was rising to national status and through the Chinese War and the Russian war, despite rivalry with Germany, Russia and Great Britain, she achieved a new status in the world, which only the United States refused to recognize. All this I began to realize was but a result of the expansion of Europe into Africa where a fierce fight was precipitated for the labor, gold and diamonds of South Africa; for the gold, cocoa, raw materials and labor of west Africa; for the exploitation of the Belgium Congo."

The Pan-African Congress of 1900, the first of five such events that would occur on European soil before the independence of Ghana in 1957, was convened by the London-based barrister, H. Sylvester Williams, at Westminster Hall in London. David Levering Lewis tells us that at this first Pan-African Congress, "DuBois was in the company of racial equals for a change: Benito Sylvan of Haiti, a Pan-African reincarnation of Talleyrand and former aide-de-camp to the Ethiopian emperor, Samuel Coleridge Taylor of London, a musical prodigy; John Alcindor of Trinidad and London, an Edinburgh trained physician and chief collaborator in Williams's African Association; and Henry Box Brown, aged hero of the Underground Railroad." There were other Afro-Americans in attendance too, including Anna Julia Cooper, Ada Harris, and AME Zion Bishop Alexander Walters.

DuBois's great moment came when he gave his speech before the Congress. Titled "To the Nations of the World," it began, "In the metropolis of the modern world, in this closing year of the nineteenth century, there has been assembled a Congress of men and women of African blood, to deliberate solemnly upon the present situation and outlook of the darker races of mankind." Then he uttered the prophetic lines that continue to underpin his reputation as a seer: "The problem of the Twentieth Century is the problem of the color line, the question of how far differences of race, which show themselves chiefly in the color of the skin and the texture of the hair, are going to be made, hereafter, the basis of denying to over half the world the right of sharing to their utmost ability the opportunities and privileges of modern civilization."

He looked on the world as it was at the dawning of this new century that promised routine miracles, and reflected on the vicissitudes of history: "To be sure the darker races are today the least advanced in culture according to European standards. This has not, however, always been the case in the past, and certainly the world's history, both ancient and modern, has given many instances of no despicable ability and capacity among the blackest of men." DuBois then offered another prophetic statement, the full meaning of which is being revealed to us as I write: "In any case, the modern world must needs remember that in this age, when the ends of the world are being brought so near together, the millions of black men in Africa, America, and the islands of the sea, not to speak of the brown and yellow myriads elsewhere, are bound to have great influence upon the world in the future, by reason of sheer numbers and physical contact. If now the world of culture bends itself towards giving Negroes and other dark men the largest and broadest opportunity for education and self-development, then this contact and influence is bound to have a beneficial effect upon the world and hasten human progress. But if, by reason of carelessness, prejudice, greed and injustice, the black world is to be exploited and ravished and degraded, the results must be deplorable, if not fatal."

There can be but little doubt that if the imperial nations of Europe—who ruled the world at the time—had followed the principles here outlined by DuBois, embracing the humanist and Christian values, the present terror that threatens disaster for the rich overdeveloped western nations might never have come to pass. For the world would surely have been a different place, and the real grievances of the Islamic peoples would have been a non-issue. However, even now, in the midst of the present crisis, far too many befuddled intellectual apologists—mostly white with a contingent of misguided coloureds—continue to offer up amoral social Darwinist arguments for western aggression against the "Third World." In this sense, the vision of the western intelligentsia as a class must be considered at best short sighted, and at worst morally blind, when compared to prophetic insight of Dr. DuBois.

D.L. Lewis got it right when he argued: "Pan-Africanism came with the Zeitgeist, an inevitable, derivative idea, at once circumspect and revolutionary. It was another movement exploding into the twentieth century like a stick of dynamite—Pan-Hellenism, Pan-Germanism, Pan-Slavism—with the Irish, Africaners, Armenians, Serbians, and other historic 'races' already lighting fuses for the new century." In other words, how could it have been otherwise? How could Africans and their kinsmen whom plantation slavery had scattered throughout the new world not have tried to build a transnational movement to resist the common disaster?

The wisdom of this effort is verified by the fact that the leaders fronting the movements that toppled the European colonial regimes on the African continent emerged from the Pan-African movement. And although honest and visionary African leaders have been consistently overthrown by western intelligence agencies (who then installed fakers, fools and murderers in their stead so long as they were willing to serve the interest of European and American multi-national corporations), the triumphant formation of the African Union during the continental congress held in the new South Africa last July 2002, vindicates the Pan-Africanist vision of a united Africa.

Thus DuBois had gained wisdom, experience, and accomplishment by the time most of his white countrymen met this erudite, mystical, poetic, and prophetic voice speaking from behind the veil, inviting them to peer into the soul of black America. "Between me and the other world there is ever an unasked question: unasked by some through feelings of delicacy; by others through the difficulty of rightly framing it. All, nevertheless, flutter round it. They approach me in half-hesitant sort of way, eye me curiously or compassionately, and then, instead of saying directly, How does it feel to be a problem? They say, I know an excellent colored man in my town; or, I fought in Mechanicsville; or, Do not these southern outrages make your blood boil? At these I smile, or am interested, or reduce the boiling to a simmer, as the occasion may require. To the real question, how does it feel to be a problem? I answer seldom a word."

With these poignant and quizzical lines from "Of Our Spiritual Strivings," the essay that begins *Souls,* DuBois affords us a chance to experience the texture of relations between even intelligent and sensitive Americans on different sides of the color line. Written during the nadir, with the trees of his southern homeland bearing strange fruit, DuBois addressed his words to the "better class" of educated whites—those who made political decisions, funded education, and hired people for the vast array of jobs being generated in an expanding industrial economy—and he hoped they had a heart as well as a brain. Thus his argument was aimed at the conscience as well as the intellect. "And yet," he tells them, "being a problem is a strange experience—peculiar even for one who has never been anything else, save perhaps in babyhood and in Europe"— which is to say before he was old enough to understand his social environment, or beyond the jurisdiction of his white countrymen.

Having seized the reader's attention with just the right dose of mystery and a hint of revelation, he recounts the moment that he came to grasp that he was a member of America's untouchable caste. "It is in the early days of rollickingly boyhood that the revelation first bursts upon one, all in a day as it were. I remember well when the shadow swept across me. I was a little thing, away up in the hills of New England. . . . In a wee wooden schoolhouse, something put it into the boys' and girls' heads to buy gorgeous visiting cards—ten cents a package—and exchange. The exchange was merry, till one girl, a tall newcomer, refused my card,—refused it peremptorily, with a glance. Then it dawned upon me with a certain suddenness that I was different from the others; or like mayhap, in heart and life and longing, but shut out from their world by a vast veil."

The young DuBois's response to this first encounter with white chauvinism would mark his reaction to white impertinence his entire life. Over half a century later, he would write of his life: "I did not seek white acquaintances, I let them make the advances, and they therefore thought me arrogant. . . . I deliberately refused invitations to spend weekends with Henry James and H.G. Wells. I did not follow up on an offer of the wife of Havelock Ellis to meet him and Bernard Shaw."

Having declared himself at the outset to be a fighting man who could take white folks or leave them, DuBois charged straight ahead with fourteen essays, each one a masterpiece. The essays can be classified by theme, and some themes have emerged as more important than others over the years. At the time of publication, the essay that sparked the most intense debate was "Of Mr. Booker T. Washington and Others," but the most enduring theme is the metaphor of "double consciousness." Adolph Reed points out in a recent study of DuBois's political thought that he abandoned this notion in his writings a few years after he introduced it, yet the idea is still debated a century later. Dr. Gerald Early has edited an entire volume examining the question of double consciousness, exploring it from the perspective of natural science, social science, law, and literature. But if Reed is right, and he has searched DuBois's *oeuvre* extensively, then this whole long discussion is much ado about nothing.

I believe the double consciousness metaphor has endured because it speaks to the enduring question of black identity in a predominantly white, racist society that has used all of its resources—political, economic, religious, and police power—to deny Afro-Americans their human rights for the first 250 years of the nation's history, and the benefits of citizenship for the next hundred years, and even now attempts to deny the consequences of this criminal history in order to avoid a just remedy. The "double consciousness" construct follows upon DuBois's discussion of his discovery of racism, as he takes the reader further into the experience of the untouchables in the America's color caste system.

> After the Egyptian and Indian, the Greek and Roman,
> the Teuton and Mongolian, the Negro is a seventh son,
> born with a veil, and gifted with a second sight in this
> American world—a world which yields him no true

self-consciousness, but only lets him see himself through
the revelation of the other world. It is a peculiar sensa-
tion, this double consciousness, this sense of always
looking at one's self through the eyes of others, of meas-
uring one's soul by the tape of a world that looks on in
amused contempt and pity. One ever feels his
twoness—an American, a Negro; two souls, two
thoughts, two unreconciled strivings; two warring ideals
in one dark body, whose dogged strength alone keeps it
from being torn asunder.

Although the language is weighted with mystical allusion, graphic
metaphor, and other literary devices used by poets, it seems to me that
his intent is clear. He is describing the tortuous experience of being subjected to continuous psychological warfare as a minority group member
and despised other in one's native land. The horror of the experience is
such that he resorts to folklore—"A seventh son born with a veil and
gifted with a second sight"—and symbolic language, in order to try to
make such a bizarre experience intelligible in human terms to his white
countrymen, who erected and maintained the racial caste system. In
other words, what it felt like to be black in America in 1903. It strikes
me as a no-brainer, really.

Perhaps the reason it seems so clear to me is because I spent nearly
a third of my life living behind the veil erected by the *Plessy vs. Ferguson*
decision (legalizing segregation in 1896), and I still feel a sense of
twoness, which is to say ambivalence about being black and American.
Furthermore, in relation to white Americans I feel that I definitely possess "a second sight" in terms of the realities of American society. The
great majority of my experience with white Americans reveals that they
have little or no understanding of the life that I, and black Americans
in general—have lived in America. And this is true of the best and
brightest whites.

In fact, what passes for history teaching in most American schools at this very hour amounts to little more than white racial mythology. That's why the overwhelming majority of white Americans, and black Americans too, know nothing of Dr. DuBois—the most interesting and consequential American humanist intellectual of the twentieth century. So, from the moment I read DuBois's "double consciousness" analysis, I felt as if he was reading my mind. Most of the convoluted discussion around the meaning of this revelatory declaration strikes me as just so much academic busy-work, churned out by academic careerists who must publish or perish.

However, there are some obvious changes in the Afro-American predicament in the U.S. at the dawn of the twenty-first century. To be sure the tendency on the part of some whites to employ pseudo-science to try and prove the biological inferiority of the "Negro race" still plagues us—at least before they completed mapping the human genome—and the predominately white media yet prefers a tale of black pathology to a story of black heroism. But there are myriad images of black mastery and genius in various fields that intrude into the heads of all who watch television, listen to radio, or read the newspapers. For instance, at the end of the nineteenth century, whites universally believed themselves to be naturally superior athletes to blacks. It seems ludicrous now, but in 1903 it was conventional wisdom—backed by a large body of "scientific" theory—that white males were superior physical specimens to black males.

Therefore it was assumed that they would easily win at any sport, including track and especially heavyweight boxing, which is why Jack Johnson's easy knockout of "White Hope" Jim Jefferies sparked murderous pogroms against black men by white mobs throughout the nation. And sprinter/hurdler Jesse Owens's multiple world records and four Olympic Gold medals set the pundits and the scientists to work manufacturing racist explanations for his achievement. Today, however, white heavyweight champion boxers and world-record sprinters—distance runners too—are about to join white running backs and wide receivers on the road to near extinction. And based on the performances of the Williams sisters, Tiger Woods, and the saber fencers in the Peter Westbrook Foundation of New York City, it's getting harder for white American athletes to compete in these sports which until recently were lily-white preserves. In a sports-mad society, the symbolism of black excellence and prowess arising from these spectacular victories on the playing fields, performed by articulate intelligent athletes, is impossible to suppress.

Moreover, there are many other conspicuous examples of Afro-American excellence, such as Colin Powell and Condoleeza Rice—the son of poor Jamaican immigrants and a black American female who grew up in Birmingham, Alabama, which was then a violently racist apartheid society—who run the foreign policy establishment in the most powerful nation in the world. With all his prophetic powers, DuBois could not have imagined such a thing. Nor could he have imagined a black C.E.O. of the largest communications conglomerate in the world, or of one of the largest brokerage firms on Wall Street, nor Dr. Allen Counter researching and teaching the biological sciences at Harvard, or Wynton Marsalis—arguably America's greatest musician—directing a jazz department at Lincoln Center, the world's greatest performing arts emporium, while recording the most acclaimed masterworks of the European classical tradition. Given the world in which he was writing a century ago, the achievements of Afro-Americans at the start of the twenty-first century are beyond DuBois's most hopeful imaginings.

The outstanding performances of Afro-Americans in a range of fields, plus the expansion and democratization of media coverage for the great of all races—though the depictions of blacks in the media are not ideal, they are light years ahead of the portrayals in DuBois's time—have altered his analysis regarding the relationship between the racist perceptions of white society and the way Afro-Americans form their self-conception. However, even considering the tenor of his time, I take exception to much of DuBois's contention that "Here in America, in the few days since Emancipation, the black man's turning hither and thither in hesitant and doubtful striving has often made his very strength to lose effectiveness, to seem like the absence of power, like weakness. And yet it is not weakness,—it is the contradiction of double aims. The double-aimed struggle of the black artisan—on the one hand to escape white contempt for a nation of mere hewers of wood and drawers of water, and on the other hand to plough and nail and dig for a poverty-stricken horde—could only result in making him a poor craftsman, for he had but half a heart in either cause."

Even taking into account that he was trying to appeal to the hearts and minds of the white majority, DuBois should have noticed that this analysis failed to take into account the excellence of his own works, as well as that of other black Americans whom he celebrated in his "Talented Tenth" essay, written earlier in the year. However, I suspect that while "the would-be black savant" might well be immobilized by a shaken self-confidence due to white contempt for his ambition and competence, the carpenter, painter, blacksmith, and mason viewed the matter differently. This is in the nature of the tasks. In my family there were many skilled craftsmen when I was a boy; they were masters of their trades and they all had black and white clients. They knew that they were superior at their crafts, and they commanded their price.

They were too happy at having escaped the fate of hod carriers and other common laborers to fret over their fortune. And, having worked on big-time construction jobs in New York, I witnessed the same cocky self-assurance on the part of skilled craftsmen, black and white. So I don't think my uncles were unusual for their class. After all, these are not men who aspire to change the world; they just want to mind their business, do a good job, and take their rest and recreation when the workaday tasks are done. Over the course of my life, I have been a professor and a member of the Society of Master Painters, and in my experience academics are more insecure about the quality of their work and how it will be received than are journeyman mechanics.

This is equally true of Afro-American performing artists—especially musicians, singers, and dancers. Hence, it does not ring true to my ears as a former bandleader who has delved in the joyous communion of music making off and on since I was a young boy, and sought the society of musicians of all sorts throughout my life, when DuBois claims that "The innate love of harmony and beauty that set the ruder souls of his people a-dancing and a-singing raised but confusion and doubt in the soul of the black artist; for the beauty revealed to him was the soul beauty of a race which his larger audience despised." While his description of the nature of the revelation experienced by musicians, which they convert into art, is true enough, he misses the mark totally in describing their feelings about their role as artist, or how the "larger audience"—who were not their primary audience anyway—received it.

In order to get the real deal, DuBois—who was stuck in Wilberforce, Ohio, Philadelphia, or Atlanta—should have been on the scene at the Marshall Hotel in mid-Manhattan, the home of James Reese Europe's Cleft Club, and the headquarters of his great contemporary James Weldon Johnson—an Afro-American Renaissance man who was a lawyer, diplomat, poet, novelist, memoirist, librettist, founding member of ASCAP, and the first black executive secretary of the NAACP. During the period at the end of the 19th century when DuBois was writing the essays that would evolve into *The Souls of Black Folk,* J. W. Johnson was helping to shape the American popular song as lyricist to the music of his composer brother J. Rosamond Johnson; together they produced popular hits like "Under the Bamboo Tree," and the immortal "Lift Every Voice and Sing," an eight-stanza art song that is as good an example of an authentic American lieder—as opposed to a European imitation—as one is likely to find.

As far back as I can remember, this song was sung at the opening of all important events in the Afro-American community, often in the place of the "Star-Spangled Banner," since it was popularly known as "The Negro National Anthem." And, by the way, it is a far more beautiful and humanistic song than the jingoistic "Star-Spangled Banner." The widespread acceptance of this composition as the national anthem for black folk, lends the lie to those who argue that before the rise of "identity politics" in 1960s black Americans saw themselves as one with white Americans.

In any case, by the end of the 19th century, Afro-American musicians knew that they were on to something unique and something grand. Noble Sissle, who would hook up with the great pianist composer Eubie Blake and produce such early twentieth-century standards as "Memories of You" and "I'm Just Wild About Harry"—which Harry Truman would use as his presidential campaign song several decades later—recalls that Afro-American music began to dominate the New York music scene to the extent that black musicians were preferred even by the high society crowd. The center of this creative flowering (which reached its apex two decades before the Harlem Renaissance) was the area of mid-Manhattan known as San Juan Hill—an Afro-American enclave established after they were driven out of Greenwich Village, where black new Yorkers had previously converted a malarial swamp into a livable area of Manhattan—particularly within a two-block area know as "Black Bohemia." This community of Afro-American performing artists congregated at the black-owned Marshall hotel, which was the nerve center and staging area for this artistic community.

James Weldon Johnson offers an insider's view of the creative milieu in Black Bohemia in his autobiography *Along This Way:* "The Marshall gradually became New York's center for Negro artist. For a generation that center had been in Negro Bohemia, down in the Tenderloin. There, in various clubs, Negro theatrical and musical talent foregathered. The clubs of Negro Bohemia were of diverse sorts . . . there were clubs frequented particularly by the followers of ring and turf, where one got a close-up of the noted Negro prize fighters and jockeys; there were 'professional' clubs, that served as meeting places and exchanges for Negro theatrical performers. Among the clubs . . . were some that bore a social aspect corresponding to that of the modern nightclub. These had their regular habitués, but the also enjoyed a large patronage of white sight-seers and . . . white theatrical performers on the lookout for 'Negro stuff,' and, moreover, a considerable clientele of white women who had or sought to have colored lovers."

Johnson also describes the work schedule they kept as creative artists generating material for the performing artist. "Bob Cole lived two doors from the Marshall, and that made it convenient for the trio to work together. We worked according to a schedule. We rose between nine and ten o'clock, breakfasted at about eleven, and began work not later than twelve. When we didn't go to the theater, our working period approxi-mated ten hours a day. We spent the time in actual writing or in planning future work. In our room and without stopping work, we snatched a bite to eat. . . . Always we went downstairs for a midnight supper. . . . Sometimes it consisted of planked steak or broiled lobster . . . the gay air of the dining room, gayer around midnight than at any other hour, stimulated us." Sounds just like heaven to me. Although DuBois clearly dropped the ball in his characterization of the inner yearnings, or spiritual strivings, of Afro-American musicians as a class, his location in black academia rather than Black Bohemia provides a clue to his pessimistic vision.

Whereas the academic musician situated in the black college was hired to teach a curriculum developed by the professional association of music teachers, which was totally devoted to European art music, the musical artists in New York were involved in creating a new music which was quintessentially American. This emerging musical art employed different song forms, instrumental technique, orchestral instrumentation and voicings, and especially the syncopated rhythms, or "ragged" time signatures. This was the golden age of live perform-ance. Television, radio, records and talking movies had yet to be invented. But the theater, concert and dance halls were booming and New York was rapidly emerging as the show business capitol of the world. Hence the greatest performers congregated in New York City, from whence shows were assembled and shipped out to the hinterland and across the ocean to Europe.

Thus the musicians that gathered at the Marshall Hotel were broadly trained, several—like Will Marion Cooke, Harry T. Burliegh, J. Rosamond Johnson, et al.—were thoroughly conversant with European classical music. Cooke, who was arguably the greatest American violinist at the turn of the century, had studied with Joseph Joachim, whom many considered Europe's reigning master of the violin and the greatest interpreter of the scores of Brahms and Schumann, and Burliegh had studied with the great European master Antonin Dvorak. In fact it was Burliegh who introduced the famous Bavarian composer to the spirituals, and the effect of this music upon Dvorak's own compositions can be clearly heard in the hauntingly beautiful theme of Symphony From the New World.

With the blessing of Dvorak—who declared to the dismay of white American cultural chauvinists that Afro-American music contained all the ingredients necessary to the development of a national, fine–art music—these musicians had put aside their involvement with European forms and were consciously searching for a uniquely Afro-American voice in western music; while their counterparts, stuck in conventional college music departments, agonized over trying to repeat the achievement of Beethoven or Bach. Thence lay the source of the angst that DuBois saw. This attitude was alive and well over half a century later when the writer Imiri Baraka, a.k.a. Leroy Jones, attended Howard University. In an essay entitled "Philistinism and the Negro Writer," Baraka recalls the attitude of the music department during his student days in the 1950s: "For instance, the teacher in charge of the music school there told professor Sterling Brown, and some others who wanted to organize a jazz concert at Howard, that jazz never, never would be played in the Music and Art building." The tragic irony was that this great American art music that Dvorak had prophesized would grow from the black tradition was rejected by a black professor and dean in the top black university in the world.

This must have scandalized Sterling Brown, a poet, critic, and professor of literature who was fond of inviting jazz pianist to perform for his students, and whom Leadbelly praises in his classic blues "Washington Is a Bourgeois Town." Yet there was one great body of Afro-American music that would command the attention of the cultural nationalists in the New York avant-garde and the academicians in black colleges, the body of sacred slave music that DuBois immortalized in "Of the Sorrow Songs," the most moving essay in *The Souls of Black Folk*.

While the great Afro-American musicians transcribed these songs and arranged them in the grand choral and operatic style—Harry Burliegh and Roasmond Johnson both published volumes of scores that set the standard—and every classically trained Afro-American singer—from the great contralto Marion Anderson, who named her autobiography after one of these songs, to the peerless Wagnarian soprano Jessye Norman— has performed them, no one has ever written of their meaning with the passion, eloquence, and clarity of the young DuBois.

In an essay redolent with wisdom and beauty, DuBois explained the relationship of the spirituals to the inspiration and design of his book: "They that walked in darkness sang songs in the olden days—Sorrow Songs—for they were weary at heart. And so before each thought that I have written in this book I have set a phrase, a haunting echo of these weird old songs in which the soul of the black slave spoke to men." This declaration tells us from the outset that he conceived of these songs as the musical texts of an epic drama played out on American soil for two and a half centuries, and that this drama—a titanic struggle between righteousness and evil, master and slave—was a force in shaping the character and sensibility of the new American nation called the United States.

Furthermore, for DuBois, the best and most humane expression of the sensibility arising from that great moral struggle came from the black slaves and is embodied in the "Sorrow Songs." "Little beauty has America given the world save the rude grandeur God himself stamped on her bosom; the human spirit in this new world has expressed itself in vigor and ingenuity rather than in beauty. And so by fateful chance the Negro folk-song—the rhythmic cry of the slaves—stands today not simply as the sole American music, but as the most beautiful expression of human experience born this side of seas . . . the singular spiritual heritage of the nation and the greatest gift of the Negro people."

Although DuBois apologizes for his lack of musical knowledge in the explication of these songs, I find his grasp of music superior to the majority of literary lions and social scientists—Albert Murray, Stanley Crouch, and George Bernard Shaw being notable exceptions. But when one is capable of capturing the spirit of an art form as DuBois does in the following passage, specialized knowledge is irrelevant. "What are these songs, and what do they mean? I know little of music and can say nothing in technical phrase, but I know something of men, and knowing them, I know that these songs are the articulate message of the slave to the world. They tell us in these eager days that life was joyous to the black slave, careless and happy . . . but not all the past south, though it rose from the dead, can gainsay the heart-touching witness of these songs. They are the music of an unhappy people, of the children of disappointment; they tell of death and suffering and unvoiced longing toward a truer world, of misty wanderings and hidden ways."

It is clear that DuBois's discussion of this music is not some cold intellectual exercise, but a revelation of the heart. Indeed this passion, which can only come from an engaged intellectual, informs all of his work. The power of DuBois's prose is a product of his involvement in the fight to vindicate the humanity of black people against the barrage of racist propaganda, and to uplift the race. This kind of engagement is beyond the comprehension of many highly paid contemporary black intellectuals, whose narcissistic obsession with being accepted as an equal by their white colleagues saps so much of their emotional energy that there is nothing left to expend on the kind of issues that so moved DuBois.

A classic example of this emotional vacuousness is on display in Gerald Early's book, *Daughters*. As the director of Afro-American

Studies at Washington University, a major white academy in the Midwest, a celebrated essayist, and ubiquitous commentator on African American affairs, Early tells us, "Naturally, as a college professor who runs a black-studies program, my house is filled to the rafters with books by and about black people. I probably own more such books than anyone else in St. Louis. . . . Yet there is, with rare exception, something dispassionate, detached, something that seems curiously without the intensity of identification. My children are awash in exposure to African American culture. . . . But this has little emotional impact on them—perhaps because there is little emotional impact of any of this knowledge on me." It is no wonder, as he tells throughout the book, that his daughters have no black friends and can think of no reason why they should.

In contrast to deracinated, wishy-washy bourgeois colored savants like Professor Early, DuBois was committed to his people and felt their joy and pain in his soul. Upon first hearing the spirituals, for instance, he tells us, "Ever since I was a child these songs have stirred me strangely. They came out of the South unknown to me, one by one, and yet at once I knew them as of me and mine." To cultural assimilationists like Early, this probably sounds like "race memory," a thoroughly discredited concept in their eyes. But I felt the same way when I heard these songs many years later. I broke out in gooseflesh as I listened to the pathos evoked by the minor keys in which they are pitched, and though I was yet a child could feel the pain of its authors, whom somebody told me had lived "back in slavery times."

Thereafter I thought of them when I walked by the old slave market, which still stands in the town square in St. Augustine, Florida, where I grew up. And when I heard the blind chorus from the State School for the Deaf and Blind sing "Nobody Knows the Troubles I've Seen," I wept like the Union General who heard the ex-slaves sing it at Port Royal, South Carolina, after he announced that the government intended to return the land they were tilling to their former masters—who had only recently committed treason against that very government. Even as I write, tough guy that I am, tears well in my eyes while reading DuBois's discourse on the meaning of the message in these slave songs, while Marion Anderson sings "I Couldn't Hear Nobody Pray" in that deep, rich, unspeakably beautiful contralto voice which the late Maestro of he great Philadelphia Symphony Orchestra Leo Stokowski declared "is heard once in a century."

If hard-boiled Euro-American soldiers like Thomas Wentworth Higginson could feel the spirituals in their souls, then any black American who can boast of having no emotional reaction to the experience that gave birth to them sure has a hole in his soul! It is over-privileged, self-absorbed, emotionally remote, prima donnas like Professor Early and others of his ilk—such as Harvard's Randall Kennedy, author of the recently published book *Nigger*—and intellectual quislings like Uncle Justice Thomas, that prompted Dr. DuBois to eventually reconsider his previous hopes that the "Talented Tenth" would lead the untutored masses to the promised land of freedom and equality in their American house of bondage.

But in 1903, DuBois could never have imagined the development of soulless careerists without empathy for struggles of the striving masses. Early, for instance, tells us that his newfound bourgeois life in the white suburbs alienated him from his own family who remained in Philadelphia and were "poor or working-class, who seemed loud and crude, who lived in tiny houses in run-down neighborhoods. Unwed mothers, people who spoke the word nigger, who liked to jive around." And his daughters, "ran away from my uncle George, deeply frightened by his raucous laughter . . . I stood guard over them, over protective and wary, as if I thought my relatives might wound them, might injure them in a clumsy 'niggerish' way. Perhaps my children's awkwardness and unhappiness merely mirrored my own." Yet he wonders in this same text why his black students don't like him; perhaps it's because they see what I see.

What is especially irritating about Gerald Early's discussion of his family is that I knew three of his aunts, Lois, Laura, and Vickie, and his sister Lenora, well. These aunts were public school teachers and his sister would later become a teacher. During the sixties when I lived in Philadelphia, I often had occasion to work with them on cultural projects in the black community. I met no more charming, intelligent and community-minded ladies in Philadelphia than them, and although I have not spoken with them in years I imagine that they must be deeply wounded that "Jerry"—as he is known to his family—does not mention them or their work in his disdainful, sneering, portrait of the family. Although he admits in the book that they were not all damaged goods, he chooses to allow these splendid ladies to stay invisible.

Perhaps it is because they were "Afrocentric," being founders of the Yoruba Temple and the great annual African Odunde celebration in Philadelphia, and "Jerry" makes a point of telling us: "I am not Afrocentric. I do not celebrate 'African' ceremonies, so African American culture is not celebrated in my house." Well, I am not Afrocentric either, in the academic sense of the term, but we do celebrate African-American culture in my house. Of course, Professor Early has the right to think and do whatever he pleases, so long as he is not breaking the law. But one cannot help wondering why he is directing a black studies department? It would seem to me on the basis of his own testimony that he would be better suited to teach in some other department where he feels some real commitment to his subject, such as chairman of Bloomsbury studies. But it is doubtful that he could have the power elsewhere that he has in his present position, which affords him the opportunity to live in a mansion and get lucrative consultant jobs as an "authority" on "black" issues. Sounds like old-fashioned pimping to me, especially since he often has nothing of substance to say. A case in point is the comment he makes in Ken Burns's PBS series *Jazz*. On this occasion, Professor Early informs us that the only things the U.S. "has invented is baseball and jazz." I wondered how he could have overlooked Atomic energy, moon shots, skyscrapers, and the assembly line for starters.

At various points in his later years, DuBois warned that certain members of the black bourgeoisie were starting to ape the class snobbishness among white Americans. And "Jerry Early" is so far gone that he has no shame. Ironically, Early grew up in the Seventh Ward, where DuBois did his study half a century earlier, attended the University of Pennsylvania, and thus became one of the "Talented Tenth"—an idea about which we will have more to say—on whom he had placed the hope of the race in 1903. At the time, neither he, nor any other sane person, could have foreseen the advent of a class of neurotic black intellectual lickspittles such as Gerald Early, Clarence Thomas, Walter Williams, Thomas Sowell, et al., because DuBois was cut from different and better cloth.

The reader can feel the love in DuBois's remembrance of how he felt when he arrived at Fisk, the home of the world-famous Jubilee Singers, and his description of how the nation first came to hear of the "Sorrow Songs." After recounting how the "Spirituals" had bewitched him as a boy, he goes on to tells us: "Then in after years when I came to Nashville I saw the great temple builded of these songs towering over the pale city. To me Jubilee Hall seemed ever made of the songs themselves, and its bricks were red with blood and dust of toil. Out of them rose for me morning, noon and night, bursts of wonderful melody, full of the voices of the past. . . . Away back in the thirties the melody of these slave songs stirred the nation, but the songs were soon half forgotten. . . . Then in war-time came the singular Port Royal experiment after the capture of Hilton Head, and perhaps for the first time the North met the Southern slave face to face and heart to heart with no third witness."

Then, in a passage of uncommon erudition and eloquence, he tells of the meeting of soldier, slave, and tutor amid the destruction and dislocation in the aftermath of civil war. "The Sea Islands of the Carolinas, where they met, were filled with a black folk of primitive type, touched and moulded less by the world about them than any others outside the black belt. Their appearance was uncouth, their language funny, but their hearts were human and their singing stirred men with a mighty power. Thomas Wentworth Higginson hastened to tell of these songs, and Miss McKim and others urged upon the world their rare beauty. But the world listened only half credulously until the Fisk Jubilee singers sang the slave songs so deeply into the world's heart that it can never wholly forget them again." Here DuBois is alluding to the poignant descriptions of Afro-American singing in Higginson's classic text *Army Life in a Black Regiment.* An abolitionist who commanded Afro-American troops in the Civil War, Higginson heard black singing in a way that was rare for northern whites. And Lucy McKim, who was a trained musician, had tried to notate the songs using the Aeolian harp, but was as bewildered by the unusual tones as later conventionally trained musicians would be when trying to notate the solos of Theolonius Monk.

DuBois then relates the fantastic tale of the rise of the Fisk Jubilee Singers, an epic that begins with a Euro-American man, George L. White, who heard the spirituals sung by ex-slaves and found his destiny. A native of New York State, White fought in the Union Army, experiencing combat in several major battles, and after the war became an administrator for the Freedman's Bureau in Nashville. "Here he formed a Sunday-school class of black children in 1866," writes DuBois, "and sang with them and taught them to sing. And then they taught him to sing, and when once the glory of the Jubilee songs passed into the soul of George L. White, he knew his life-work was to let those Negroes sing to the world as they had sung to him." The essay goes on to chronicle their journey from ragtag ensemble who were called "Nigger Minstrels" in the New York newspapers, and denied accommodations in northern hotels—southern hotels were out of the question—to triumphant command performances "across the sea, before Queen and Kaiser. . . . Seven years they sang, and brought back a hundred and fifty thousand dollars to found Fisk University." This college later became the Alma Mater of DuBois and later his Pulitzer-

Prize-winning biographer David Levering Lewis, among countless other Afro-American, West Indian, and African professionals.

While the Jubilee Singers yet continue to sing these songs, continuing a tradition of 131 years of performance, by the early twentieth century the artists who became most identified with the spirituals were the world-renowned, classically-trained tenor Roland Hayes and the basso profundo Paul Robeson, who developed his art in the vernacular tradition of the black community. In his book, *Slave Culture,* a uniquely learned treatise that explores the African roots of Afro-American culture, Sterling Stuckey observes that Hayes and Robeson differed from the Jubilee Singers in that they were soloists singing only with an accompanist on piano. But he also observes a crucial difference in the approach each artist brought to the interpretation of the music: "In contrast to Roland Hayes, the greatest interpreter of the spirituals after Robeson, Robeson wanted to preserve the beauty of the 'black voice,' which could not be done by employing the techniques of another tradition." Although I appreciate the point that Stuckey is trying to make here, I would argue that the black voice does not lose its unique beauty because the singer studies classical technique.

Let the academics holler and scream about the evils of "racial essentialism" all they like—and often they are right about the devils that lurk in the details of such arguments—I insist that the black voice has unique qualities which remain even after years of classical training, and the musically tutored ear can hear it. Some folks believe the special sound produced by black singers like Marian Anderson, Leyontine Price, Simon Estes and Robeson results from the thickness of the lips—a feature that was long a subject of ridicule by white folks before collagen injections became all the rage—while other folks believe it is the special timbres and blues intonations absorbed from a life time of listening to other singers in the black tradition.

While I am not prepared to resolve the controversy here, after a half century of listening to great singers—first in my aunt Marie's parlor as she gave voice lessons to a host of gifted singers from the high school, the local black college, and assorted church singers, then as a member of choral ensembles, later on the recital stage, and finally on the band stand with Jean Carn—I know there is a special warmth and beauty to the black voice. Some would confine this gift to Afro-American singers alone, but anyone who has heard the great Afro-Puerto Rican soprano Martina Arroyo, or the virtuosi of the Afro-Cuban Son like Arsenio Rodriquez and Celia Cruz, or the fabulous South African songstress Miriam Mekeba, knows it isn't so.

Furthermore, while Paul Robeson did indeed have a black sound, his approach to singing had more to do with the recital hall than the gospel tradition of the black church or the blues tradition of the dance hall—as the disastrous recording of Richard Wright-authored blues with the great Count Basie Band will verify. Anyone who has heard marvelous gospel virtuosos like Mahalia Jackson and Rev. James Cleveland, or authentic blues shouters like Jimmy Rushing, a.k.a. "Mr. Five by Five," or Joe "Everyday I Got Tha Blues" Williams, accompanied by the hard swinging Basie band, will see that Robeson was way out of his element.

Stuckey's analysis of how the residual African elements in the New Jersey black communities where Robeson grew up shaped his approach to singing the spirituals is impressive. However, Zora Neale Hurston, a folklorist—trained by Columbia University anthropologist Franz Boaz, the founder of American anthropology—who grew up in the far more African milieu of all-black Eatonville, Florida, thought that Robeson's rendition of the spirituals was no more authentic than Roland Hayes. In fact, she ridiculed them both for what she considered their Eurocentric style, and bragged that there was "a potato head man" down in Eatonville who would run them all off the stage singing spirituals. Hence I think it best to say that there is a black sound that all black singers who grow up in black cultural environments manage to acquire by some artistic alchemy, whatever style of music they sing. When I worked with Jean Carne for instance, she was singing rhythm and blues songs written by the Hall of Fame Philadelphia songwriters Gamble and Huff, but she had won a national Opera contest at eighteen, and was making superb jazz recordings when I first heard her, plus she was an arresting gospel singer too. Yet in whatever genre she sang, I heard that special magic that makes the great black female voice a beautiful vocal instrument that moves the spirit to dance.

These are the voices that DuBois heard at Fisk, and it was this experience, which occurred before the "emergence" of Robeson as a concert artist, that inspired DuBois to become "a major interpreter of the spirituals" as Professor Stuckey rightly puts it. The real reason the spirituals had such a hypnotic effect on the world—wide audiences before whom Robeson sang, was that he was so much more than a singer; he was the personification of DuBois's ideal of the "Talented Tenth." In fact, Robeson, a quintessentially West African phenotype, was the Greek ideal of human perfection: a magnificent athlete with a brilliant mind. A gifted actor, singer and orator, men of many races admired him and women of all nations adored him. And just as DuBois set the standard for the engaged intellectual in twentieth-century America, Robeson was a paragon of the engaged athlete and artist.

On many occasions, Robeson would testify to the defining influence DuBois had on his own intellectual and political development. The only person with a stronger influence was his father, the remarkable Reverend William Drew Robeson, a brilliant Ibo who escaped from slavery as a teen and acquired a classical education, growing fluent in Greek and Latin, which he passed on to his son. Robeson idealized this learned and heroic man with the melodious bass voice, who danced around in his pulpit like an African shaman when the spirit of the Lord moved him, and was driven from his beloved church for standing up to the rich white folk of Princeton on behalf of his flock. When no longer allowed to make a living as a preacher, the Rev. Robeson bought a horse and wagon and began to haul ashes, maintaining the same unassailable dignity. Paul would later say of him in his 1957 memoir *Here I Stand*: 'That a so-called lowly station in life was no bar to man's assertion of his full human dignity was heroically demonstrated by my father."

In an article published in the winter 1965 edition of *Freedomways,* Robeson would write of DuBois's effect on him and his generation of Afro-Americans. "Casting my mind back," he recalls, "my first clear memory of Dr. DuBois was my pride in his recognized scholarship and authority in his many fields of work and writing. In high school and at college our teachers often referred us to standard reference works on sociology, race relations, Africa and world affairs. I remember feeling great pride when the books and articles proved to be by our Dr. DuBois, and often loaned them to my fellow students, who were properly impressed." He and fellow students joined the NAACP and read the journal *The Crisis,* of which DuBois, their Professor and their Doctor, was a gifted editor.

These are the kind of young people DuBois had in mind when he argued so passionately in favor of a liberal academic education for black youngsters who showed the intellectual capacity to succeed, in "Of Mr. Booker T. Washington and Others," the most controversial essay in *Souls,* which, along with the Reverend Thomas Dixon's hysterically racist screed, *The Leopard's Spots,* was one of the two most incendiary books published in 1903. And they came from diametrically opposed positions on the question of race in America. While I cannot say for certain, I believe that there does not exist another essay in which so much of consequence is said in a mere seventeen and a half pages—or said so well. The essay is broadly learned, relentlessly honest, courageous to the point of bravado, and exhibits the same scrupulous evenhandedness that DuBois first displayed in his Harvard baccalaureate address. And if it seems all these things to me now, a century after its publication, one can imagine what a powerful impact it must have had on the debate over race and rights at the beginning of the last century.

When DuBois published this learned polemical essay, the white power elite, in the north and south, was backing Booker T. Washington as the lone spokesman for black hopes in America. And this backing was not simply lip service, but supported by cold cash and political clout. In fact, so committed was the American Plutocracy to the success of Washington's approach to "industrial" education, that they richly endowed Tuskegee while much older, and much better, black colleges struggled to survive. While the South was yet binding up its wounds from the economic devastation wrought by the Civil War, the northern industrialists were pouring capital into the underdeveloped region. A basic goal was to establish racial peace, because businessmen like to conduct their transactions in a tranquil social environment.

Hence Booker T., whose counsel of patience and humility to his fellow Afro-Americans, was their man. And they backed his projects by pouring money into Tuskegee Institute, located in the violent black belt of Alabama. By the time DuBois spoke out against the "Tuskegee Machine," Washington was considered the sole legitimate leader of black America, and his powerful white patrons were willing and able to wreck the careers of any Afro-American who vocally opposed his ideas, and buy out newspapers that criticized Washington's program—which seemed to offer the only alternative to permanent race war in the former Confederate states. And the mind of the South was becoming the mind of the nation, causing the status of black folks in the north to decline as the white backlash against the gains of "Radical Reconstruction" spread. Hence publishing an essay like "Of Mr. Booker T. Washington and Others" in 1903 was an act of singular courage, further demonstrating the extent of DuBois's commitment to the uplift of his people, whose position in America was fast losing ground.

The essay begins with DuBois's generous acknowledgement of the success of Booker T. Washington: "Easily the most striking thing in the history of the Negro since 1876 is the ascendancy of Mr. Booker T. Washington." Then he describes the historical context of Washington's rise to prominence: "It began at the time when war memories and ideals were rapidly passing; a day of astonishing commercial development was dawning; a sense of doubt and hesitation overtook the Freedman's sons,—then it was that his leading began." The great virtue of all the essays in this collection is the delicate balance between the voices of the poet, prophet, historian, and social scientist in the narrative. But, depending upon the question to be explicated, some voices are naturally more prominent than others. Hence, although the sociologist and economist take the lead in the present essay, the poet and prophet are ever present.

From the outset, DuBois seeks to portray Washington's success as the product of a man who is consistent with his times, a man whose approach to the nation's most vexing social problem—race relations—embodied the zeitgeist of the era. "Mr. Washington came with a simple definite programme, at the psychological moment when the nation was a little shame of having bestowed so much sentiment on Negroes, and was concentrating its energies on dollars." DuBois went on to show that the ideas which melded into the philosophy of the Wizard of Tuskegee—"industrial education, conciliation of the south, and submission and silence as to the question of civil and political rights"—came from various sources and were "not wholly original." Nevertheless, DuBois argues, "Mr. Washington first indissolubly linked these things; he put enthusiasm, and unlimited energy, and perfect faith into his programme, and changed it from a by-path into a veritable way of life." These principles, as DuBois points, out were succinctly stated in Washington's 1895 speech at the "World Exposition of Cotton Growing State," in which he said, "In all things purely social we can be as separate as the fingers, and yet one as the hand in all things essential to mutual progress." A native southerner who had risen from slavery—an epic American success story chronicled in his autobiography *Up From Slavery*—Washington understood the mentality of southern whites, particularly their obsession with "social equality" for Afro-Americans, hence he alleviated their fears with two well-placed lines. So potent was this southern white male obsession (that black men would be viewed by women as equals with white southern males) that Ralph Ellison, who attended Tuskegee in the 1940s, would parody this fear in the Battle Royal scene at the opening of his novel *Invisible Man,* a canonical text in twentieth-century American literature.

Assessing the reaction of the nation to Washington's ideas, DuBois tells us: "It startled the nation to hear a Negro advocating such a programme after many decades of complaint; it startled and won the applause of the South, it interested and won the admiration of the North; and after a confused murmur of protest, it silenced if it did not convert the Negroes themselves." DuBois points out that the success of Washington's program required him to first win the approval of the various factions in southern society, then gain the support of the ruling elite in the North. And he observes: "Others less shrewd and tactful had formerly essayed to sit on these stools and had fallen between them; but as Mr. Washington knew the heart of the south from birth and training, so by singular insight he intuitively grasped the spirit of the age which was dominating the North."

This portrait of Washington as a quintessential man of his age, and DuBois's insistence that it was key to understanding Washington's philosophy and leadership style, was echoed by Kelly Miller, a black scholar who taught mathematics and sociology at Howard University, and had become a dean by 1908, when he published the essay "Radicals and Conservatives" in his book *Race Adjustment.* In an effort to show how the character of radical and conservative tendencies in Afro-American leadership reflected the tenor of the times, Kelly contrasts the leadership style of Frederick Douglass with that of Washington: "Douglass lived in the day of moral giants; Washington lives in the era of merchant princes. The contemporaries of Douglass emphasized the rights of man; those of Washington, his productive capacity. The age of Douglass acknowledged the sanction of the Golden

Rule; that of Washington worships the Rule of Gold. The equality of men was constantly dinned into Douglass's ears; Washington hears nothing but the inferiority of the Negro and the dominance of the Saxon." This argument, published five years after *Souls,* was a convincing elaboration of DuBois's theory of Washington's leadership style. Kelly also had some things to say on the DuBois/Washington controversy, which we will examine later.

As an intellectual with an elite education, DuBois is appalled by the fact that Washington had "so thoroughly" absorbed the "speech and thought of triumphant commercialism, and the ideals of material prosperity, that the picture of a lone boy poring over a French grammar amid the woods and dirt of a neglected home soon seemed to him the acme of absurdities." He then muses in disgust: "One wonders what Socrates and St. Francis of Assisi would think of this." With the objectivity he always brought to the observation of human behavior, he observes: "And yet this singleness of vision and thorough oneness with his age is a mark of the successful man. It is as though nature must make men narrow in order to give them force. So Mr. Washington's cult has gained unquestioning followers, his work has wonderfully prospered, his friends are legion, and his enemies are confounded."

However, while respectful of Washington's achievements on behalf of the race, DuBois felt that there were aspects of the "Tuskegee Philosophy" that demanded criticism from educated and thoughtful members of the race, and failure to do so, either because of cowardice or a false sense of racial solidarity, was a dereliction of their duty to Afro-Americans and the nation. But he still thought, in 1903 at least, that such criticism should be carefully targeted. "And yet the time is come when one may speak in all sincerity and utter courtesy of the mistakes and shortcomings of Mr. Washington's career, as well as of his triumphs, without being thought captious or envious, and without forgetting that it is easier to do ill than well in the world." It must have come as quite a shock to most white Americans, who had been convinced by a well-coordinated and persistent press blitz that Washington was some sort of black Moses who would deliver America from the race problem, to learn that many Afro-Americans strongly disagreed with him.

"Among his own people, however," DuBois wrote, "Mr. Washington has encountered the strongest and most lasting opposition, amounting at times to bitterness, and even today continuing strong and insistent even though largely silenced in outward expression by the public opinion of the nation." Although he conceded that "Some of this opposition is, of course, mere envy; the disappointment of displaced demagogues and the spite of narrow minds," he still felt that silencing Washington's critics through various forms of intimidation was a far graver offense. "But the hushing of the criticism of honest critics is a dangerous thing. It leads some of the best of the critics to unfortunate silence and paralysis of effort, and others to burst into speech so passionately and intemperately as to lose listeners."

Here DuBois would offer an observation on the relationship of unvarnished criticism to the success of democracy, a link that those who lived through Stalinist Russia, the Chinese Cultural Revolution, successive African and South American dictatorships, and the American South, would also discover. "Honest and earnest criticism from those whose interests are most nearly touched—criticism of writers by readers, of government by those governed, of leaders by the led—this is the soul of democracy and the safe guard of modern society." And in a fascinating display of balanced judgment he observes: "If the best of the American Negroes receive by outer pressure a leader whom they had not recognized before, manifestly there is a certain palpable gain. Yet there is also irreparable loss—a loss of that particularly valuable education which a group receives when by search and criticism it finds and commissions its own leaders."

In his inimitable way, DuBois calls upon his vast knowledge of Afro-American history and presents a capsule analysis of Afro-American leadership styles and ideological objectives from the middle of the eighteenth century to the dawn of the twentieth. We learn that "Before 1750, while the fire of African freedom still burned in the veins of the slaves, there was in all leadership or attempted leadership but the one motive of revolt and revenge." But, "The liberalizing tendencies of the latter half of the eighteenth century brought, along with kindlier relations between black and white, thoughts of ultimate adjustment and assimilation." However, at the turn of the 18th century, after the Revolutionary War in which thousands of black soldiers fought to establish the new nation, DuBois tells us: "The disappointment and impatience of the Negroes at the persistence of slavery and serfdom voiced itself in two movements." One movement took the form of armed slave revolts, the other expressed itself in institution building such as the African Methodist Episcopal church—"an organization still living and controlling in its various branches over a million men." After tracing black leadership through the 19th century, DuBois says: "Then came the new leader. Nearly all the former ones had become leaders by the silent suffrage of their fellows, had sought to lead their own people alone. . . . But Booker T. Washington arose as essentially the leader of not one race but two,—a compromiser between the South, the North, and the Negro."

The nature of this compromise, DuBois argued, was that Afro-Americans would sacrifice political and civil rights in return for economic gains. "This is an age of unusual economic development, and Mr. Washington's programme naturally takes an economic cast, becoming a gospel of work and money to such an extent as apparently almost completely to overshadow the higher aims of life." The dangers to the moral and intellectual development of the nation posed by the single-minded obsession with making money, is a recurrent theme in these essays. One finds it in "On the Wings of Atalanta," a poetic allegory based on Greek mythology, in which DuBois warns, "Atlanta must not lead the south to dream of material success; already the fatal might is beginning to spread; it is replacing the finer type of southerner with vulgar money-getters; it is burying the sweeter beauties of southern life beneath pretence and ostentation. For every social ill the panacea of wealth has been urged. . . . wealth as the end and aim of politics, and as the legal tender for law and order; and, finally, instead of truth, beauty, and goodness, wealth as the ideal of the public school."

Nowhere is DuBois's gift of prophecy more clear than in this passage on Atlanta. For as I write, the stock market is crashing after an unprecedented period of prosperity in which it seems virtually everyone who bought stocks possessed the Midas touch. But now, as the dirty deeds of "creative accountants" done in the dark of corporate counting rooms come to light, we see that much of the wealth of the blue chip multi-nationals is an illusion, bred by the smoke and mirrors of white-collar gangsters. It seems that every month brings sad tidings announcing the implosion and impending bankruptcy of a giant corporation, because the top executives have looted the company and lied about its profits. And according to press reports, most of these corporate thieves get to keep the money even as poor pensioners postpone retirement and others face a future of poverty after a lifetime of employment and responsible citizenship.

In a civilization which exalts the businessman above the poet, scholar, artist, or statesman who is to teach public morality to the youth? The ethical culture of America is rapidly decaying—and all for the love of money. Decay does not stop at the top; it infects the entire body politic and even corrupts the art of the folk. We need look no further than the new Sorrow Songs, the art of Hip Hop.

Hip hop is an art form that, like the spirituals, began as a gift from the most oppressed class of black Americans, a wonderful highly democratic art that composes narratives of the trials, tribulations, and triumphs of real life wholly in verse—like Shakespeare. From the beginning much of the verse was crude by the best standards of posey, or the divinely inspired poetry of the spirituals, but like the "Sorrow Songs," they told tales from a wide spectrum of human experience "and spoke to the hearts of men." But now, driven by the imperatives of soulless marketing men with their eyes on the bottom line, Hip Hop—like movies and television—has degenerated into twisted melodrama that increasingly celebrates greed, violence, misogyny, and myriad debaucheries. All of this represents the moral disaster DuBois saw on the horizon and warned the nation against a century ago. Although reworded in his own unique poetry, the question posed by DuBois regarding the sanctification of money grubbing is the same as that asked in the Bible: "What does it profit a man to gain the world but lose his soul?"

Aside from Washington's genuflection before the high priests of Mammon, DuBois believed Washington's passivity in the face of militant white racists mocked any historical gains and could only sap the manhood of the race. Hence he boldly told his fellow black Americans: "In the History of nearly all other races and peoples the doctrine preached at such crises has been that manly self respect is worth more than lands and houses, and that a people who voluntarily surrender such respect, or cease striving for it, are not worth civilizing." Here DuBois echoed Benjamin Franklin's revolutionary maxim: "Any people who will accept temporary security in place of basic liberty deserves neither!" Thus, after all was said and done, DuBois called on black Americans to reject Washington's demand that they "give up, at least for the present, three things,—first political power; second, insistence on civil rights, Third, higher education of Negro youth."

Witnessing the decimation of the civil rights Afro-Americans had gained from laws passed by the Reconstruction era congress, as a result of the Supreme Court decisions of 1883, then the *Plessy vs. Ferguson* decision legalizing segregation in 1896, the nullification of black voting rights starting with the Grandfather clause in the Louisiana constitution of 1898, and the increasing shift of funds from academic to industrial education, DuBois concluded: "As a result of this tender of the palm-branch…(three things) have occurred. (1) The disfranchisement of the Negro. (2) The legal creation of a distinct status of civil inferiority for the Negro. (3) The steady withdrawal of aid from institutions for the higher training of the Negro." In this fair critique, DuBois admits, "These movements are not, to be sure, direct results of Mr. Washington's teachings; but his propaganda has, without a shadow of a doubt, helped their speedier accomplishment."

Finally, DuBois poses this question to the backers of Booker T. Washington: "Is it possible, and probable, that nine millions of men can make effective progress in economic line if they are deprived of political rights, made a servile caste, and allowed only the most meager chance for developing their exceptional men? If history and reason give any distinct answer to these questions, it is an emphatic No." DuBois concludes that Washington's philosophy for black advancement in America is built upon a complex paradox that is impossible to resolve and is thus a sham. DuBois calls upon thinking black men who value higher learning and cherish their self respect to speak out against the Tuskegee program, "men like the Grimkes, Kelly Miller, J.W.E. Bowen, and other representatives of this group . . ." Five years after DuBois had become an activist with the Niagara movement, a group of black intellectuals who met in 1906 to answer DuBois's call to raise their voices in opposition to Washington's philosophy of non-resistance to the rising tide of white racism, Kelly Miller finally spoke his mind.

Miller's answer came in the essay "Radicals and Conservatives." After berating William Monroe Trotter, the firebrand editor of the *Boston Guardian,* Harvard graduate, and stalwart Niagarite, he turns his attention to DuBois. First, he celebrates DuBois's virtues: "The author of the "Souls of Black Folk" is also a Harvard man, and possesses extraordinary scientific and literary talent. . . . He is a man of remarkable amplitude and contrariety of qualities, an exact interrogator and a lucid expositor of social reality, but withal a dreamer with a fantasy of mind that verges on 'the fine frenzy . . .' Then Miller critiques DuBois's misguided ways and calls him back into the society of pedagogues. "When DuBois essays the role of the agitator, and attempts to focus the varied energies of his mind upon a concrete emergency, it is apt to result, as did his 'Atlanta Tragedy,' in an extravaganza of feeling and a fiasco of thought. His mind being cast in a weird and fantastic mold, his place is the cloister of the reflective scholar. He lives behind the veil; and whenever he emerges to mingle with the grosser affairs of life we may expect to hear, ever and anon, that bitter wail. Dr. DuBois is passionately devoted to the welfare of his race, but he is allowing himself to be exploited in a function for which he is by nature unfit. His highest service will consist in interpreting to the white people the needs and feeling of his race in terms of exact knowledge and nice language, rather than an agitator or promoter of concrete achievement."

Since we have the historical record before us, it would be easy to dismiss Kelly Miller as a pompous fool and pay him no mind. But this essay, and "As to the Leopard's Spots," his brilliant and trenchant critique of Thomas Dixon's best-selling racist manifesto, reveals Kelly Miller as one of the most learned and literate Americans of his time. But, alas, to the good of his posterity, he failed to heed Mark Twain's warning: "It is far better to be thought a fool that open your mouth and remove all doubt." As an activist/intellectual, Dr. DuBois would go on to play a pivotal role in the liberation of African peoples on the continent and the U.S., as a founder of the NAACP and the Pan-African movement. Hence it is his name that is revered among freedom-loving people around the world, it is his story that is the subject of two Pulitzer Prize winning volumes, and it is DuBois's book *The Souls of Black Folk*—a treatise that has remained in print for a hundred years and is the subject of this edition.

Finally, I have kept extensive discussion and commentary to only a few of the essays that comprise *The Souls of Black Folk;* two of these were chosen because they contained ideas that are still passionately debated a century after they appeared, and another because of its sheer beauty and enduring cultural significance. However, while alluding to others of the essays, I think it best to allow readers the joy and wonder of exploring them on their own and arriving at their own conclusions. Needless to say, reading this text again after many years has been a marvelous experience for me, as I have grown older and wiser and thus better equipped to appreciate the timeless wisdom and soul stirring eloquence therein. My task in this introductory essay is to give the reader some sense of the historical context in which this work was created, as well as introduce them to the life and work of W.E.B. DuBois, whom I believe to be the most important American humanist intellectual—as well as one of the most interesting personalities—of the twentieth century.

What the reader should always bear in mind, however, is that *The Souls of Black Folk*—written just three decades after the Civil War ended the system of chattel slavery—represents firsthand reportage from the front line, documenting the struggles of a people emerging from 250 years of life, such as it was, under one of the worst forms of bondage endured by any people in the history of the world—a crime against humanity, in which all the power of European Americans was used to stamp out the humanity of African Americans and reduce them to the level of beasts of the field, while preaching that "all men are created equal." These essays then, form a record of how black folk kept their humanity, and attempted to raise themselves against all odds to the level of full citizenship in an American civilization committed to consigning them to the bottom of a caste system based on skin color.

X: A Note on Life After *Souls*

With the publication of *Souls,* Dr. DuBois, who had been known mostly within scholarly and social policy circles, moved into the wider arena of opinion makers. Having witnessed, to his disappointment, the fact that his scientific studies of Afro-America life were not having the positive effect on public opinion and social policy he had expected, DuBois appended "The After-Thought" to this text, which, in spite of his agnosticism, sounds suspiciously like a prayer for *Souls.* "Hear my cry, O god the reader;" he prays, "vouchsafe that this my book fall not still-born into the wilderness. Let there spring, Gentle One, from out its leaves vigor of thought and thoughtful deed to reap the harvest wonderful. Let the ears of a guilty people tingle with truth, and seventy millions sigh for the righteousness which exalteth nations, in this drear day when human brotherhood is mockery and a snare. Thus in thy good time may infinite reason turn the tangle straight." Judging by the response to *Souls,* DuBois's text was anything but still-born.

For instance, Ida B. Wells, who would have her share of spats with DuBois in the future, wrote him upon the publication of *Souls* with heartfelt praise, ecstatic about his critique of Booker T. Washington. Born during the Civil War in Holly Springs, Mississippi, Wells had experienced war, pestilence, racism, and natural catastrophe before she was twenty years old. And by the time DuBois published *Souls,* she had been a school teacher, crusading journalist, civil rights activist, and editor of her own newspaper. And what's more, her theater of operations was the Deep South.

There was at that time, for sure, no more heroic figure in America— male or female, black or white—than Ida. B. Wells. Such was the caliber of her intellect and the quality of her service in uplifting an Afro-American community in crisis, that many, including herself, thought she should have been the natural successor to Frederick as leader of the race in America. After all, when DuBois was a college student in Germany, Wells was touring England telling the tall tale of her life and struggles, lecturing on the epidemic of public crucifixions of black men, and exposing the U.S. government's rising hostility to the civil rights of Afro-Americans—the shameless sell-out of half a million loyal black men who fought to preserve the Union was the price of rapprochement with their white southern brothers who had lately committed treason. Hence what Ida Wells thought of *Souls* is a barometer of opinion among the most politically astute, morally advanced, and militant sector of black America in 1903.

In a letter dated May 30, 1903, about a month and a half after the publication of *Souls,* Ida Wells Barnett—she had by now married the Chicago lawyer and publisher Ferdinand L. Barnett—told DuBois about a dinner party held to discuss his book. Hosted by Mrs. Celia Parker Woolley—a club woman, author, and ordained Unitarian minister whom Wells describes as "a very good friend of the race"—the affair was attended by "some of the most literary folk here among white folks," and six distinguished black folk including the scholar Monroe Work. "Mrs. Bentley had a fine review about which she doubtless told you," Wells wrote DuBois. "Most of the others, save my husband and myself, confined their reviews solely to your criticisms of Booker T. and thought the book was weak because of them. Of course you know our sentiments. There was not much time for the white side of the audience to present its view. Of one thing I am certain," she assures DuBois, "the discussion stimulated a curiosity to read the book. . . . We are still reading your book with the same delighted appreciation. I am arranging myself for a meeting of our best brained, to have a discussion thereon, within the next two weeks. Am only sorry that you cannot be present with us."

A June 27 letter from Charles Chestnutt, a successful Ohio businessman and the premier black literary figure in turn-of-the-century America, gives us another look at where the black intelligentsia stood on the Washington/DuBois controversy. A quadroon like the NAACP's Walter White—who appeared so white he infiltrated southern lynch mobs without being detected—Chestnutt's novels and short story collections: *The House Behind the Cedars, The Marrow of Tradition, The Wife of His Youth,* and *The Conjure Woman,* present an insider's view of the status anxieties that marked the precarious existence of America's near-white middle class at the turn of the century, when racial identity and adjustment were still unsettled questions for many. Chestnutt, who, like Walter White, was urged to slip across the color line by white friends and other mixed bloods who were "passing," chose to be a

"Negro." In his letter he told DuBois, "The South is suffering a great deal more from malignity of the whites than the ignorance of the Negro. I have wondered whether your book on the 'Souls of Black Folk,' had any direct effect in stirring up the peonage investigation in Alabama; it might well have done so." Clearly, Chestnutt thought DuBois's book would have a salutary effect on the race problem.

This was the case with J. Douglas Wetmore, a Jacksonville, Florida, attorney—and James Weldon Johnson's college roommate—who wrote DuBois in a letter of October 20, 1903, "My Dear Doctor, I have just finished reading 'Souls of Black Folk,' for the second time, and am so much impressed with it, I feel compelled to write you, and thank you in the name of the race, for writing so able a book on the Negro's condition in this country, and especially in the south. I believe that you are the only Negro we have, who is in any way worthy to be classed with the lamented Douglas, as an advocate of equal rights and justice for our race." These, and many other letters, were preserved in the DuBois papers, which the W.E.B. DuBois Department of Afro-American Studies fought to persuade the University of Massachusetts to acquire and make available to scholars. The indefatigable Herbert Aptheker, who knows the papers perhaps better than anyone, has edited several volumes of these remarkable letters.

David Levering Lewis, who has also spent a great deal of time digging about in the collection, offers a panoramic view of the responses to *Souls*. He tells us that the well-to-do Princeton-educated Mulatto Francis Grimke, who like Philadelphia's Robert Purvis was the son of a prominent southern white man, "hurried to his writing desk to his writing desk to tell DuBois, 'More than ever do I feel that God has raised you up at this juncture in our history, as a race, to speak to the intelligence of the country on our behalf.'" And just as other black men in Africa and the Caribbean testified to the inspirational effect *Souls* had on them, Lewis tells us that J.E. Casely-Hayford of the Gold Coast, a lawyer, publisher, author, and leading intellectual of

Anglophone west Africa, believed if there were more black intellectual virtuosity of the sort DuBois offered up in *Souls,* "This century would be likely to see the race problem solved." Viewing this wildly optimistic testimony with historical perspective, it is easy to dismiss much of it as naive. But seen in its historical context, *Souls* must have read like a divine revelation to many thoughtful and deeply religious black folk wherever they happened to be in the world. And, as we can see, the responses to the text often say as much.

But it was not blacks alone who felt that DuBois was an inspired thinker offering another way to wage the struggle against an escalating racist reaction that was producing a set of racial exclusion laws. Ida Wells tells us in her autobiography that Rev. Patricia Woolsley was so moved by the book that she "announced he determination to give up her pleasant residence, surrounded by literary friends, and come over to Macedonia to help black folks with their problems." The next year, Mrs. Woolsley acted on her convictions and founded the Frederick Douglass Center in the heart of the black ghetto of Chicago, and she took up residence there, serving the poor black community until her death in 1918.

Other whites offered moving testimony to the inspirational and educational virtues of the text, although none responded in so dramatic a fashion as Ms. Woolsley, and added their voices to the swelling chorus of accolades for *Souls.* Lewis tells the story of D. Tabak, whose letter he excavated in the voluminous *DuBois Papers,* and who upon reading *Souls* felt "overpowered by a peculiar pain that was so much akin to bliss." He also said that his engagement with the text made him "ashamed of being white," and that he "envied the despised and abused." This letter raises some interesting questions about an important theme in Afro-American history, and that is their relationship with the American Jewish communities.

It is a question that comes up for discussion willy-nilly as the interests of the two ethnic groups clash, but at such times passion often subjugates reason and what we get is a contemporary version of the

Tower of Babel. But there is little dispassionate and systematic discussion of this relationship. While it is far too complex a subject to tackle here, we cannot simply pass over it in silence either. Suffice it to say that the experience of the Jews of Eastern Europe, especially Poland, has much in common with the experience of Africans in America. And, for all the talk about how great things were for the Jews of Germany before the rise of Hitler, one need only read the theological writings of Martin Luther, the patriarch and prophet of the German church, to see how deeply ingrained anti-Semitism is in the religious culture of Germany.

Indeed Ottilie Assing, who came of age during the 1840s in bourgeois German society, where her family was at the center of the intellectual and artistic life of Germany, has written quite frankly about the persistent anti-Semitism even among the most enlightened and progressive elements of the German cultural elite. Some of the anti-Jewish incidents that she describes sound like events in the early Nazi period. There is one incident that she describes in Maria Deidrich's *Love Across Color Lines,* which sounds remarkably like *Kristallnacht.* The anti-Semitic persecution, even when subtle, could be maddening. For instance, Assing's father, a talented poet and able lawyer was a Jew, but her mother was Lutheran German artist. Her father tried so hard to be accepted by his wife's family and friends, and completely assimilate into the Christian population, that when his efforts failed, and his neighbors began referring to him as "The Lutheran Jew," he committed suicide.

If one examines the descriptions of the arguments over language—Polish or Yiddish—and Zionism vs. assimilation, that I.B. Singer describes in *A Young Man in Search of Love,* they sound remarkably like the often-passionate cultural debates within black America in the twentieth century—Ebonics vs. standard English, integration vs. nationalism. This is why some Eastern European Jews, like D. Tabak and the munificent Julius Rosenwald, deeply identified with the tragic Afro-American predicament at the end of the nineteenth century. A case in point is the story told me by Dr. Al Lewis, the feisty 93-year-old talk show host on New York's WBAI-FM. While working in a clothing plant as a boy, he befriended the black janitor and discovered that the man held a college degree and was highly intelligent but had the lowliest job in the factory.

When he told the black man's story to his mother—a Russian Jewish immigrant with little formal education, who was a union organizer in the garment industry which was the scene of many bitter battles between German and eastern European Jews—told Al: "He should come into work with a gun one day and kill them all!" It is no wonder that Al would one day "ride shotgun" for DuBois during the fifties when his life was threatened by right-wing warmongers, who were enraged because of DuBois's consistent call for a detente with Soviet Russia, and his circulation of the Stockholm Peace Appeal calling for nuclear disarmament.

It is also of some interest that Zionism, Pan-Africanism, and Nazism has intellectual roots in the Romanticism that was rampant in the 19th century German universities where, Robert Herschel, the ideological father of modern Zionism, W.E.B. DuBois, one of the architects of Pan-Africanism, and the German nationalist intellectuals who would nurture Nazism, all studied. This is why DuBois supported the founding of the state of Israel in 1948, citing his reasons in a 1948 essay entitled "The Case for the Jews." I doubt that any Jew made a better case.

But, as we saw with Mrs.Woolsley, Jews were not the only white Americans to be deeply moved by the pathos and heroism of the Afro-American odyssey in the United States. Lewis points out that William James called *Souls* "a decidedly moving book" when he sent a copy to his brother, the great novelist Henry James, in London, and the president of the American Missionary Association, Reverend Washington Gladden, who was known as "The father of the Social Gospel," commanded his audiences to read *Souls* from his pulpit. But the prestigious

New York Times published an insulting unsigned review by a white southerner—who remained anonymous to escape injury to his own literary reputation for having slandered a transparent masterpiece. And other influential white publications like *Collier's Weekly* and *The Outlook* attacked the book with a "how dare he?" attitude. Yet other whites compared the emotional impact of *Souls* to *Uncle Tom's Cabin,* the 19th-century novel Abraham Lincoln blamed for starting the Civil War. However, *Uncle Tom's Cabin* was a best-seller—in fact, the biggest-selling book ever at the time—and DuBois sold under 10,000 copies of *Souls* when it initially appeared. In terms of sales, it was another book on race in America published in 1903, *The Leopard's Spots,* by Rev. Thomas Dixon Jr. that carried the day, selling 100,000 copies within six months.

Yet what made *Souls* so important was the caliber of people who read the book. The fact that he had called Booker T's racial accommodation strategy into question, commanded the attention of thoughtful Americans black and white who were concerned about the future of the nation. The widely read and respected New York *Evening Post* praised the book, as did the *Nation* and the *Independent.* The endorsement of the *Post* and *Nation* bore significance beyond literary considerations because they were both owned by Oswald Garrison Villard, the grandson of the great abolitionist William Lloyd Garrison, who had been a strong supporter of Washington before reading *Souls.* Even at the end of the twentieth century, *Souls* was still receiving lavish praise.

Mike Thelwell, SNCC organizer during the Civil Rights struggle, novelist, essayist, critic, Professor of Literature at the University of Massachusetts, and also the first Chairman of the W.E.B. DuBois Department, says of *Souls:* "Every essay is a masterpiece—and like James Baldwin and Frederick Douglass, you can always find a great quote in Dr. DuBois's writings to address any problem that may confront us." The prolific novelist and professor of literature, John Edgar Wideman, the only two-time recipient of the PEN/Faulkner Award, says: "If I could assign only one book for my students to read, it would be *The Souls of Black Folk*," and David Levering Lewis offers this assessment: "For the first time in the brutal, mocked, patronized and embattled history of Negro life on the North American continent, there was now a revelation of the race's social, and psychological realities and prospects of such lyricism, lucidity, and humanity as to leave its mark on a white America guilty of evasion, obfuscation and hypocrisy."

As impressive as are these accolades from the latter-day members of the Talented Tenth—the intellectual spawn of DuBois—the panegyric of his great contemporary and NAACP comrade Joel Spingarn sounds as if he were reading the deepest sentiments of my own soul. In a 1918 letter to DuBois in commemoration of his 50th birthday Spingarn, a professor of literature at Columbia University, wrote, "I know that some people think that an artist is a man who has nothing to say and writes in order to prove it. The great writers of the world have not so conceived their task and neither have you. Though your service has been for the most part the noble one of teacher and prophet (not merely to one race or nation but to the world), I challenge the artist of America to show more beautiful passages than some of those in Darkwater and *The Souls of Black Folk*." It is a challenge that I boldly reiterate here, 81 years later, because I believe it still to be true! But, aside from the artists, I challenge anyone to name a work that combines innovative social science and art on the level of *Souls*.

Like Joel Spingarn and Garrison Villard, many of the people who praised *Souls* when it first appeared were actively seeking solutions to the race problem and helped spur DuBois into assuming an activist role outside of the cloistered environs of the academy. He had begun to move in this direction as he began to question the power of scientific truth in deterring lynch mobs, or their apologists in politics and the pulpit. Two years later DuBois would call the Niagara Conference, a convention of black college men who gathered to forge a new agenda for Afro-Americans, a counterstatement to the Tuskegee philosophy. By this time the split between DuBois and Booker Washington had become open and permanent. But it didn't happen overnight as legend would have it.

When DuBois gave his baccalaureate address at Harvard in 1890, he praised the virtues of the "submissive man," but now that he had him in the flesh, he didn't look so good. These two men were once not so far apart in their view of the "Negro Problem" and its possible solution. They had also worked together in the Afro-American Council, under whose auspices DuBois designed the National Negro Business league, an organization whose invention was attributed to Washington. Furthermore Washington had visited DuBois's Negro Conferences at Atlanta University and even made him a generous offer to do his research on the black belt at Tuskegee, where the school owned a state of the art printing press, which means they could have published the studies at Tuskegee.

Lewis suggests that DuBois's ego may have hindered the two men getting together, because Washington really wanted DuBois at Tuskegee after observing his research, which he thought was truly valuable. But he wanted DuBois in the capacity of a happily detached scientist going about his business doing research—and possibly as a ghostwriter for Washington—not agitating on the politics of race relations or critiquing his leaders. It seems clear to me why DuBois had to turn down Washington's generous offer to join him at Tuskegee on principle.

Possessing a sense of hubris born of one great success after another— the latest being a recent fundraiser at Madison Square Garden that made Tuskegee one of the richest colleges in the nation, white or black— Washington thought he could recruit anybody, with a prestige job or cold cash, so he invited DuBois down to Tuskegee to dine with him and his third wife, Margaret James Murray, DuBois's old classmate at Fisk, just a few months after the publication of *Souls*. Furthermore, Washington needed DuBois in his camp because his recruitment would weaken and disorient the radicals, whose ranks were growing among college men and their criticism of his leadership was becoming increasing shrill. And with the publication of *Souls*, DuBois was fast becoming their spokesman. At the time the leading voice and moving spirit of the radicals was William Monroe Trotter, the Boston firebrand who published and edited the Boston *Guardian*—the most anti-Washington paper in the country.

An example of the routine treatment of Washington in the *Guardian* can be seen in a description of "The Wizard" composed by the Harvard–educated editor, and resurrected by professor Stephen R. Fox, in the *Guardian* of Boston: William Monroe Trotter. Written during a 1902 visit by Washington to Boston, Trotter describes him thus: "His features were harsh in the extreme … his forehead shot up to a great cone; his chin was massive and square; his eyes were dull and characterless, and with a glance would leave you uneasy and restless during the night if you had failed to report to the police such a man around before you went to bed."

In a time when the attitudes of even the most enlightened section of the "better class" of whites were vulgar racial paternalist, Trotter's intellectual stance—which, simply put, was that he insisted on black men being regarded as men like white males and accorded the same respect—was anathema to virtually all white men of whatever class. But it was particularly odious to the rich white men supporting Washington. Yet Washington and his inner circle of advisors felt that a swelling chorus of sharp criticism from the best minds of the race might eventually shake the faith of the white industrialists who were bankrolling the Tuskegee machine. This fear, above all, was the reason for Washington's persistent attempts to recruit DuBois.

For his part, DuBois believed there was much virtue in Washington's efforts to train the former slaves in useful trades, as he made clear over and over in *Souls* and elsewhere. But he found it intolerable that this should be used as a guise to deny a liberal education to intellectually capable black youths who sought it. And of course, he insisted upon the right to participate in American democracy as a voting citizen. After all, it was the birthright of all Americans, guaranteed in the U.S. Constitution, and he well knew that black men had fought every time white men fought to preserve it. Thus he was not about to allow Booker T. Washington, or anyone else, to barter it away.

Furthermore, when the Afro-American Council met at Carnegie Hall on January 6-8, 1904, DuBois was offended by the racist condescension of the white industrialists, and other Washington backers who addressed the Carnegie financed conference. He would later recall in the *Autobiography*, "About 50 persons were present, most of them colored and including many well known persons. There was considerable plain speaking but the whole purpose of the conference seemed revealed by the invited white guests and the tone of their message. Several persons of high distinction came to speak to us, including Andrew Carnegie and Lyman Abbott. Their words were lyric, almost fulsome in praise of Mr. Washington and his work, and in support of his ideas." But, he observes, "Even if all they said had been true, it was a wrong note to strike in a conference of conciliation."

Yet, it seems to me, the spirit of conciliation was severely compromised when Monroe Trotter was not invited. What this conference actually represented was Washington's attempt to let the "great white fathers" know that he was still in charge of the plantation and could still keep the darkies in line. Instead, it served to convince many radicals that Washington was little more than a lickspittle for the rich white elite. And to be sure, it was the beginning of the end of any hope of DuBois and Washington working together. DuBois and Washington gave the closing speeches and both were selected to set up a Committee of Twelve, to coordinate the work of the Conference. But this collaboration was very short lived. DuBois recalls that the committee "was unable to do any effective work as a steering committee for the Negro race in America." And he was direct as to the reason why: "first of all, it was financed, through Mr. Washington, probably by Mr. Carnegie." After analyzing the set up DuBois tell us: "I therefore soon resigned so as not to be responsible for work and pronouncements over which I would have little influence." Thus the die was cast, and DuBois would begin to move away from Booker T. Washington for good.

The catalyst that led DuBois to issue a call for a conference of black men who opposed the "Tuskegee Machine" was a 1905 incident in Boston. Trotter and some cohorts disrupted a meeting where Booker T. Washington was speaking. Trotter later got a sentence of thirty days in jail for disturbing the peace, and signs of the Tuskegee Machine's manipulations were everywhere. This proved to be the straw that broke the camel's back. "I did not know beforehand of the meeting in Boston," DuBois recalls in "Dusk of Dawn," nor was he aware "of the projected plan to heckle Mr. Washington. But when Trotter went to jail, my indignation overflowed. I did not always agree with Trotter then or later. But he was honest, brilliant, unselfish man, and to treat as a crime that which was at worst mistaken was an outrage." Then DuBois would take a decisive step that would radically change the course of his life as he metamorphosed from a dedicated academic researcher to an activist intellectual and master propagandist of rare passion and skill. "I sent out from Atlanta in June, 1905, a call to a few selected persons 'for organized determination and aggressive action on the part of men who believe in Negro freedom and growth.' I proposed a conference during the summer to oppose firmly present methods of strangling honest criticism; to organize intelligent and honest Negroes; and to support organs of news and public opinion."

The Conference was held in early July 1905, in a Canadian hotel near Niagara Falls across the river from Buffalo, New York (where the delegates would have been subjected to the indignities of American racism). The 29 delegates who attended the conference—fifty-nine had originally answered DuBois's call—hailed from fourteen states and considered a range of issues critical to the advancement of blacks in the United States. Six months later the "Niagara Movement" was incorporated in the nation's capitol and issued a set of eight written principles which repudiated racism, affirmed the right of universal suffrage, demanded an "unfettered and unsubsidized press," affirmed the right to full educational opportunities for black youths and acknowledged "the dignity of labor." While these demands may seem pedestrian to contemporary readers, DuBois tells us, "The Niagara Movement raised a furor of the most disconcerting criticism. I was accused of acting from motives of envy of a great leader and being ashamed of the fact that I was a member of the Negro race."

This last charge is indicative of how twisted the thinking of most white Americans was at the start of the twentieth century. The implication here is that proud Negroes "know their place" and don't sass white folks or aspire to "live like a white man." And this pathological view of African-Americans was not confined to the untutored white mob. Indeed, DuBois points out: "The leading weekly of the land, the New York *Outlook,* pilloried me with scathing articles." Yet he refused to be whipped into silence; as the old hymn says: "Like a tree planted by the waters, he would not be moved" All the criticism—much of which he understood to be emanating from a press whose writers and publishers were either partisan to, or paid by, Booker Washington and the Tuskegee Machine—seemed to stimulate his resolve, which was already formidable. So the Bookerites yelled, "But the movement went on." Indeed it did. "The next year, 1906," DuBois continues, "instead of meeting in secret, we met openly at Harpers Ferry, the scene of John Brown's raid, and had in significance if not numbers one of the greatest meetings that American Negroes have ever held. We made pilgrimage at dawn bare-footed to the scene of Brown's martyrdom and we talked some of the plainest English that has been given voice to by black men in America."

The ritualistic and dramatic character of the conference—an event rich in symbolic acts—reveals DuBois's gift for propaganda, which in this case meant the use of carefully crafted language, buttressed by symbolic acts and imagery, to inspire masses of people to action. The power of propaganda—that, as a class of phenomena is value free and thus can be employed for good or evil—can be observed in the extreme example of the monumental madness orchestrated by the evil genius of Dr. Joseph Goebbels and Leni Reifensthal. While Goebbels used radio broadcasts to drive the German masses into murderous anti-Jewish frenzies, Reifensthal's documentary film *Triumph of the Will,* with its stunning lighting designs by "Hitler's architect," Albert Speer, captured by a hundred cameras, turns the Nazis into Wagnerian warrior/gods and remains the masterpiece of its genre. Their evil works raised German nationalist propaganda to a high art informed by the science of mass psychology. Goebbels, the Third Reich's Minister of Propaganda, and Riefensthal, the era's premier cinematic artist, made full use of the expanding technology of the mid-twentieth century such as radio and motion pictures, which proved to be incredible tools of mass indoctrination when backed by the resources of a modern state.

The obvious difference between DuBois and these master German propagandists, aside from the scope and technological disparities, is in the nature of their projects. The Germans committed their talents to the elevation of the "Strong Man" to the enduring sorrow of humanity. DuBois, on the other hand, by placing his art and science at the service of the oppressed elevated humanity—a commitment that would mark the pattern of his long life and good works. The perceptive Kelly Miller recognized DuBois's talent as a propagandist, even if he did not agree with its aims or find it totally persuasive. This is evident in Kelly's response to DuBois's choices of locale for the inaugural convocations of his new movement. "We need not feel surprised, therefore, that such picturesque points as Niagara Falls and Harper's Ferry figured in the 'Niagara Movement' under the guiding mind of DuBois. They were planned by a poetic mind. It is a poet's attempt to dramatize the ills of a race with picturesque stage settings and spectacular scenic effect. At the call of DuBois a number of men met at Niagara Falls . . . and launched the 'Niagara Movement' amid the torrential downpour of the mighty waters. In this gathering were some of the ablest and most earnest men of the Negro race." Although Miller, a sometime Bookerite whose ideological stance Washington referred to as "mushy," was unmoved by DuBois's theatrics, he recognized the art of it all.

It was an art that first revealed itself in *The Souls of Black Folk,* which finds a musical analogy in the *Transcendental Etudes* of Franz Liszt, a series of short masterpieces that combine great passion and virtuoso technique; manifested again in the obvious Wagnerian echoes in the grand opera of the Niagara Movement's conclaves, and would come to full flower in the musical pageants he wrote and produced to put the genius and beauty of afro-America on display, and especially the twentieth-five years he served as editor and columnist with *The Crisis,* a perch from which he orchestrated the consciousness of black America and much of the African world, during the critical years of the twentieth century in which the world-wide African resistance movement to European oppression was born. Given his myriad gifts and moral commitments, it is no surprise that DuBois emerged as the key figure in the Pan-African liberation struggle.

Yet due to his prodigious intellect, broad learning, insatiable quest for truth, and unshakable integrity that could neither be coerced with the threat of hunger, nor seduced with the promise of gold, DuBois would eventually come to a forced parting of the ways with the NAACP, and a knockdown, drag out ideological brawl with Marcus Garvey, the Jamaican immigrant who built a mass movement based on Pan-African nationalism in post-World War I America. Lest we give a false impression however, let me hasten to add that DuBois's ideological battles were not confined to the liberal Constitutionalists of the NAACP and the black nationalists of Garvey's Universal Negro Improvement Association; during the turbulent Harlem Renaissance period of the 1920s, he also had his share of intellectual melee's with young Afro-

American Marxists—like A. Phillip Randolph and Chandler Owen—who edited and wrote for *The Messenger*—as well as Richard B. Moore, Cyril Briggs and other young West Indian Marxist intellectuals in the African Blood Brotherhood.

In other words, Dr. DuBois, the Paterfamilias of them all, had occasion to chastise his progeny now and then when he concluded that they were ranging far a-field in their analysis of the "race problem," or in the policies they prescribed to solve it. Thus his many ideological battles with adversaries, inside and outside of the race, was a natural consequence of his unwavering commitment to the shepherding of black folks to the promised land of freedom, justice and equality in a racist planetary caste system. *The Souls of Black Folk* was, therefore, his "shot heard around the world," and once having taken the field of battle he never for one moment removed his intellectual armor for the next 60 years. Finally, after all is said and done, it was a performance we are not likely to see again.

XI: SOME REFLECTIONS ON THE LEGACY OF W.E.B. DUBOIS

Assessing the legacy of Dr. W.E.B. DuBois is a daunting task. It seems not quite enough to say that he was a central figure in the shaping of movements that resulted in the death of apartheid in the U.S., and the end of colonialism in Africa. Thurgood Marshall, who headed the NAACP Legal Defense Fund during the critical years of the struggle against the legal caste system that relegated Afro-Americans to a subservient position in American life, once said: "Martin Luther King didn't desegregate a damned thing!" That honor, Marshall argued, belonged to the stalwart and learned lawyers in the NAACP. And as we well know, DuBois was a founding member and pivotal figure in the work of that venerable institution. From his office, where he served as editor of *The Crisis,* a weekly magazine, he shaped the consciousness of and inspired a fighting spirit in educated and thoughtful African and neo-African peoples, at home and abroad, for more than a quarter of the twentieth century. His many columns call to mind James Joyce's declaration, "I intend to forge in the smithy of my art the consciousness of a race." And through a series of Pan-African conferences—most of which were organized by him—he helped the young Africans who would one day free the motherland from the European invaders to define a course of action that would result in liberating their land. Hence, one could well argue that he was the most influential figure in the black liberation movement of the twentieth century.

Of course the remarkable Trinidadian intellectual duo, George Padmore and C.L.R. James, also played key roles in the African liberation movement, having personally tutored most of the political activists who led the first Anglophone African nations to independence. Yet neither was as important as DuBois to the black liberation movement on two continents. And we can say with certainty that he has no peer among today's intellectuals—although many have written about him in essays of varying depth and duration. The most striking thing about these essayists is how much their vision of Dr. DuBois is shaped by the particular academic discipline in which they are trained. For instance, political scientist Adolph Reed is principally interested in DuBois's politics, sociologist Paul Gilroy is interested in the role of DuBois's ideas in shaping the world view of the "Black Atlantic," a kind of sociology of knowledge that seeks to understand the formation of racial consciousness in the world behind the veil, and Gerald Horne, the foremost revisionist historian of the black left, is most concerned with DuBois's relationship to the struggles on the left, especially during the cold war. Cornel West, a philosopher and radical Christian democrat, is essentially interested in DuBois's prophetic vision.

The extent of the bias of DuBois's critics is nowhere clearer than in the writing of Cornel West who, along with his colleague Henry Louis Gates, Jr., has authored a book of essays with the ambitious title *The Future of the Race.* It is fitting to begin the discussion of DuBois's legacy by examining the views of West and Gates, because they are ubiquitous in academic and media circles as Ivy League-trained scholars, and key figures in the DuBois Institute at Harvard—the late scholar's Alma Mater. In his essay "Black Strivings in a Twilight Civilization"—a pessimistic polemic reminiscent of Oswald Spengler's *The Decline of the West*—Dr. West, then still a professor in the DuBois Institute, begins with praise: "W.E.B. DuBois is the towering Scholar of the twentieth century. The scope of his interest, the depths of his insights and the sheer majesty of his prolific writings bespeak a level of genius unequaled among modern black intellectuals."

I, for one, wish that Professor West had told us who among today's white intellectuals working in the humanities can measure up to Dr. DuBois? Especially when his entire *oeuvre,* coupled with a long history of activism, is taken into account. But alas, no such wisdom was forthcoming. Instead he tells us the obvious as if it were a profound insight: "like all of us, DuBois was a child of his age. He was shaped by the prevailing presuppositions and prejudices of modern European civilization." Then West sets forth a puzzling bit of analysis that appears to suggest a paradox where none is evident: "And despite his life long struggle—marked by great courage and sacrifice—against white supremacy and for the advancement of Africans around the world, he was in style and substance, a proud black man of letters primarily influenced by 19th century Euro-American traditions."

I fail to see what West finds so exceptional about the character of DuBois's education and love of the written word, and the fact that he was also committed to black liberation. The same could be said of Frederick Douglass, who, although an autodidact like Abraham Lincoln, was in love with the written word, and was also nurtured on the 19th century European/American intellectual traditions that were *au courant* in his time. The same can be said of redemptionist intellectuals such as Alexander Crummel, Edward Wilmont Blyden, Martin Delany, and all of DuBois's predecessors who fought for the liberation of African peoples at home and abroad in the 19th century. And who, in spite of their commitment to an ideology of African national Wilson J. Moses—the authority on the subject—have shown themselves in their Anglophile writings to be committed to a Eurocentric concept of cultural assimilation. So what, pray tell, is the point of the professor's observation about DuBois's education and love of letters?

I begin to feel uneasy about this essay early on, especially when the construct discussed above is followed by other observations that don't add up. West tells us: "For those of us who are interested in the relation of white supremacy to modernity . . . the scholarly and literary work of DuBois are indispensable. . . . For those of us obsessed with alleviating black social misery, the political texts of DuBois is the Brook of fire through which we must all pass in order to gain access to the intellectual and political weaponry needed to sustain the radical democratic tradition in our time." All this is true enough, but then he quickly follows with "Yet even this great titan of black emancipation falls short of the mark." Here the thoughtful observer is forced to wonder if the learned Prof. West is lamenting the fact that DuBois wasn't the *Ubermensch* that he, like his fellow philosopher Friedrich Nietzsche, was evidently searching for? When he goes on to declare, "The grand example of DuBois remains problematic principally owing to his inadequate interpretation of the human condition and his inability to immerse himself fully in the cultural depths of everyday black life," then poses the question: "Are these simply rhetorical claims devoid of content—too abstract to yield conclusions and too abstract to evaluate?" I want to scream a resounding yes. When he writes that "DuBois was never alienated by black people—he lived in black communities where he received great respect and admiration. But there seemed to be something in him that alienated ordinary black people," it is clear, from the oxymoronic nature of this statement, that I am dealing here with a bit of pretentious mumbo-jumbo.

To begin with, DuBois spent far more time living and working in black communities, and struggling in their behalf against unspeakable odds, than does Cornel West, a pampered bourgeois intellectual for whom the "struggle" is mostly a series of oratorical exhibitions, the spouting of stock sermons for which he is scandalously overpaid—if his compensation is based on the extent to which these performances actually lead to substantive change in the status of the black masses in whose interest he affects to labor. However, I would venture the speculation that the fees West collects on the stump—ranging between 15 and 20 thousand dollars a speech—are determined by forces in the academic/public intellectual marketplace, and bear no relationship to his actual contribution to advancing the cause of the "ordinary black people" to whom he claims DuBois did not properly relate. DuBois, however, showed again and again over the course of a long and productive life that he didn't give a damn about money—the incident with the NAACP secretary being a striking case in point. As I read further into this poorly organized, badly argued, self-righteous screed, I was reminded of Adolph Reed's observation that Professor West is a mile wide and an inch deep!

The fact of the matter is that DuBois had a greater grasp of the struggles of "ordinary black people" than West because, like William J. Wilson—about whom more will be said later—DuBois grew up as a member of a small and poor black community surrounded by white folks, and later as a highly educated scholar he actually lived in the poorest black communities while studying their needs. Then he published the results, with policy recommendations. In spite of the vast academic resources at his command, I have seen no similar works from West, who was ensconced in a suite in the plush "Four Seasons" hotel in Cambridge during his tenure at Harvard. The fact is that West's idea of addressing the needs of "ordinary black folks" was to advise black people to vote for Ralph Nader in the 2001 presidential race. I had always held Professor West in high regard, and on more than one occasion rose to his defense when others accused him of rank opportunism.

However, my assessment of the man as an activist/intellectual began to change when I heard an actual black worker in New York City try to explain to the learned professor that working people like her could not afford to gamble on a longshot like Nader. She said there were life-and-death, bread-and-butter issues involved with who got into the White House. Instead of listening to what she had to say, West chose to try and talk her down with a flurry of condescending preachment. He sounded like a pompous fool who was totally out of touch with the pressing concerns of the "ordinary black people" he claims to know so well, and I wrote as much at the time. In a commentary entitled "On Choosing the Lesser Evil," delivered on the Pacifica radio network on the eve of the election, I said: "Do Cornel West, Columbia University's Manning Marable, Randall Robinson, and other black Naderite intellectuals really believe it is in the best interest of the black community to engage in a protest vote at the expense of a Republican victory? Instead of telling black voters that while the Democrats are far from perfect, the Republicans will murder their dreams, they are counselling the black community to cast votes for a pipe dream. I have no doubt that these pampered, privileged intellectuals will do just fine under four or eight years of Republican misrule, just like their upper-middle-class white counterparts."

Aside from supporting utopian political causes, West's idea of addressing the problems of "ordinary black people" is to serve as chairman of Rev. Al Sharpton's presidential campaign committee! A fool's errand for sure. And I am certain that DuBois would have seen an Al Sharpton presidential candidacy the same way as he saw the utopian schemes of Marcus Garvey—another badly educated meglo-maniac—when he wryly concluded that Garvey was "cuttin' the fool before the world." (An apt description of both men and their schemes.) For Sharpton has about as much chance of becoming President of these United States as Garvey had of becoming "Generalissimo" of all Africa. And given that he was *persona non grata* in Liberia, which was founded by black Americans who emigrated to West Africa, and was one of only two "independent" African nations at the time, Garvey's chances of success were about equal to those of a snowflake in the African sun. Yet the presidential is the kind of outlandish scheme to which Prof. West chooses to commit his time and efforts, while having the unmitigated gall to suggest that Dr. DuBois was out of touch with the "spiritual strivings" of "ordinary black people."

The sad truth, I fear, is that West knows that these efforts are headed nowhere—unless he is the world's most highly educated fool—and that his posturings will add up to nothing concrete in terms of changes in the life chances or living conditions of the "ordinary black people." But he also knows that it will keep his name in the press—and he seems to have been well tutored by the Revs. Al Sharpton and Jesse Jackson in this tactic—and ensure that the fat honorariums will continue to roll in. When we consider that West has probably made more money in a year than DuBois made in ten years, his self-righteous put-down of DuBois as an elitist reveals itself to be the most odious form of hypocrisy. But for the sake of clarity, lets look at the basis of West's charge that DuBois was an "elitist," for the facts will reveal that this is a classic case of the pot maligning the kettle.

We should note at the outset of any discussion of West's charge that DuBois was suffering from elitist alienation—which as I have noted before is contradictory double talk—is that much of it is subjective and impressionistic. Hence he presents nothing in the way of evidence; we must just take it on faith the professor knows what he is talking about. A case in point is West's contention that while DuBois "certainly saw, analyzed, and empathized with black sadness, sorrow, and suffering. But he didn't feel it in his bones deeply enough, nor was he intellectually open enough to position himself alongside the sorrowful, suffering, yet striving ordinary black folk." What patent nonsense and gross hypocrisy. Unlike Professor West, DuBois was based in black colleges his entire academic career, and as we have seen, building a strong black university was a goal to which he had a deep intellectual and professional commitment.

West, on the other hand, does not seem to have ever considered teaching at a black college. When recently driven out of Harvard Yard by a president who was unimpressed by his academic output or his efforts as a rapper, he fled back to Princeton—perhaps the least likely place on earth where one could "position himself alongside the sorrowful, suffering . . . ordinary black folk." Anyone so committed to such a proposition would surely have moved to Howard—which would have welcomed him with open arms—and set up housekeeping among the common black folk of D.C. In fact, when the Harvard fiasco hit the news, George Curry, a well known black journalist and commentator and himself a product of a black college—my erstwhile Alma Mater, Florida A&M—suggested that West go to a black college. But as far as I have been able to tell, West has not even dignified the suggestion with a reply. Yet this is where the majority of Afro-American students are still to be found . . . especially the sons and daughters of "the ordinary black folk."

Of course, anyone making such a suggestion will be greeted with impassioned, and self-serving, arguments about all the advantages they would lose in terms of academic standing and grant money. Such arguments strike this writer as just so much self-serving sophistry that should no more be taken as serious argument than the apologia of those who argue that elite black football and basketball players must attend big white universities in order to make it into the professional ranks. The facts inveigh against both arguments. For instance, the running back Archie Griffin played for Ohio State and won two Heisman trophies during his college career. But when he entered the professional ranks he never made it big with the Cincinnati Bengals, while Walter Payton from Jackson State—a small black college in Mississippi—went on to become the all time leading rusher in the NFL during his career with the Chicago Bears. The same is true of the leading receiver in NFL history, Jerry Rice, who hailed from even smaller and poorer Mississippi Valley College. Then there was Doug Williams, the only black quarterback to win a Super Bowl, setting an unprecedented nine records in the process. The obvious moral of this story, as Walter Payton was fond of telling young black athletes—is that if you are good enough at what you do you will be recognized. Nobody who is 6' 3", 230 pounds, and can run a 4.3—4.5 in the forty-yard dash is going to go unnoticed no matter where they go to school.

It is still true that "If a man can make a better mouse trap than his neighbor, even if he removes himself to the wilderness, the world will make a beaten path to his door." And this has not only been demonstrated in athletics. For example, the undergraduate business program at Florida A&M University is seen as one of the top five in the country. This is because the Dean, who was a professor in the top-rated accounting program at the University of Indiana, decided to relocate at Florida A&M and design a top flight business program. As a result we have a group of dynamic young black business people, like the publisher Keith Clinkscales, now making their way in the marketplace—and the lord knows we need them.

But then, it had been shown long ago that it is possible to set up centers of academic excellence at black institutions of learning. Just consider what Howard University was during the era of segregation. A few examples will suffice. Kenneth Manning, professor of the history of science at the Massachusetts Institute of Technology, tells us in his masterful book *Black Apollo of Science*—a biography of Dr. Ernest Just, professor of biology at Howard in the first half of the twentieth century, that Just was the first American scientist from any university to be appointed to a professorship in science at the Kaiser Wilhelm University of Berlin. Just's book *The Biology of the Cell Surface,* which was published some years after his sojourn in Germany, was widely regarded as the definitive treatise on the subject. Among the other outstanding scholars were men like Ralph Bunche, Rayford Logan, Sterling Brown, E. Franklin Frazier, et al.

Although these men labored in the era of American apartheid, they continued to write and publish important works which would later serve as the basis for the discipline in which Ivy Leaguers like West and Henry Louis Gates now make their living. For instance, *Blacks in Antiquity,* written by Howard's star professor of classical studies, Frank Snowden, almost forty years ago, is still the definitive work on the subject, just as Logan's *The Betrayal of the Negro* and Eric Williams's *The Negro in the Caribbean* remain key texts on their subjects. E. Franklin Frazier gained such wide recognition from his sociological studies that he was eventually elected President of the American Sociological Association, the professional organization of all American sociologists. Political Science professor Ralph Bunche went on to win a Nobel Prize for his diplomacy in the Middle East, historian Eric Williams became the first Prime Minister of an independent Trinidad, and medical professor Charles Drew invented blood plasma, saving countless lives in World War Two.

But more important for our purposes here is the work of the Howard University Law School, under the direction of its dean, Charles Hamilton Houston, a man whom Professor Stephen Carter calls, "surely one of the canniest and most subtle legal minds of the century." A Harvard Law graduate and brilliant litigator, Houston devoted himself to building a distinguished law school at Howard and using its faculty and students to dismantle the evil edifice of *de jure* segregation in America. Concentrating in the deep South, the most racially reactionary section of the country, Houston spent the rest of his life litigating case after case, guided by a legal strategy that sought to make the southern states live up to the *Plessy vs. Ferguson* decision's mandate of "separate but equal" facilities for blacks and whites, thus making the system too costly to sustain. This strategy came to fruition in the *Brown vs. Board of Education* case of 1954, when the Supreme Court effectively reversed *Plessy*. Although Houston had passed on by then, it was the faculty and former students of his beloved law school, several of whom he had recruited and worked with on prior cases, who successfully argued the case before the court. One of those faculty members, William Hastie, Harvard Law graduate and cousin of C. H. Houston, became a federal judge. And one their former students, Thurgood Marshall, who led the team of litigants in the *Brown* case, went on to become the first—some would say only—black Justice of the Supreme Court.

Furthermore, the *Brown* case employed not only black lawyers and legal scholars but academics from other fields as well. Most notable was the Harvard-trained historian John Hope Franklin, who taught for many years in black colleges before his outstanding scholarship led to his being lured by white academia, and the Columbia-trained social psychologist Kenneth Clarke, who was one of the first Afro-American faculty members at the City College of New York. In fact, according to the Justice, Clark's experiments, which he conducted with his wife Mamie who was also a psychologist, showing the psychological damage done to black children as a result of growing up in a segregated society, swayed the court in favor of Brown. Hence one could argue that this one of the finest examples of the Talented Tenth carrying out the vanguard role that Dr. DuBois had envisioned for them when he wrote almost precisely a half century earlier: "The Negro race, like all races, is going to be saved by its exceptional men." If this be elitism, then we need far more of it.

There are two important lessons we can learn from the Howard experience. First, it shows that it is possible for serious scholars to do great work in a black university—now referred to as "predominately black" due to the sprinkling of white students that dot the campuses of these "historically black colleges"—if they are capable of doing outstanding work anywhere. Furthermore, this should objectively be much easier for West and company to accomplish since they are already famous, and their fame and foundation money will surely follow them wherever they go. The second important point verified by the Howard experience is that DuBois was right in his thesis regarding the role of the "Talented Tenth" in the education of black Americans: "The problem of education, then, among Negroes must first of all deal with the Talented Tenth; it is the problem of developing the best of this race that they may guide the mass away from the contamination of the worst, in their own and other races."

The prophetic truth of this statement should now be obvious to all who are not slaves to certain notions which remain fashionable on the left. For we are living in a time when ignorant rappers like Snoop Doggy Dog, Jay Z, Tupac and Master P. amass fortunes spouting vulgar and dangerous panegyrics celebrating debauchery and murder to millions of "ordinary black folk," while Professor West and his fellow public intellectuals who have much to say of real value—ethical equipment essential to civilized life and group advancement—are known to but a small fraction of this audience of working-class, unemployed, and increasingly middle-class youths black and white. The best indication of their alienation from these youths of the Hip Hop generation, was when several of them were invited to address the Hip Hop summit sponsored by record mogul Russell Simmons and held in New York City during the summer of 2000, and virtual none of the youths showed up. However, those panels that featured rappers were over run by these same youths.

DuBois's argument that providing the most intellectually capable among Afro-Americans with a first-rate education would create the leadership and professional classes basic to uplifting a people emerging from two and a half centuries of chattel slavery, and yet facing terror and segregation on a daily basis, was revealed as prophecy by the Howard experience. For it verifies his argument that "the training of men is a difficult and intricate task. Its technique is a matter for educational experts, but its object is for the vision of seers." Had the vision of Booker T.Washington and his mentor Armstrong, who was committed to educating black "hearts and hands" while teaching his black charges "to love the white race," prevailed, such a place as Howard University would never have existed. Just as there is no counterpart to Howard in any other multi-racial society in the American Diaspora.

DuBois's Talented Tenth thesis was also validated by the experience of Dunbar High School, which was named after the famous Afro-American poet Paul Laurence Dunbar, and was also located in Washington. Here Afro-American students were trained by Afro-American teachers not for admission to Howard, but Harvard, Yale, Princeton, Brown and other elite universities—the kind of elite schools favored by Prof. West as a student and a teacher. And they sent forth Benjamin O. Davis, the first Afro-American to become a General in the U.S. Army; Dr. Charles Drew, Dr. Ralph Bunche, Dr. Rayford Logan, the novelist Jean Toomer, the poet and longtime Howard English professor Sterling Brown, Charles Hamilton Houston, William Hastie, et al. The prophetic wisdom of DuBois's concept of the Talented Tenth—which, as I have previously shown, was a demand for a first-rate liberal academic education for black youths who could qualify, a resounding counterstatement to Booker T. Washington's "Industrial Education" program—is beyond question for all unbiased observers. Hence Cornell West's reduction of the Talented Tenth thesis to "a mild elitism that underestimated the capacity of everyday people to 'know' about life . . . a descendant of those cultural and political elites conceived by the major Victorian critics during the hey day of the British Empire" is . . . well, inexplicable. The Talented Tenth argument was first and foremost an indictment of the attempt by the "Tuskegee Machine," and the rich racist white businessmen who financed them, to impose an inferior brand of non-academic education on black youths—an education designed as DuBois correctly pointed out, to "produce a race of scullions." But, as strange as it seems, there is virtually no discussion of the reactionary forces against whom DuBois was fighting in West's long-winded polemic.

Thus in an ostentatious, ahistorical essay—which suffers from bouts of presentism that further distort West's sense of history—we are subjected to 57 pages of precious prattle that tell us far more about Professor West's broad and eclectic reading habits—mostly in literary texts rather than economic, sociological, or political treatises—but nothing about how he thinks DuBois's programmatic approaches to black liberation and development can be updated for our time. Instead he rattles on *ad nauseum* about the inadequacies of DuBois's ideas, most of which were advanced early in the last century. This would be fine if he were merely writing an objective scholarly history examining DuBois's thought in that period. But this essay pretends to more—a summing up of DuBois's ideas with a view to standing on his "broad shoulders" in order to "begin where he ended." Yet, the best advice that West can offer us in these troubled times, when there are more young black males in jail than in college, is to "look candidly at the tragi-comic and absurd character of black life in America in the spirit of John Coltrane and Toni Morrison . . . continue to strive with genuine compassion, personal integrity, and human decency in the face of the frightening abyss . . . of the twenty–first century."

After all that ink and erudition, spiced with professions of solidarity with the black masses, the essay ends with a prescription for cultural products that mainly appeal to highbrow aesthetes like the author himself. Not that this is a bad thing, but the truth is that the masses are reading Terry McMillan—or sappy romances of even more questionable literary merit, if they are reading at all—while listening to Mary J. Blidge, Nas, and Puff Daddy. Furthermore, even some literature teachers do not understand Ms. Morrison's complex narratives to hold a class discussion. The eradication of music education in the public schools makes certain that few will appreciate the improvisational instrumental music of John Coltrane. In fact, Wynton Marsalis, one of the greatest musicians of our era, a master of jazz—which is to say classical Afro-American music—and the classical European trumpet repertoires, constantly complains about the absence of Afro-Americans in the audience as he travels around the country concertizing. Hence if John Coltrane and Toni Morrison are the good doctor's prescription for easing the pain and lifting the spirits of the struggling masses, he reveals himself to be out of touch with their cultural tastes and common pleasures. And, based on his chastisement of DuBois for not being willing to be instructed by the masses, I suspect the Princeton savant considers it elitist condescension to try and elevate their taste.

I turned away from the text confused and wondering if Prof. West is in reality a mystic with a cavalier attitude toward making sense in rational terms. Considering his repeated ridicule of DuBois's rational approach to the conundrums of life, one wonders. Whatever else can be said about this learned but flawed essay, it has nothing to offer "ordinary black people" fighting to keep food on the table and a roof over their heads. On the contrary, it is the kind of overly literary abstract tract that is accessible to only the most educated intellectuals, the kind of people that DuBois envisioned as the ultimate product of a liberal education. Hence Cornel West, and all black intellectuals in America, virtually owe their existence to the ideas advanced by DuBois a century ago, when the educational agenda for black Americans was being decided by rich racist paternalist white folks who thought his rightful place was behind a plow or at a work bench, and wouldn't have allowed him in the room, let alone be involved in a discussion of his fate.

Thus the irony of West's case against the Talented Tenth—the class responsible for most of the good and constructive things that are currently happening in black communities throughout the United States—especially since he is a quintessential representative of this class in spite of his psuedo-Marxist rhetoric and Christian mysticism. In comparison to this kind of muddled thinking, DuBois's rationalism sounds like divine revelation. And, alas, Professor West has accomplished what for most thinking folks seems the impossible: He has written an essay that is at once erudite and nonsense.

On the other hand, the interpretive essay of Henry Louis Gates Jr., "A Parable of the Talents" represents a far more insightful reading of DuBois's texts. This is partly because Professor Gates, who took a degree in history at Yale before earning a doctorate in English literature at

Cambridge University in England, possesses a historian's grasp of context. And unlike West, although literature is his primary field of study, Gates cites important texts from the social sciences and economics that can provide us with specific data and analysis, which is essential to understanding the complexities of the Afro-American predicament in contemporary society. Thus from his readings we get a fuller perspective on the life and ideas of Dr. DuBois, and their relevance for our time. Moreover, the vicissitudes of the struggle for bread, which DuBois understood to be the bedrock issue that must be solved before a people could build a higher civilization, has also been a major concern of Professor Gates for some time—at least in his public utterances. I have heard him speak to this issue with passion and clarity in the loftiest intellectual assemblages, whether in Harvard Yard, the Sorbonne in Paris, or the Spanish Canary Islands.

No matter how literate the audience, "Skip"—as he is affectionately known to his friends and colleagues—always puts before them the swelling tragedy of the black urban proletariat and lumpenproletariat, the working class and their unemployed counterpart. He is appalled at the widening class stratification in the black community made possible by the end of *de jure* segregation and, like DuBois, wonders how the new black rich will relate to the plight of the black poor. And he challenges all within the range of his voice to ponder this question because he believes, and rightly so, that the black community as we have known it will disintegrate if remedies are not found to the most grievous problems facing the black poor. Hence his concern with these matters in the present essay is no fluke. I cannot say with certainty that he ponders these questions more that Cornel West, but in *The Future of the Race,* his discussion of the problems that threaten to decimate black America is more coherent, and so more useful in thinking about finding our way out of the present crisis. Pointing to economic data questioning the much-lauded black economic ascendancy in Atlanta, he tells us: "In fact, inner-city blacks were shut out of the emerging job market, which was largely to be found in outlying areas, and which drew upon workers from outside their neighborhoods."

Gates also goes on to show how the fall from grace of Talented Tenth members upon whom DuBois had placed the historical imperative of leading the race—ranging from the disgrace of former NAACP head Ben Chavis, to the black congressman/Rhodes Scholar Mel Reynolds due to sexual harassment of adult female colleagues or consorting with a minor, to the Republican assault on Secretary of Agriculture Mike Espy (the charges against him proved to be unfounded) to the sad spectacle of a crack-addicted Marion Barry, the mayor of Washington D.C.—has left the field open to a new group of pessimistic black leaders whom he calls "a band of sad-eyed prophets bewailing the so-called leadership crisis in America." First among this group is Louis Farrakhan, "who took center stage, having convened the best attended black gathering in the nation's history." And he sums the situation up thusly: "The mighty have fallen; the fallen have become mighty." Gates observes that many of those who agonize over the crisis of black leadership argue that if we could straighten out that problem then Afro-Americans could effectively tackle the problems that confront the masses, but correctly observes that "The trouble is, no one can agree on what that leadership should look like; no one ever could."

As evidence of the crisis in leadership that plagues contemporary black society, Gates cites a 1985 survey of Afro-American opinion that revealed a striking dichotomy in the views of black leadership and the masses they purport to represent. On critical issues such as the death penalty, school busing for the purpose of facilitating integration, prayer in schools and abortion the survey showed that the black leadership establishment is at odds with the majority of their constituents. The survey also revealed that blacks are more conservative than whites on "many key social issues." Hence Gates wisely cautions black progressives that "If the numbers of black Republicans are on the rise, as these opinion surveys suggests, it would be unwise to dismiss the phenomena." He senses danger here regarding the political direction of the black community—which has traditionally been left of center and progressive—because "Given the breach between the black leadership and its putative constituency, we shouldn't be surprised at the motley company who seek to fill it." Here he is suggesting that blacks who advocate policies and hold positions that are detrimental to the best interest of the Afro-American community—*à la* Clarence Thomas, Roy Innis, and the members of the "Black Leadership Council," whose members include Shelby Steele and Ward Connelly—could gain sympathy from uninformed and misguided Afro-Americans. And he is right; so long as the untutored masses tend to applaud any black person who manages to gain a lofty position, the specter of them rallying behind black reactionaries a possibility.

However, Professor Gates's analysis of the black leadership paradigm becomes confused as he ventures into the issue of the historic split between those leaders who chose a nationalist/separatist path on the one hand, and those who backed integration with white Americans on the other. By far the most striking thing about Professor Gates's discussion of what he labels the "integrationists and accomodationists" is its superficiality. It is no more correct to describe Dr. DuBois as an "integrationist," as it is to label Marcus Garvey and Louis Farrakhan "accommodationists." Gates says that Garvey and Farrakhan are the heirs of Booker T. Washington's accomodationist strategy—a formulation Gates no doubt borrowed from Harold Cruse, whose seminal text *The Crisis of the Negro Intellectual* was assigned reading along with *The Souls of Black Folk* in several of his Afro-American classes at Yale.

At the time *The Crisis* was published in the mid-sixties, it came as a sort of revelation to confused activist intellectuals trying to develop a theory of black liberation—of whom the present writer was one—as well as those career academics who were just starting to dig into the newly emerging field of "Black Studies." But Cruse's analysis of nationalist vs. integrationist leadership was itself was flawed, as anyone who has read two later and deeper studies of the subject by W.J. Moses: "The Golden Age of Black Nationalism," and "On the Wings of Ethiopia," will agree.

To begin with, Cruse locates the origin of the split in the ideological debate between Fredrick Douglass and Dr. Martian Delaney, in the mid-nineteenth century. He extends this analysis to DuBois and Booker T. Washington, and further to DuBois and Garvey. There are several problems presented by this analysis: First, Cruse apparently did not understand that the discussion about whether to emigrate to Africa began in the early national period, when Afro-Americans actually began to settle elsewhere; secondly he makes no attempt to analyze the thought of nationalist intellectuals like Alexander Crummell and Edward Wilmont Blyden, both of whom were far more important to the nationalist project than Delaney, and finally he ignores the fact that DuBois was never the total integrationist that Douglass was.

Unfortunately for Gates, however, Professor Cruse would have a change of heart about his assessment of DuBois's place in the nationalist/integrationist polarity that upsets the ideological apple cart. In a letter from Cruse to political scientist Adolph Reed, dated June 11, 1986, Cruse writes: "You quote me as identifying DuBois with the 'Integrationist tendency' in the history of Afro-American thought . . . maybe I did, but that was because DuBois willingly allied himself with a white liberal dominated 'civil libertarian' protest movement because he had no other choice in 1909-1910 . . . DuBois was calling for 'economic cooperatives,' and 'self-help organizations' among blacks as 1918-1920. You are quite right in highlighting DuBois's preoccupation with 'race pride.'"

On the contrary, Douglass was the mixed-blood progeny of an out-of-wedlock union between a white plantation owner and his black slave mistress; he was a conscious mulatto who insisted that the idea of inherent racial differences that determined human character or culture was a fiction. When he took a white woman as his second wife, he dismissed the criticism of those who opposed the union by reminding them, "My first wife was of my mother's race; my second wife is of my fathers." Hence he was convinced that racial unity was a step in the wrong direction and eschewed what contemporary academics call "racial essentialism." Douglass summed up his feelings on the matter with the comment: "I thank God for simply having made me a man, but Delaney always thanks god for having made him a black man." From this description DuBois sounds more like Delaney than Douglass.

Not only did Douglass lack pride of race as such—notwithstanding feelings of solidarity for his fellow victims of white American oppression or his opposition to the theory and practice of white supremacy—but also he opposed the building of separate black institutions. His view on the latter was that there should be no black school unless the alternative is no school at all. This was in sharp contrast to Martin Delaney, who was a "race man" that at one point even advocated blacks emigrating from America and founding a nation elsewhere. Alexander Crummell, a leading intellectual among Douglass's Afro-American contemporaries, was so offended by Douglass's assimilationist attitudes—which he expressed with a succession of devoted white lovers and finally his marriage to a white woman much his junior after the death of his black wife of decades—that Crummell referred to him as "that mulatto showman." On the contrary, we see that Crummell was fond of DuBois and vice versa. Perhaps that was because they were in many ways soul mates on questions of race. Indeed, Moses makes a compelling case for inclusion of DuBois in that strain of black nationalist thought that he calls "Mystical Ethiopianism."

Hence the clear difference between Delaney and Douglass on the question of race, does not apply to Garvey and DuBois. After all, DuBois was a far more important figure in the Pan-African movement that nurtured the leadership of emergent Africa than was Garvey, who never set foot on African soil. DuBois's disagreements with Garvey had more to do with theory and practice of African liberation, and the transparent folly of Garvey's advocacy of Afro-American emigration to the

African "motherland," than any beliefs DuBois held regarding "integration" with white Americans. Unlike Garvey, however, DuBois had visited Liberia and held no illusions about African realities. Furthermore, to cast Booker T. into this ideological morass on the nationalist side is to worsen the confusion.

The fight between Booker T. Washington and DuBois was over how blacks could advance in society, hence the battle was over tactics: militant protest vs. accommodation to the imperatives of southern caste etiquette. Washington's accommodationist stance was a far cry from the militant race pride of a Garvey or Farrakhan; the former saw whites as pillagers of the honor and treasure of the African race everywhere in the world, and Louis Farrakhan, following the lead of his spiritual leader and teacher Elijah Muhammad, sees whites as the "Devil." And both of them have repeatedly said so in countless public forums, using blunt language. Thus, while neither Garvey nor Elijah Muhammad believed that agitation for equal rights in the U.S. would solve the problems of black Americans—and both thought it a fool's errand to pursue them—they were hardly accommodationists in the tradition of Booker T. Washington.

The fact is that Garvey and Muhammad were advocates of total separation from white folks. What they truly had in common with Washington was his preaching regarding black economic development, because economic self-determination in the U.S. was a basic goal of both leaders. A desire to foster economic development among the black peasantry of the Caribbean was the catalyst that inspired Garvey to travel to the U.S. in the hope of studying the Tuskegee experiment and moving it to the Caribbean. DuBois, however, shared their views on joint economic efforts among black folk—although the organization he was affiliated with, the NAACP, was committed to a program of legal redress based on constitutional law, and non-economic liberalism. It is easy to see from this brief review of the history of the "integration/accommodation" controversy that Gates has grossly oversimplified the issue and misrepresented where DuBois stood in the nationalism vs. integration debate. Reading Gates's argument, I thought of Adolph Reed's charge that many scholars are appropriating DuBois's legacy for their own projects, at the expense of his own. Therefore, students of DuBois's ideas should follow Cruse's advice and read DuBois's *oeuvre* for themselves.

There are other missteps in this essay, such as his description of the black summit conference called by Benjamin Chavis, when he was the executive director of the NAACP. This was an honest attempt to organize a national black united front in which all ideological and religious factions in the Afro-American community could work in concert in order to deal more effectively with the crisis that is engulfing black America. The fact is that persons holding a wide variety of opinions were present there, and the nationalist element was a distinct minority. Yet Gates views this historic gathering, held under the imprimatur of the nations oldest civil rights organization, as a retro-convocation of "aging remnants of a bygone era's nationalist vanguard."

I can say that this is a lie, because I covered the event as a columnist for the New York *Daily News.* This is but one of many blunders and lies that mar an otherwise intelligent discussion of the legacy of DuBois, the scope of which dictates that a more expansive critique must await another forum. Suffice it to say, however, that anyone reading DuBois's correspondence with Washington, or his biographical ruminations, regarding the conferences on Afro-American leadership that the Tuskegean was organizing, will note that the Doctor's main criticism was that the list was not broad enough in terms of promoting diversity of opinion. Hence there is every reason to believe that he would have welcomed the kind of ideological ecumenicism represented by the summit.

Given all the wit and wisdom displayed in his discussion of the arts, life at Yale, and early portraits of scholars like Armistead Robinson— who would go on to become the first black historian to teach the history of the Civil War at the University of Virginia, in the very heart of the old Confederacy—Gates's failure in this essay to recognize an affinity between Chavis's summit and DuBois's wish for a conference including a spectrum of black opinion in this essay, and his misreading of some crucial aspects of DuBois's essay "The Talented Tenth" elsewhere in the book, remind me of the proverbial cow that gives a good bucket of milk, then kicks it over. Yet, in spite of his critics, some of whom accuse him of acting like Booker T. in his power over funding of research in Afro-American studies, and his will to use that power to support the work of scholars who share his ideological biases, which tend to the assimilationist *à la* Frederick Douglass, Gates is carrying on the tradition of DuBois in his promotion of research and publication of studies on Afro-American history and culture.

For many years, DuBois struggled in vain to find a source to fund an *Encyclopedia of the Negro,* and by the time the government of Ghana offered to fund the project he was already past ninety years old, the project had been renamed the "Encyclopedia Africana," and DuBois's research design projected 70 volumes. He died working on the *Encyclopedia,* and the reactionary, culturally backward, military junta that seized power dropped the project, and it was soon forgotten—until Professor Gates resurrected and completed the *Encyclopedia,* making it available to the world on CD-ROMs. Its completion was a great tribute to the intellectual legacy of DuBois, and there is every reason to believe that had he lived to see it he would have been ecstatic. But the *Encyclopedia,* as impressive as it has proved to be, is but one of many publications produced by the DuBois Institute.

This scholarly project was made possible by Gates's entrepreneurial talents, which are the most impressive displayed by an academic since Dr. Carter G. Woodson's "Association for the Study of Negro Life and History" was organized in the 1920s. Considering the fact that Woodson's organization conducted original research and published books without the benefit of any university affiliations—since no research university was interested in black historical projects—Professor

Gates should produce more important studies due to his affiliation with Harvard. It should be pointed out, however, that aside from conducting historical studies, Woodson's association also formed Negro history clubs in the black community in which working-class folks got together to read and discuss works in Afro-American history. Woodson, an early voice of the "Talented Tenth" that DuBois called forth, had also earned a Ph.D. in history from Harvard a decade and a half after DuBois took his, and like DuBois, his base of operations was in the black community.

But, ironically, the most scathing criticism of the DuBois Institute's activities comes from community activists in Boston, just a hop and skip from Harvard Yard, and it is voiced by the Reverend Eugene Rivers, an activist clergyman who works among the poorest and most endangered black youths. In Reverend Rivers's view, Skip Gates and company—including Cornel West—are a bunch of bourgeois Negro poseurs who are fakin' the funk. According to Rivers, they are missing in action in the life-and-death struggles of the young black people who languish in the ghettoes of Boston. Rev. Rivers's charge is especially ironic in view of the pompous prattle from West in his essay about Dr. DuBois's inability to relate to "ordinary black people," especially since one cannot get more ordinary than the people Rev. Rivers has chosen to serve as minister. I cannot say if Rev. Rivers is right about these guys, but his views are important in any case because he represents the voice of the "ordinary black people" right in their back yard.

Here two clichés will suffice: "Charity begins at home then spreads abroad" and "people who live in glass houses shouldn't throw stones." Frankly, I cannot imagine what Professors West and Gates could do to measure up to the standard set by Dr. DuBois. This conclusion is meant as no slight to them, just a statement of opinion—which I am sure they will understand, because it's the same critical enterprise in which they are engaging. Perhaps it is their fate to live in a time when there are fewer opportunities for heroic action, or maybe a life lived behind the

ivy walls of elite academia simply cannot provide the challenges that living and acting in the wider world of activity in which W.E.B. DuBois
found his calling.

The idea of DuBois as an elitist is a persistent theme in discourses
about DuBois's socio/political thought, but in the erudite polemics of
Adolph Reed it takes on the character of obsession. He even goes so far
as to accuse him of preferring royalty based on the dialogue of a character in DuBois's Harlem Renaissance novel, *Dark Princess.* This, despite
the fact that DuBois often denounced all forms of hereditary aristocracy in his many essays, articles and books. Reed, a professor of political
science at the New School of Social Research who also taught at Yale, is
the opposite of Gates in temperament and outlook. And, predictably,
they offer different views on DuBois's life and work. Whereas Henry
Louis Gates is a liberal academic at home living the life of the mind in
privileged academia, and apparently as content as a Carnation cow with
his project of advancing Afro-American Studies in general and literary
studies in particular, Reed comes across as a pugnacious misanthrope
who missed his calling as leader of the American socialist revolution—
well, on the theoretical level anyway. When his fascination with Marxist
theory and cultural assimilation is added to his combustible intellectual temperament, what we get is an odd mix of status anxiety, political
correctness, and a near-martial stance toward his intellectual adversaries
that often clouds his judgment.

Indeed, his critique of the works of Skip Gates and his fellow literary
critic/theorist Houston Baker, Professor of English and Afro-American
Studies at the University of Pennsylvania, is often so vitriolic that it is
often hard to tell if Reed simply disagrees with their ideas or thinks they
have sinned. Some passages are so caustic they seem fitting for child
molesters, or some other reprobate, not a colleague with whom he has
intellectual differences. (And as anyone who has read thus far in this essay
will note, the present writer is no shrinking violet when it comes to tough
criticism.) Although he has written about them elsewhere, his major cri-

tique is to be found in a curiously organized book entitled *W.E.B. DuBois and American Political Thought: Fabianism and the Color Line.*

Reed claims to be interested primarily in DuBois's political thought, which is what one would expect from a political scientist, but after a brief workmanlike discussion of DuBois's place in the political trends of his time, the book soon ranges far afield and we soon find the author engaged in tortuous polemics about highly esoteric literary and philosophical theories that have meaning only for the most ivory tower academics, and appears to be motivated by a burning desire to prove that virtually every line that Baker, West, and Gates have ever written is superficial and fallacious, or is part of a giant reactionary plot to throttle the socialist revolution, or at the very least, remove DuBois's intellectual *oeuvre* from its historically ordained role to serve such political interest. At times, the book grows so bogged down with polemics about critical literary theory, it seems the first part of the book has no tie to the second part.

To make matters worse for the reader seeking to understand and be enlightened, Reed conducts these abstruse polemics in an arcane academic language that is at best an unpleasant experience to read, and at worse is undecipherable to all but the academic specialist. It appears that Reed's philosophy of writing is "Never use elegant English vocabulary where obscure polysyllabic technical jargon will suffice." In this regard he obviously missed one of the most important lessons that he should have learned from DuBois: It is quite possible to write about the most complex social phenomena with eloquence and high literary style. This assumes, of course, that the writer wishes to be read and understood outside of a small group of academic specialists, which was certainly the goal of DuBois who, as Reed points out, was always motivated by a political project and policy concerns—which, incidentally, Reed claims as the driving force for his own scholarly endeavors.

Anyone who has followed the career of Professor Reed and is familiar with his essays in the *Nation,* and especially the *Village Voice,* will attest that the man is able to write readable prose when he sets his mind to it. And on those rare occasions when it is possible to read him without getting a headache, it becomes all too obvious that Reed is a learned man with some things to say. Hence the thoughtful and sensitive reader must detect a hint of tragedy here: Are these exercises in academic obscurantism motivated by a desire to be taken seriously as a scholar by his white colleagues, most of whom are committed to a different intellectual project from his? This is no picayune issue, because anyone reading the texts of many forty-something black academics, the first generation of black scholars who were actively recruited into white academia—often to the chagrin of their white colleagues who are ticked off by the fact that some friend or classmate of theirs didn't get the faculty position they wanted—cannot help but notice the angst that appears to hang over many of their spirits like a cloud.

The basis of this angst lies in the suspicion that their white colleagues do not really like them or take their scholarly projects seriously—a theme in the Yale law professor Stephen Carter's 700-page novel, *The Emperor of Ocean Park*, a fable about the "Talented Tenth," circa 2001. In an interview on National Public Radio's Sunday Edition of June 21, 2002, Carter said that while it was not true of him, many members of the black upper class suspect that their white colleagues secretly hold them in disdain and harbor animosities. This may well be true in some cases, but as the old saying goes: "Just because someone is following you doesn't mean you are not paranoid." But even if the racist condescension they detect on the part of white colleagues is real, so what? Get over it guys and just do great work. And if you still feel that you are not getting the promotions your scholarly output merits, they take your employer to court the way workers in less glamorous jobs who feel that they have been discriminated against are forced to do—or better still organize and follow Frederick Douglass dictum: "Agitate! Agitate! Agitate!"

But enough of the *Sturm* and *Drang* already. Anyone who is familiar with the marvelous works of E. Franklin Frazier, John Hope Franklin,

Benjamin Quarles, Rayford Logan, St. Clair Drake, Eric Williams, C.L.R. James, and of course W.E.B. DuBois, knows that they were too busy producing path-breaking work to be consumed with angst over the irrelevant opinions of ignorant white colleagues about subjects on which they were the authority. While that much celebrated mediocrity Shelby Steele, along with Gerald Early, a gifted essayist and solid literary scholar, have set the standard for soul rending angst, Reed seems to suffer from his fair share.

Interestingly enough, the main thing about Gates's writings on DuBois that sets Reed atwitter is the fact that Gates is interested in DuBois's texts as literary creations, not as political polemics. But, after all, Gates is a professor of literature and a first-rate critic/theorist regarding the Afro-American literary canon. Thus it is as natural, and logical, for Gates to be interested in DuBois as a literary presence as it is for Reed to examine his politics. But somehow this simple logic appears to escape Reed, who talks as if by concentrating on the literary rather the political aspects of DuBois's work Gates has betrayed the legacy of the great man. But, ironically, the critique that Reed offers here is perhaps the most compelling argument for political scientist sticking to political theorizing and literary critics confining their theoretical postulations to the province of literature. Thus far, they way I see it, Reed's assault on the lit/crits has been like the Tyson-Lewis heavyweight championship fight, maybe he won a round.

As evidence of Gates's evil intention to distort DuBois's legacy, Reed points out, "Gates cites *Souls* reviewers and others among DuBois's contemporaries to support his view of the book's principally literary significance. He draws on Aptheker's survey of reviews selectively, however, not mentioning the extent to which they—as Aptheker notes—revolved around DuBois's challenges to Washington. Gates also adduces William Ferris, Langston Hughes, and James Weldon Johnson." Well, no surprise here, since all three are cosmopolitan men of letters. But Reed is having a hissy fit because Gates does not accent the political dimensions of the book. Yet many black literary critics think that there has already been far too much emphasis of the political significance of black texts.

This is the main criticism that Albert Murray has leveled against Richard Wright, one of the most important American men of letters in the last century, in his book *The Omni-Americans:* "Sometimes Wright also gave the impression that he felt that the writer's basic function was to politicize everything."

The same can be said of Reed, who launches a scathing attack on John Edgar Wideman, Gates, and Houston Baker because they found the literary aspects of *The Souls of Black Folk* more important to their intellectual project than the political ones. He even goes to the trouble of analyzing the various editions published over the years to see how many of the introductory essays concentrate on the "double consciousness" metaphor in the essay "Of Our Spiritual Strivings," in preference to the ideological conflict discussed in "Of Mr. Booker T. Washington and Others." And he selects Gates out for special flagellation, arguing disdainfully, "Gates is concerned with it only as a literary device. In fact, he annexes the entirety of *The Souls of Black Folk* to his literary/theoretical project by contending that the volume is a 'classic' not because of the phase of DuBois's ideological development that it expresses but because of the manner in which he expressed his ideology." In other words, as Reed makes clear in his argument, Gates and the other lit/crits have misappropriated DuBois's text.

XII: The Legacy (Pt. II)

Although I agree that given the *gravitas* of the issue in 1903, "Of Mr. Booker T. Washington and Others" was the most important essay in the book, Reed's argument strikes me as silly. Especially since it is clear from the evidence that Reed's own reading of the reviews of *Souls* by DuBois's contemporaries is biased in favor of his disciplinary and

political interests. For instance, several prominent American intellectuals commented on the exquisite prose in which the book is rendered.
David Levering Lewis tells us that "The sometimes grumpy Albert
Hart loved it. Fourteen years later, he was still insisting that his finest
Ph.D. student's collection was 'the only literature published by a
Harvard graduate in forty years.'" When Professor W.D. Hooper of
the University of Georgia read the book in the fall of 1909, he wrote
to DuBois to remark that "even the pure English was very refreshing
in this day of slovenliness." Indeed, it is an assessment of the banal
state of academic prose that our present critic would do well to heed.
Ironically, if Prof. Reed had stuck to his subject, "W.E.B.DuBois and
American Political Thought," a subject he appears better equipped to
handle, we might have learned some really interesting things.

A major problem in trying to assess who among contemporary
American intellectuals best represents the legacy of Dr. DuBois lies in
the fact that he was so many things: sociologist, historian, economist,
essayist, novelist, occasional poet, master of several languages, political
polemicist, editor, columnist, and a political organizer/activist on three
continents—America, Europe, and Africa—for nearly three quarters of
a century. Beyond all this, he was a man of unflagging integrity and
commitment to the liberation and "development of the colored peoples
of the world." Hence, to try to match such a towering legacy is a tall
order indeed. It is safe at this point to say that no one has succeeded in
equaling it.

XIII: The Historians

Many people have furthered aspects of DuBois's legacy in their life and
work, however. A full accounting of such persons is beyond the scope
of this essay, so those chosen for recognition here reflect my biases as
well as their actual achievements. To begin with, there are the revisionist historians who walked in DuBois's footsteps, scientifically

reconstructing the real story of the African experience in American civilization. Thus, for the first time rendering the whole American story as it was actually experienced on these shores, setting aside the "feel good history" and white racist mythology that has too often masqueraded as the American saga. First among these is Carter Godwin Woodson, an eccentric loner who in his way was cut from the same heroic mold as DuBois. And although they had a long acquaintance, there is reason to believe that they were never good friends. Based on DuBois's descriptions of Woodson, they don't seem much alike either. To those who wish to portray DuBois as an uptight puritanical prig, they should take a look at Woodson.

A big, powerfully built man possessed of an iron will, both of which traits had formed in the coal mines of West Virginia, where he spent what should have been his high school years digging coal, Woodson was twenty years old when he began high school. Nevertheless he soon earned his high school diploma and enrolled in Berea College in Kentucky, where he received his Bachelors, and then he took a Masters from the prestigious University of Chicago, and after some study in Europe, earned his Ph.D. in history from Harvard in 1912, sixteen years after DuBois became the first Afro-American to do so. Faced with racial barriers that restricted his opportunities to do scholarly research, Woodson would go on to create his own opportunities by founding the Association of Negro Life and History in 1915, the same year DuBois published his history *The Negro.*

However, while Woodson was just as committed to uplifting the race as DuBois, unlike DuBois, he saw his role strictly as a scholar committed to excavating the history of the race and thereby arming blacks with the intellectual weapons to defend themselves against the psychological warfare being waged on them by the white cultural apparatus. This attack seemed to come from everywhere: newspapers and magazines, blackface minstrel shows, novels, "scholarly" history books, museums, denigrating images on the boxes of many products that stocked the shelves of stores, and especially the racist pseudo-scientific treatises that were flowing from the colleges and universities. The denigration of the African branch of the human family was complete, black inferiority was preached from the pulpits of white churches in the tale of the curse of Ham, and taught in the nation's schools as social Darwinist ideas grew fashionable.

With the invention of the motion picture, a new and monstrous weapon joined the arsenal of the white supremacists. Thus with the appearance of D. W. Griffith's assault on the character, competence, and humanity of Afro-Americans, *The Birth of a Nation,* Dr. Woodson decided to organize the Association. Since this movie—based on the second volume of a trilogy of novels by the fanatical North Carolina racist Thomas Dixon Jr. purporting to tell the truth about the Reconstruction—glorified the Ku Klux Klan, it was like pouring gas on a smoldering fire in a country where African American men had been murdered in public crucifixions at the rate one every two and a half days since 1881.

These uniquely American terrorist tactics were designed to ensure black submission to white power. And when the technical virtuosity of Griffith the cinematographer added to the explosive literary propaganda of Dixon's novel, *The Klansman,* the effect was like the Nazi Minister of Propaganda Joseph Goebbels's discovery of the power of radio waves to intoxicate the masses and breed murderous racists. Even President Woodrow Wilson, a learned man with a Ph.D. who had been a classmate of Dixon's at Johns Hopkins University, praised the film profusely, calling it "history written with lightening."

Woodson saw an organic relationship between the devaluing of African humanity through racist propaganda, and the wanton murder of innocent black people whose skin color was a crime to many whites. He could clearly see that the ideological underpinnings of this racist propaganda were based on a falsification of history. And as a Harvard-trained historian who had also studied in Europe, he clearly understood that once you had written people out of human history it paved the way for their extinction. The evidence was everywhere, from Australia and Tasmania, to the Native Americans called "Indians." Hence, like the erudite and perpetually imaginative novelist Ishmael Reed—a man whose wit and broad historical reading DuBois would have enjoyed— Woodson believed "writin' is fightin'." Hence he approached his goal, "to save and publish the records of the Negro, that the race may not become a negligible factor in the thought of the world," like a Christian soldier marching to war.

In "A Portrait of Carter G. Woodson," an essay written on the occasion of Woodson's death on April 3, 1950, DuBois tells us that "he never married, and one could say almost that he never played; he could laugh and joke on occasion but those occasions did not often arise. I knew him for forty years and more, and have often wondered what he did for recreation, if anything. He had very little outdoor life, he had few close friends. He cared nothing for baseball or football and did not play cards, smoke, or drink. In later years his only indulgence was over-eating so that after fifty he was considerably overweight." As DuBois and others describe Woodson, his only passion in life was writing the untold story of black people and through his scholarship boost the spirits of his oppressed race and refute the lies that sought to deny their humanity and supply an intellectual justification for the lynchers.

DuBois tells us that Woodson "made up his mind that he was going to devote himself to the history of the Negro people as a permanent career. In doing that he knew the difficulties he would have to face. Study and publication, if at all successful calls for money, and money for any scientific effort for or by a Negro means abject begging; and at begging Woodson was not adept. . . . Most people, even historians, would have doubted if there was enough of distinctly Negro history in America to call for publication. . . . For thirteen years at Atlanta University we had tried to raise money for research and publication of studies in Sociology; five thousand a year, outside my salary. We had to give up the attempt in 1910. But one thing that Woodson's career had done for him was to make him stubborn and single-minded. He had no ties, family or social; he had chosen this life work and he never wavered from it after 1922."

Woodson would enjoy the largesse of white philanthropists, namely Julius Rosenwald, the majority shareholder in the giant Chicago merchandising house Sears and Roebuck, that served the nation by its mail-order catalog. Rosenwald, a Russian Jew who identified with the Afro-American struggle against oppression and became their primary benefactor, spending millions on projects to advance blacks in America. For more than a decade, he gave money to Woodson's project. Five years after *The Journal of Negro History* began publication, Woodson received funds from the Carnegie Foundation and later the Rockefeller backed Spelman Memorial Fund, which offered him $5,000 a year for ten years. However, Woodson's relationship with these funding institutions was short-lived because, though he was from West Virginia like Booker T. Washington, he was not a Washington man and could not be trusted to back the program of the Tuskegee machine.

Thus Woodson's relationship with the white moneymen foundered on the rocks of his independence and integrity, just as DuBois's had done. DuBois would write in his eulogy of Woodson that "he was fiercely determined to be master of his own enterprises and final judge of what he wanted to do and say. He pretty soon got the reputation of not being the kind of 'trustworthy Negro to whom help should be given . . . but if Woodson had anticipated their wishes and conformed to their attitudes, money would have poured in.'" It was an old story: become a propagandist for white interest in America and you will be well paid, dare to be independent-minded and face the destruction of your dreams. DuBois had faced the same problems as an independent minded black scholar trying to employ his gifts in the service of the oppressed. But the hostility or indifference Woodson received from the white folks didn't stop him or deter him from his lofty goal, for Woodson proved to made of far sterner stuff. So he combined the functions of scholar, teacher, editor and publisher.

He would organize the Association and solicit paid memberships, then sell subscriptions to the *Journal,* and establish a publishing company, Associated Publishers, which issued his 800-page survey, *The Negro In Our History,* in 1922, which was widely used in the segregated black schools of the era. It would remain the standard text on Afro-American history until John Hope Franklin's masterful "From Slavery to Freedom" came out in 1948. Woodson would publish a series of scholarly histories through Associated Publishers—along with an invaluable visual record of the colorful diversity of black life in America. These include *Education of the Negro Prior to 1861, A Century of Negro Migration, Negro Orators and Their Orations, Free Negro Owners of Slaves in the United States in 1830, Free Negro Heads of Families in the United States, The Mind of the Negro as Reflected in Letters During the Crisis, 1800-1860, African Heroes and Heroines,* etc. But interestingly enough, the best-known work by Woodson among literate black Americans today is his controversial polemic *The Mis-education of the Negro.*

Actually, this work was somewhat out of character for Woodson, who usually wrote works of history that were coldly objective in spite of his uplifting agenda. Indeed, DuBois would say of his work: "There was in him no geniality and very little humor. To him life was hard and cynically logical; his writing was mechanical and unemotional. . . . As a historian Woodson left something to be desired. He was indefatigable in research" . . . but "His book reviews were often pedantic and opinionated." Here one feels compelled to ask, "Whose isn't?" Certainly not DuBois's. Finally he says: "Woodson himself lacked background for broad historical writing; he was almost contemptuous of emotion, he had limited human contacts and sympathies; he had no conception of the place of women in creation. . . . Much of his otherwise excellent research will have to be reinterpreted by scholars of wider reading and better understanding of the social sciences, especially in economics and psychology; for Woodson never read Karl Marx."

This assessment of Woodson, a fellow Harvard man and the first major historian of black America to follow in the path DuBois had blazed, suggests intriguing possibilities for the critical reader. First of all, suffice it to say that DuBois's comment about Woodson's attitude toward women in his historical writing is untrue, as *African Heroes and Heroines* will verify. This is not to say that he was all he might have been regarding the role of women in his historical scholarship, but then DuBois has come under attack for his relations with women too.

For instance, the firebrand activist and muckraking journalist Ida B. Wells (whom many saw as the logical successor to Frederick Douglass based on her actions in the movement) complained about getting short shrift from DuBois regarding her role in the struggles against racism. And Anna Julia Cooper, a remarkable woman who was born a slave but went on to earn a Ph.D. in French civilization from the Sorbonne at 66 years old, would protest her exclusions from the American Negro Academy, an organization in which DuBois was prominently involved. Furthermore his texts are full of references to "Men" when speaking of issues that involve the interest of both genders. And while I believe the criticism of some young feminist scholars such as Joy James is compromised by presentism, that discussion will, unfortunately, have to await another venue, for I am running out of both time and space and, in any case, the topic deserves an essay of its own.

What is readily apparent in the divergent approaches to writing history taken by Woodson and DuBois is that the paths these men chose presage a debate that would flare up among American historians in the late sixties and that continues even as I write. That argument has to do with whether or not the discipline of history is a social science or a narrative art. This argument has its roots in earlier debates around the turn of the nineteenth century, when DuBois studied at Harvard and the field of history was professionalizng, and thenceforth historians would be "scientist" rather than frustrated literary men or learned divines. However, most historians who adopted the more reliable documentary methodology and accepted the new canons of the profession still thought of historical writing as a narrative art. And this was no less true of DuBois when he wrote *The Suppression of the African Slave Trade*. Yet he was well trained in the methods of two social science disciplines and in later years he came to believe that *Suppression* would have been better had he read Marx and Freud first.

This presages those historians who argue for "social science" and "psycho-history" almost two thirds of a century after the publication of DuBois's book. I suspect, however, that had Woodson been around he would have sided with the traditionalists who thought it a bad idea for historians to get entangled with the theoretical speculations of social scientists, which involves all sorts of comparative analysis and generalizations about "classes of phenomena" whose laws of development remain constant across time and place. Woodson, like most historians, would probably have invoked the profession's abiding fear of loose analogy and opted to study discrete events in specific time frames.

He also thought dispassion to be key to uncovering historical truth, while DuBois displayed the passion of the advocate—though Woodson was no less an advocate, and could hardly have been otherwise under the circumstances. John Hope Franklin speaks to this issue in a learned and insightful historiographical essay entitled "On the Evolution of Scholarship in Afro-American History." He notes that, "one could be extremely critical of Woodson's preoccupation with the achievements of Afro-Americans, but one should remember that Woodson was hurling historical brickbats at those who had said that Afro-Americans had achieved nothing at all."

It is tempting to view DuBois's criticism of Woodson as being inspired by competition between the men for the limited funding available for Afro-American research, as Adolph Reed suggests—at Harold Cruse's urging—in considering the split between DuBois and Booker T.

Washington. However, Janken, who did a bit of rummaging through the papers of DuBois and Woodson in the course of researching his biography of Rayford Logan—since his subject worked for both of them at different times—convincingly dismisses this argument. He argues that "the altercation between Woodson and DuBois was not a war over turf. The nub of the disagreement was the proper role for philanthropy in the production of African American scholarship."

Janken then quotes from a 1931 letter written by DuBois to Woodson, warning him that they had better get their heads together on the "Negro Encyclopedia" project (which both were itching to edit) because the white officials of the main funding institutions really didn't want either one of them. Neither were invited to the original meeting— in spite of the fact that they were the two authorities on Afro-Americans—and were included only at the insistence of Walter White and James Weldon Johnson of the NAACP. "The enemy has the money and they are going to use it. Our choice then is not how that money could be used best from our point of view, but how far without great sacrifice of principle, we can keep it from being misused." Woodson's terse response cut right to the heart of the matter as he saw it: "I never accept the gifts of Greeks," he said, alluding to the Trojan horse. "Woodson did not accurately characterize the attitude of DuBois and Logan," Janken observes, "but he did capture the flavor of the philanthropies disposition toward the project with his peppery comment" that *The Encyclopedia of the Negro* "'is now being worked on by traducing whites and hired Negroes.'"

What all of this boils down to is the fact that both men, in spite of their intellect and character, which would have won them prominence and power except for the accident of color, were powerless to affect the disbursal of funds in order to fund work that could assist in elevating their downtrodden and despised kinsmen. By now, DuBois was 63 years old and Woodson was in his fifties. Both men had been raking and scraping, begging and borrowing just to get the wherewithal to do their work. The result of all this must be a weariness of the spirit. It is no wonder that they found themselves at odds with each other, and it is a wonder indeed that they did not hate all white Americans—excepting those who had been given special dispensation by virtue of some magnanimous act on behalf of the race.

My colleague Stanley Crouch has written repeatedly of his shock that the followers of Louis Farrakhan have concluded that "The white man is the Devil." But after reading countless scholarly histories on race relations in the modern world, I find it a miracle that far more black people have not reached that conclusion—especially since so many still display Leonardo da Vinci's blond-haired blue-eyed icon of Jesus on their walls. While DuBois continued to try to reason with racist whites—which included virtually all whites in the late nineteenth and early twentieth centuries, who made it a crime for even the most accomplished black people to seek the kind of life that the lowliest whites took for granted—he tells a different story regarding Woodson, who "did develop a deep seated dislike, if not hatred, for the white people of the United States and of the World. He never believed in their generosity or good faith. He did not attack them; he did not complain about them, he simply ignored them so far as possible and went on with his work without expecting help or sympathetic cooperation from them. However, it was DuBois who wrote in "A Litany At Atlanta," a poem composed in the aftermath of a racist atrocity: "I hate them god/I hate them well/I hate them god as you hate hell/If I were god I'd sound their knell/this day!"

John Hope Franklin, however, offers a different view of Woodson. "I believe that Carter G. Woodson would have been pleased with this involvement of white historians in the third generation of scholarship. When he founded the *Journal of Negro History* in 1916, he invited white scholars to sit on the editorial board and to contribute articles. He was, nevertheless, a man of shrewd insights, and I am not suggesting for a moment that he would have approved of or even tolerated whites . . . whose motives were more political than scholarly. Even so, he would have welcomed papers for publication in the *Journal of Negro History,* whether submitted by whites or blacks, so long as they were the product of rigorous scholarship and were not contaminated by the venom of racial bias. I knew him well and spent many hours with him each year between 1940 and 1950, when he died. He would have been appalled at the bickering that engulfed the association in the 1960s over the question of white historians should be permitted to participate in the work of the association. He had always insisted that men and women should be judged strictly on the basis of their work and not on the basis of their race or the color of their skin."

Whatever happens to be the truth of Woodson's feelings about white folks, there is one thing about which there can be no controversy: he made a contribution to the scholarly study of Afro-American history. It is a many-faceted contribution, but surely at the top of the list are the training of young historians and the creation of "Negro History Week," which has evolved into "Afro-American History Month." After establishing the Association and the *Journal,* Woodson began to mentor budding young black historians. Among those he tutored were Alrutheus A. Taylor, Luther P. Jackson, Lorenzo Greene, Rayford Logan, Charles Wesley, and John Hope Franklin.

Together these men initiated the serious revision of American history and established Afro-American history as a scholarly discipline. And they did it from the history departments of black colleges—with the exception of Woodson himself, who despite a stint at Howard remained an independent scholar/entrepreneur. A.A. Taylor conducted studies of the Gullah peoples who populate the Sea Islands off the coast of the South Carolina and studies of Reconstruction, Lorenzo Greene wrote *The Negro in Colonial New England,* which is perhaps still the definitive study of the subject. Rayford Logan, a Harvard man like DuBois and Woodson, wrote several definitive studies. Fluent in Spanish and French, he became a respected Latin Americanist and a scholar in American history. Among his works is *The Diplomatic Relations of the United States*

With Haiti, The Senate and the Versailles Mandate System, Howard University: The First Hundred Years, and his magnum opus, *The Negro In American Life and Thought: The Nadir.* This last book remains indispensable for anyone seeking to understand how the gains black Americans made during the Reconstruction period was nullified in an orgy of racist violence and defamation. Logan also worked on many projects with Woodson, including *The African Background Outlined,* or *Handbook for the Study of the Negro.*

John Hope Franklin, also a Harvard Ph.D., remains the premier historian of the Afro-American tradition, with many pioneering studies on African American history. And while his relationship with Woodson was more collegial than that of mentor and student, Woodson also influenced Franklin. Especially his study of the fascinating George Washington Williams; the soldier, preacher, politician, lawyer, African explorer, and self-trained historian who wrote the first books of Afro-American history: *A History of the Negro Race in America from 1619 to 1880,* published in 1882, and *A History of Negro Troops in the War of the Rebellion,* published in 1887. Franklin's biography of this 19th century black historian, who had become so obscure that he had never heard of him when he began *From Slavery to Freedom,* was inspired by an invitation from Woodson to present a paper on him at the annual meeting of the Association. Franklin would later offer his assessment of Woodson's importance to the field.

Speaking of the second generation of Afro-Americanist to follow DuBois's lead he says: "Woodson was the dominant figure of the period. He was not only the leading historian but also the principal founder of the association, editor of the Journal, and executive editor of the Associated Publishers. He gathered around him a circle of highly trained younger historians whose research he directed and whose writings he published in the *Journal of Negro History* and under the imprint of the Associated Publishers. . . . The articles and monographs reflected prodigious research and zeal in pursuing the truth and that had not been the hallmark of much of the so-called scientific historical writing produced in university seminars in this country some years earlier." In the same essay he would say of W.E.B. DuBois, the intellectual ancestor of them all: "As he roamed across the fields of history, sociology, anthropology, political science, education and literature, DuBois became one of the few people ever who could be considered truly qualified in the broad field of Afro-American studies. Likewise it is impossible to confine DuBois to one generation. His life spanned three generations, and he made contributions to each of them."

While DuBois had some criticisms of Woodson's approach to historical writing, he respected his achievement in forcing the nation to take another look at the experience of the black folks in their midst. Hence he would write, "and then the crowning achievement, he established Negro History Week. He literally made this country, which has only the slightest respect for people of color, recognize and celebrate each year, a week in which it studied the effect which the American Negro has upon life, thought and action in the United States. I know of no one man who in a lifetime has, unaided, built up such a national celebration. . . . He did not usually attend meetings of scientists in history; he was not often asked to read papers on such occasions; for the most part so far as the professors in history of this country were concerned he was forgotten and passed over; and yet few have made so deep an imprint as Carter Woodson on thousands of scholars in historical study and research."

Among those who are following in the tradition of DuBois and Woodson, energetically combing the archives in search of the real American story, and the part black folks played in it, a few demand honorable mentions. Gerald Horne has been indefatigable in researching and rewriting the history of Afro-American participation in the radical struggles of the left. His biographies of DuBois and Benjamin Davis— Black and Red, and Black Liberation/Red Scare—along with his monographs on the Civil rights Congress and the Watts Rebellion constitute a Major contribution to American historiography. Furthermore, like DuBois, Horne is involved in African affairs. A lawyer and sometimes professor of law, he is a political activist whose work with the black lawyers committee helped to topple apartheid in South Africa. Running on the strength of his message, and virtually no money, he won over a quarter of a million votes in his 1992 bid for one of California's seats in the U.S. Senate. He has also served as special counsel for local 1199, New York's mammoth hospital workers union.

XIV: THE LEGACY (PART III)

Manning Marable, who now heads the Afro-American studies department at Columbia University, and formerly taught history and economics at Fisk, straddles history and social science as DuBois did. He has published considerable work in both fields. His radical democratic socialist stance is also reminiscent of DuBois's leaning late in life. He is also a columnist whose work is syndicated in the black press, and thus speaks to the black community about critical issues confronting them just as DuBois did in his columns in the *Crisis*. He is also an who is a founding member of the Black Radical Congress.

Wilson Jeremiah Moses and David Levering Lewis are not radical activists, but they exemplify DuBois's commitment to rigorous scholarship. Like DuBois, Moses is fluent in German, and he makes regular forays into German universities to work on various scholarly projects. Like DuBois's work on the slave trade, Moses's studies of black nationalism in America have been a pioneering effort, especially his work on major nineteenth century thinkers like Alexander Crummell, who fell into obscurity as integrationism became the dominant ideology in black America. David Levering Lewis—who has written that Moses's "mind is a gift to the field of black studies"—is himself the star of his generation of Afro-Americanist historians. John Hope Franklin, who has now reached his eighties and must be considered the Dean of American historians, has called Lewis the finest scholar writing American history today. And I think he's right.

Whether the book is *Harlem Renaissance, When Harlem Was in Vogue, The Race to Fashoda: Colonialism and African Resistance,* or a life of Martin Luther King or W.E.B. DuBois, Lewis's work shows a breadth of learning about the historical milieu, rendered in lucid prose. Some years ago, I happened to be sitting in a seminar full of American historians at Columbia University, where the subject was the difficulty involved in writing a biography of DuBois because of his long life and varied interests and activities. Some wondered if one scholar could pull it off. But like the bumblebee who doesn't know that he isn't supposed to fly, Lewis jumped on the job and got in done. And in such grand fashion that he won the Pulitzer Prize for both volumes. It is an achievement that will make his study the standard work on DuBois for years to come.

However, it must be pointed out that DuBois's influence is not confined to Afro-American historians. Euro-American scholars like August Meyer, Herbert Aptheker, Phillip Foner, Eric Foner, Herbert Gutman, et al., have also been influenced by the work of DuBois. His influence is obvious in the recent study of reconstruction by Eric Foner. Herbert Aptheker—whose *American Negro Slave Revolts* single-handedly destroyed the myth of the happy docile slave—worked so closely with DuBois in the latter part of the master's career that DuBois made him the executor of his papers. While the historians mentioned here do not exhaust the list of those whose work is worthy of consideration— Darlene Clark Hines, Robin D.G. Kelly, and Nell Painter spring to mind—they do exhaust the limits of this essay.

XV: The Sociologists

The sociological study of urban and rural America and the black populations who live there, may well be even more indebted to DuBois's pioneering efforts. The most obvious successor to his sociological investigations in Philadelphia, and the black belt of the South, is Charles

Johnson's 1920 study *The Negro in Chicago,* and his studies of the rural South, such as *Shadow of the Plantation* and *Growing Up in the Black Belt,* which he published in 1941. *The Negro in Chicago* was inspired by the 1919 race riot in that city, which occurred while Johnson was a graduate student in sociology under Robert E. Park at the University of Chicago. And he had studied the methodology and insights of *The Philadelphia Negro,* which had been published just 22 years before.

"In this vein," writes Professor Elijah Anderson, "but particularly in regard to methodology, *The Philadelphia Negro* anticipates the 'Chicago School of Sociology' Led by Robert E. Park in the 1920's through the 1950's." And the clear imprint of DuBois's thought on the rural studies carried out by Dr. Charles Johnson, under the auspices of the sociology department at Fisk, is everywhere. In fact, the titles of his two most important studies of rural black southerners was literally taken from two essays in *The Souls of Black Folk:* "Of the Black Belt" and "Of the Quest of the Golden Fleece." Much has been made of the difference in the demeanors and political stances of the fiery DuBois and his mellow fellow sociologist Charles S. Johnson, but when we take into account the fact that Johnson was a protege of Robert E. Park, his ability to remain calm in the face of racist insult should be considered a rite of passage.

Although Park was a pioneer in studying the sociology of race relations in America, he was also a white southerner who had worked as a ghostwriter and publicist for Booker T. Washington, and a strong believer in "gradualism" as the strategy for Afro-American advancement toward civic equality with whites. When the Phelps Stokes Fund, in conjunction with the Carnegie and Rockefeller Foundation decided to finance an *Encyclopedia of the Negro* in 1931—a period of economic depression when work of most sorts was scarce—they appointed DuBois Senior Editor. Whereupon they quickly rejected his request for an all black editorial board and foisted Robert Park upon him as an Assistant Editor. Janken, points out that Ansen Phelp

Stokes, the moving spirit behind the project, wanted to attract funding from the General Education Board but understood that the Board had a "jaundiced view of any project touched by radical African Americans . . . " Therefore they felt the project needed the restraining influence of a "representative white southern scholar," strategically placed to oversee the project.

DuBois was given no choice in the matter, and perhaps he accepted this humiliation because he was already sixty-three years old, and this could well be his last chance to work on a scholarly project of such magnitude. Woodson, however, would have no part of it. Yet in spite of DuBois's willingness to endure insult and humiliation for the sake of the project, in the end it was rejected by an all white board, "whose principle skill was in the fields of paternalism and racial meliorism," says Professor Janken. Rayford Logan was with DuBois when he received the bad news and Janken provides this remembrance from Logan: "Dr. DuBois ordered a bottle of champagne and a bucket of ice so that we could celebrate in his office in the Atlanta University Administration Building the confidently expected approval by the full board of the GEB. The hours passed, the ice melted, and we grew apprehensive. Finally, the word came that the full board had not approved the project. Dr. DuBois had suffered so many disappointments that he appeared hardly ruffled."

So the *Negro Encyclopedia* ended as it began, with the exclusion of Dr. DuBois and Dr. Woodson, both Harvard Ph.D.'s and the preeminent scholars on the history and sociology of black folks, from any serious scholarly project regarding their people. When the Committee representing the funding institutions first met to discuss the Encyclopedia project, neither DuBois nor Woodson was invited to participate. It required a revolt by James Weldon Johnson and Walter White of the NAACP, and Howard University President Mordecai Johnson, in order to force the board to invite the two black scholars. The men who made the decision to exclude them were considered the enlightened sector of white society, and some who opposed the *Encyclopedia* once DuBois was named its Senior Editor were among the most vocal white liberals.

For instance, the celebrated Afro-Americanist anthropologist Mellville J. Herskovitz, who had been in the forefront of anti-racist social science, represented the National Research Council on the board and, according to Janken, bragged, "I was the hatchet man." Herskovitz, a Germanic/American Jew, typified the paternalism of even the best-educated class of white Americans toward Afro-American aspirations. It is no wonder that both men, Woodson and DuBois, who wanted only to employ their talents in service to Afro-Americans in ways that would redound to the good of the nation, eventually grew embittered toward America.

DuBois remembers the *Encyclopedia* fiasco in his "Portrait" of Woodson. Recounting the progress toward producing the work once he had finally been invited aboard, DuBois writes: "I attended the subsequent meetings but Woodson refused. I and many others talked to him and begged him to come in; but no; there were two reasons: this was, he considered, a white enterprise forced on Negroes; and secondly, he had himself culled enough data eventually to make an encyclopedia. We demurred, not because we were unwilling to have him work on the *Encyclopedia;* indeed we were eager; but because we knew that one man and especially one man with a rather narrow outlook which had been forced upon him, could not write a scientific encyclopedia of sufficient breadth to satisfy the world. Eventually the Phelps stokes project was unable to collect sufficient funds chiefly, I am sure, because I had been named Editor-in-Chief."

While refusing funding to Woodson and DuBois's scholarly projects, however, the Carnegie Foundation would fully fund the massive study of American race relations by the Swedish social economist Gunner Myrdal, which was published as "An American Dilemma." Clearly, the white cultural elite that controlled the research dollars was terrified of having American society examined by competent black scholars working independently. However, the reason generally given for importing a Swede to do the work black scholars were begging to do was that Myrdal would be more objective.

In a 1944 essay/review of *An American Dilemma,* Ralph Ellison—who would write a great American novel, *Invisible Man,* ten years hence—argued that $300,000 had been squandered on a study that "has failed to even state the problem in . . . broadly human terms . . . Much has been made of Dr. Myrdal's being a foreigner . . . and while this undoubtedly aided his objectivity, the extent of it is apt to be overplayed." And the erudite literary and cultural critic, Albert Murray, Ellison's longtime friend and literary compadre, later declared that the book had missed the mark in terms of capturing the real Afro-American experience. Murray pointed out a failure in method and sensibility, resulting in a massive investigation into the quality of Afro-American life that made no attempt to interrogate the meaning of the blues—the dominant art form produced by Afro-American culture.

Since Murray well understood that an art style is the refinement of a lifestyle into "aesthetic statement," this embarrassing blunder led him to question the methods of modern sociological research and its efficacy as a tool for analyzing the deeper nuances of Afro-American experience. After reading *An American Dilemma* and Kenneth Clark's socio/psychological treatise on Harlem, *Dark Ghetto,* Murray—who is also a former professor of aviation and understands the scientific method well—concluded: "There is . . . no compelling reason at all why Negroes should not regard the use of the social science statistical survey as the most elaborate fraud of modern times." While this is an understandable reaction to the way some investigators—black and white—have misused and abused the sociological method, Murray's position amounts to throwing the baby away with the bathwater.

In the hands of the right investigator, scientific sociology is a tool for our grasp of the structure and function of modern social formations in all their variety. Although many of DuBois's scholarly projects failed to find backing in the lily-white philanthropic establishment thanks to his militant reputation—they had fled from Woodson much earlier—Charles Sturgeon Johnson, with his mild manner and patience, cajoled them into opening their coffers and funding his research. Based at DuBois's first Alma Mater, Fisk University, Johnson would expand DuBois's investigations of the rural black communities of the Deep South. With the benefit of well-funded programs, energy, mastery of modern sociological technique, youthful optimism, and bright energetic graduate students, Dr. Johnson painted a portrait of black life woven from statistics, backed by personal observation and firsthand testimony, that left no doubt about the effects of poverty, enforced by a racial caste system based on the use of violence by the white majority.

The most important difference between Johnson's methodological approach and that taken by DuBois—aside from the fact that Johnson lacks poetry—is that DuBois focused on looking closely at life in one community and using that specific body of information to generalize about similar communities, while Johnson had the resources to study the entire black belt, thus basing his policy options on a broader statistical sample. Beginning his research in the heady days of the New Deal, Johnson benefited from the largesse of the National Recovery Act and produced a series of important monographs: *The Economic Status of Negroes* (1933), *The Negro College Graduate* (1938), *Patterns of Segregation* (1943), *To Stem This Tide: A Survey of Racial Tension Areas in the United States* (1943), *Into the Mainstream: A Survey of Best Practices in Race Relations in the South* (1947). One of Johnson's most influential studies, "The Collapse of Cotton Tenancy," was supposedly co-authored with Will Alexander and E.F. Embree. However, some scholars are suspect of the claims of Alexander and Embree, suggesting that Johnson shared credit with them because they were well placed in the Department of Agriculture and the Rosenwald Foundation—two well-endowed funding sources.

Earlier, during the Harlem Renaissance of the 1920's, Charles Johnson had lived in New York and edited *Opportunity,* a magazine published by the Urban League, a moderate reply to the radical voice of *Crisis,* edited by DuBois at the NAACP. Johnson's diplomacy in dealing with powerful whites paid off on a grand scale, just as Booker T. Washington's accomodationist strategy had paid off years earlier. The generous funding that flowed into the Social Science Department at Fisk allowed Johnson to hire well-trained assistants to compile mountains of data, and buy the new calculating machines from IBM to crunch the numbers. The result was that Charles S. Johnson became one of the most prolific sociological researchers in America. So driven was he that among his students researching the conditions on the contemporary plantations in the black belt of the South, the Social Science Department was popularly known as "The Plantation," and Dr. Johnson became "Massa Johnson."

Growing Up in the Black Belt, one of Johnson's most influential works, was conducted under the auspices of the American Council on Education, who created the American Youth Commission and invested it with a mandate to look into the condition of American youths, including the ways in which life in a segregated society affected the self-concept and motivation of Afro-American youths. A number of important sociological studies in addition to Johnson's, done by black and white scholars, came out of this effort. Among the most important studies dealing with black youths were: E. Franklin Frazier's *Negro Youth at the Crossways,* W. Lloyd Warner's *Color and Human Nature,* and *Children of Bondage,* by Allison Davis and John Dollard. These studies were conducted in the upper and lower South as well as the north, and they all follow the methods of first hand observation and careful recording of the evidence begun by DuBois.

In fact these studies, as well as other major investigations into Afro-American life, correspond to DuBois's call for a hundred years of socio/economic research into the condition and development of black

Americans at the dawn of the twentieth century, thereby creating the first continuous portrait of an oppressed peasant people's acculturation into a complex modern society as free and productive citizens. Viewed from this perspective, the following are all legacies of DuBois's work: the studies of sociologists St. Claire Drake, Horace Cayton's *Black Metropolis,* a two-volume masterpiece on Afro-Americans in depression-era Chicago; the many books of E. Franklin Frazier—ranging from the monumental *Race and Culture Contacts in the Modern World,* to *The Negro Family in the United States*—a grim treatise which has been largely refuted by Gutman's *The Negro Family in Slavery and Freedom*—to *Black Bourgeoisie,* written in the mid-twentieth century, plus the late twentieth century studies of Elijah Anderson and William J. Wilson.

The Truly Disadvantaged and *When Work Disappears,* written by Wilson, are landmark works that along with the sociological investigations of Elijah Anderson, such as *The Urban Plantation,* provide a detailed model of the problems and prospects facing the majority of black urban dwellers in the post-industrial city. These studies are obvious lineal descendants of *The Philadelphia Negro,* but Elijah Anderson convincingly argues that the work of Myrdal, Daniel Patrick Moynihan, and the Kerner Commission report also owe a debt to the work of DuBois, since his work anticipated the questions they seek to answer. And I would argue that the work of Ortiz Walton and Robin Kelly on Afro-American music is firmly in the tradition begun by DuBois in "Of the Sorrow Songs."

Walton, who holds a Ph.D. in sociology, and is also a master musician who has performed on the double bass violin in symphonic and jazz orchestras, has given us a special gift in *Music: Black, White and Blue.* From his unique vantage point straddling two disciplines, the musically ambidextrous Walton offered rare insights into the sociological forces at work in the turn of the century New Orleans milieu where the art of jazz was born. In *Kickin Reality, Kickin Ballistics,* Robin Kelly has written an extraordinary treatise on the socio/economic catalysts that spurred the growth of "Gangsta Rap" in the post-industrial city. Kelly, the youngest of all the scholars I have cited, is an innovative historian from the "Hip/Hop generation" who is pioneering in research techniques that allow us to view American history from the bottom up. His book, *Race Rebels,* in which the aforementioned essay appears, is a standard bearer in this new relatively genre in American historiography. Like the young DuBois, Kelly is a pacesetter.

While DuBois's influence on the historiography and sociology of black Americans is clear, his role in setting the pace for involved artists seeking to use their art in the service of racial uplift is less well understood. Yet his fictional trilogy, *The Black Flame,* presages many of the historical novels that would later draw on Afro-American history in an attempt to clarify the black experience for a wider audience who would rather receive this wisdom as story. Some of the important works that comprise this tradition are *Jubilee,* by Margaret Walker; *The Cheyneysville Incident,* by David Bradley; *Sally Hemmings and The President's Daughter,* by Barbara Chase Riboud, and Tony Morrison's *Beloved,* to name a few. Of course, Ishmael Reed and Charles Johnson also explore Afro-American history in their novels, but their texts are experimental and thus take wild liberties with historical fact—a practice to which Toni Morrison's texts are not immune either.

Finally, the question of DuBois's legacy could well consume a sizable book, or several volumes if one is gung-ho on the matter. However, I wish to make one additional point. All those who study Africa with a view to aiding in the uplift of that continent by contributing to a deeper understanding of that continent's fascinating history and tortured present, also owe a considerable debt to DuBois's activism and scholarship. In works such as *The Negro* (1915), *Black Folk: Then and Now* (1939), and *The World and Africa* (1947), DuBois pointed out the long and complex history of African civilization and exposed the racist fictions about Africa symbolized by the wildly popular Tarzan films. Those books opened the eyes of generations of Afro-Americans—this writer included—to the real African story and raised their consciousness to the potential of African peoples.

First published in the aftermath of the second global war initiated by power-mad European imperialists, Dr. DuBois tells what inspired him to write *The World and Africa* in the foreword. "Since the rise of the sugar empire and the resultant cotton kingdom, there has been consistent effort to rationalize Negro slavery by omitting Africa from world history, so that today it is almost universally assumed that history can be truly written without reference to Negroid peoples. I believe this to be scientifically unsound and also dangerous for logical social conclusions. Therefore I am seeking in this book to remind readers in this crisis of civilization, of how crucial a part Africa has played in world history, past and present, and how impossible it is to forget this and rightly explain the present plight of mankind."

When taken together with his long years of agitation on behalf of African liberation, these texts are a priceless gift to the rebirth of the "African personality" in the twentieth century. And those among the Afro-American intelligentsia who write and struggle in behalf of African liberation since are the heirs to this aspect of DuBois's legacy. This group comprises some of the most salutary African Americans of the twentieth century; from Rayford Logan et al. in the Pan African movement early in the century, to Paul Robeson and Dr. Alpheus Hunton, in The Council on African Affairs at mid-century, to Trans-Africa, Kwame Ture's All African Peoples Party, and the Black Lawyers Committee— whose role in bringing down apartheid is less well know than Trans-Africa's, but is well documented in Gerald Horne's book, *Essays in Black*—at the end of the century. This legacy lends the lie to the argument that African-Americans have been uninterested in the plight of Africa—although international relief agencies will no doubt testify that African Americans show less interest in the plight of their kith and kin in the old world than virtually any other ethnic group. But that is a matter of education and material resources, or lack thereof.

Alas, it is once again the Talented Tenth that has produced the leadership in this critical struggle. And that is exactly the role that the Doctor envisioned for them when he wrote his essay "The Talented Tenth," at the start of the century. Given the trajectory of his life: protracted struggle for the liberation of African peoples in the diaspora and the motherland; it is both fitting and proper that he should spend the twilight of his life in Ghana, from whence his ancestors that gave greatest meaning to his life hailed, as the honored guest of a Prime Minister who had been educated at an Afro-American University. Hounded by the FBI—which was headed by the paranoid, racist pervert J. Edgar Hoover, who had personally targeted him—and subject to the same humiliations suffered by the mass of black citizens, "not everywhere but anywhere, not all the time but anytime," he joined the Communist Party and emigrated to Africa, thus turning his back on capitalism and racist America, where, he recounted in a speech delivered at the Great Wall of China: "For nearly a century I have been known as nothing but a nigger!"

Although he was already past ninety when he removed himself to Africa, his plan was to finish the *Encyclopedia Africana,* with the financial support of the Ghana government. More than a quarter of a century since the Euro-American managers of the funding institutions shot down his prized project, DuBois's beloved *Encyclopedia* found a home. Always thinking big with an eye towards to future, he planned a 72-volume set. Such was his vision and commitment right up till his death on the night before the great March on Washington.

I remember well the announcement of his passing at the great March. No matter that the movement was plagued with accusations of communist subversion, Roy Wilkins of the NAACP, courageously took time out to commemorate the passing of this great spirit, and tell the world of his contribution to the cause for which this multitude of righteous souls had gathered to speak unvarnished truths to the Princes and Powers who governed a racist and increasingly imperialistic America. I felt a deep sense of loss then; I feel it still. President Nkrumah announced, "A mighty tree has fallen in Africa!" And the old Afro-American spiritual said, "My Lord, what a morning!"

XVI: Some Parting Thoughts

As fate would have it, I am finishing this essay on Independence Day, July 4, 2002, and as I write, David McCollough, the great American historian, speaks to me from my television screen, reacquainting all those lucky enough to be tuned in, with the story of that great American patriot, John Adams, second President of the United States, and first President to sire a President. The most important point Professor McCollough makes regarding Adams is that while he thought Thomas Jefferson's declaration, "All men are created equal," was hyperbole—pointing out the obvious fact that some folks were beautiful while others were aesthetically challenged, some were swift on the cap while others were dumb as cake dough—they all are entitled to equal protection of the law.

As I reflected on this question it occurred to me that Adams had offered the more profound observation on the natural rights of man. Had the nation embraced that ethical principle from the outset, the ideological defense of slavery, and the hundred-year *de jure* cast system that followed in its wake, would have been undermined. Both systems of oppression were based upon the assumption that since European Americans were superior to African Americans and Native Americans, the genocide and slavery committed against these "inferior" sub-humans—crimes as fundamental to the birth of this nation as the war against England—were justified. Even Thomas Jefferson used this argument to justify his involvement in the massive crime against humanity that was chattel slavery.

John Adams, however, would have none of it. And his wife, Abigail, who, along with the nation Adams had helped to create, was the love of

211

his life, never tired of reminding her fellow Euro-Americans that the existence of slavery contradicted all that the revolution stood for and exposed them as hypocrites. After all, John Adams was the only one of the "Founding Fathers" who refused to own black slaves as a matter of principle.

John and Abigail Adams's arguments would be taken up over a century later by their fellow Bay Colony native, William Edward Burghardt DuBois. And DuBois would never tire of pointing out that the roots of the race conflict lay in the decision of the "Founders" to exalt money over morality. In a spectacular career—spanning parts of two centuries—as a scholar and public intellectual par excellence, he repeated his critique unceasingly in polemical and scholarly language. The most challenging ancestral imperative arising from this legacy is that the intellectual must take a stand on behalf of justice, deflating pomposity and exposing hypocrisy in service to those farthest down. DuBois's candid critique of Booker T. Washington and several U.S. Presidents during his lifetime is reminiscent of Adams's comment that George Washington was barely literate, and Thomas Jefferson was a likable fellow, so long as you did not require him to render an opinion that demanded knowledge of the real world.

Standing up for what's right and defending the poor, powerless and oppressed is also, finally, the essence of the teachings of Jesus Christ. Hence, just as Frederick Douglass inspired DuBois, he would go on to inspire Martin Luther King. I believe it is no accident that Dr. King chose the words of the New England poet, James Russell Lowell, to accent some of his most powerful speeches. It was the same verse DuBois chose as the epigraph for "Of the Dawn of Freedom": "Truth forever on the scaffold, / Wrong forever on the throne; / Yet that scaffold sways the future, / And behind the dim unknown / Standeth God within the shadow / Keeping watch above His own."

Surely Dr. King had read this essay—as had virtually every literate Afro-American of his generation—and it is reasonable to speculate that he first read Lowell's poem there. It is further evidence of a tradition of struggle among Afro-Americans, handed down to the intelligentsia and literate layman as texts, and passed on orally from one generation to the next as folk wisdom. Many Afro-Americans—this writer included—received the tradition through both media. This received wisdom had philosophic antecedents and heroic ancestors from many traditions: Shakespeare and the Bible, the Declaration of Independence and the Signifying Monkey, Langston Hughes and W.E.B. DuBois, Gut Bucket Blues, Handel's Messiah, Duke Ellington, and the "Sorrow Songs." A persistent source of conflict has been the attempt by African Americans to live out the universal human values and visions articulated in these traditions, which is simply a quest to become more fully human, because it placed them in opposition to the American racial caste system of white over black.

This was the dilemma that confronted DuBois throughout his long and extraordinarily productive life. As much a New Englander as his fellow Harvard man John Adams, although more degreed but just as feisty, DuBois fought to realize the freedom of thought and action promised in the Declaration of Independence. But he would continually discover that when he uttered such ideas they were considered dangerous subversion. This is the point he makes so poignantly in the short story "The Coming of John," where the same ideals taught to white boys as manly virtues became heresies worthy of death when embraced by a black boy. Yet DuBois continued to seek and tell the truth no matter what. This, then, is the enduring challenge the legacy of Dr. William Edward Burghadt DuBois—humanist, Pan-African patriot, and an intellectual for all seasons—poses for all American intellectuals who stand for truth and justice, and seek a better world in their time.

—ɯ—

III: A Hundred Years Hence: Blues to Be DuBois

These one hundred years after the publication of *The Souls of Black Folk* should provide us with some insights into things that were beyond the perspective or the imagining of its author at the time of its publication. They should even go beyond what W.E.B. DuBois thought as he grew more and more hostile to friends and foes, as his ideas twisted in the wind until he became a Communist, fell out with everyone on whom he should have been able to rely, and ended his life in Ghana, still sputtering the fantasies of Pan-Africanism, reviled at home but welcomed in Russia and China until his death at ninety-five. He died on Lester Young's birthday, August 27, in 1963, near the dawn of the March on Washington later that year and five years before the dusk of the civil rights movement that took place shortly after half of Martin Luther King, Jr.'s face was blown off as he stood on the balcony of the Lorraine Motel in Memphis, Tennessee, where DuBois, a New Englander at a remove from the souls of black folk, had come to first love the culture of the Negro and to appreciate the fine brown frames of the imposing pulchritude of Fisk University.

We exist in a time quite different from that in which DuBois came to maturity, insulted literally or figuratively by those who were inferior to him in far, far more cases than not. That obviously galled DuBois most when such sneers came from people below him in every objective measurement of personal development but who could become, whenever their defense of skin privilege was focused on a Negro, full-fledged white men. These dregs worked in cahoots with the whites on top who ran things and they had paid an enormous price during their service in the Civil War, which might well have been the result of the biggest con job in the history of the nation, then or now.

These crackers who were never considered as valuable as slaves, and who were brought in at bargain prices to do all jobs that overseers and masters thought too dangerous for their expensive chattel, were chumped off during the War of Rebellion. Those greasy crackers, with dirt so often in the cracks of the backs of their necks, were whipped up into believing that they were somehow defending themselves, *their* culture, *their* way of life, *their* liberties and all of the rest of it as they went on to have their heads and limbs blown off. These minor men within their own social contexts found themselves dying or maimed as a result of having defended a system that looked upon them with limitless contempt.

What redneck who lived in the vast shadow land between being a slave and being a Southern aristocrat would ever have been welcomed into the home of a plantation owner—or, as Faulkner made clear in *Absalom, Absalom!,* allowed to come to the *front* door? Which of them could have vied for the hand of one of their daughters or had their own daughters treated as more than erotic training tools for the rich plantation boys looking to sow all the wild oats they could? Who among them would not have been chastised verbally or physically for crossing plantation property without permission? Yet, bowing down before what was perverted into the romantic description of "the Lost Cause" when the time came to pretend that the war had been about anything other than maintaining slavery, those whites who came into national description as "trash" died by the thousands upon thousands upon thousands, never even once having sat on the verandah and had their hearts tickled and their souls pricked by the joy and the pathos of the darkies singing. Here and there some of them saw what the real deal was and refused to be used by wealthy men who had no regard for their kind, but the average white man down below put on his homemade gray uniform and went out there to give the Yankees hell on the tail of a rebel yell. But what they became after the devastating conflict that men such as Mississippi Senator Trent Lott now call the War of Aggression made the terrorist means of the Ku Klux Klan possible and eventually destroyed the meaning of the Civil War in daily practice.

Both Booker T. Washington and DuBois met the force that had brought the brutal means of slavery that had been reserved for plantations into ordinary life across the South. Or is anyone among us crazy enough to believe that the plantation system would have allowed for cracker trash to put slaves "in their place" with perhaps incapacitating violence when said chattels might have cost anywhere from $400 to $2,000 before 1860? Like it or not, that would have been tantamount to a redneck taking a club to an expensive racehorse because it had kicked or bitten him. More than doubtful.

What Washington learned was key to his understanding of what was to be done later, when he came to power in the world of Negro education. As a young man in the late 1860s, Washington had seen rednecks go nuts in West Virginia, even striking General Ruffner, a former plantation owner, with a brick and knocking him cold because he sought to defend some Negroes quite willing to defend themselves—and who were going about doing it when Ruffner stepped into the mess. At that moment, with Ruffner lifted from the ground and taken into his home, Washington felt that there was no hope for his people in the entire world. He had seen the future. White authority in the world of race had been usurped by those crackers at the bottom, the men who worked themselves smutty in coal mines. These were men who lived in shacks and had no plumbing, whose places, like those of the poor black people who lived right next to them, stank of garbage and human feces. No matter, they were violently intent on making sure that those who were right down there in the trash with them realized that they, the Negroes, were actually quite lower.

In "Booker T. Washington's West Virginia Boyhood" by Louis R. Harlan, published in the journal *West Virginia History*, we get a very clear report of what happened during that period of mayhem moving at the tempo of mercury in a little dirty county called Malden, West Virginia. We see that the riot was prophetically assessed in a clear investigatory reading. But we also witness an accurate reference to Homer, and what we can now see as an ironic and surely unintentional allusion to the Committee for Public Safety that functioned during the Reign of Terror and foreshadowed the kinds of central committees within the totalitarian regimes DuBois would one day support:

> There existed [in the Malden area] a secret order, members of which were bound together by solemn oaths. Its object was "to deprive the black race in our midst, of the rights now guaranteed to them by law, and by discrimination against them, in point of labor, and by depriving them of the protection of the laws and other acts of oppression, to render it impossible for this class of citizens to longer live among us in peace and safety." At a Klan meeting they put the matter more succinctly. "To clean out and finish up the niggers at Tinkersville" was, according to a witness, the whole agenda of the meeting. Reputedly under the leadership of a Malden physician, Dr. John Parks, as Grand Cyclops, the Klan was probably more a political instrument of partisan Democrats than a factor in economic competition.

DuBois never saw such men in action, though he had heard plenty of tales of their viciousness when he first went south and was well aware, as were all educated Negroes of his time, of the reports that arrived in the North whenever shocking redneck violence broke out again. Echoing the complaint that led to the Revolutionary War, DuBois wrote of the condition into which "Boards of Education" and Jim Crow laws had driven Negro life in the South: "Taxation without representation is the rule of their political life." At the same time, he could not agree with everything that Washington thought which has now been called accomodationist out of context. After all, by the time he set *The Souls of Black Folk* to paper, DuBois had not been in the middle of building anything below the Mason-Dixon line that demanded a grasp of how to avoid providing an excuse for the ever-present brutality of white Southerners to shift into high and bloody gear, which could easily result in the celebration of *full* whiteness, which meant total power, that control of the sort that the minor men who become serial killers feel when they have command over life and death. That is the primary reason why those terrorist orders had so much appeal and why, in our time, we see them inside Negro communities oppressing black people in the form of street gangs with monosyllabic names like Bloods and Crips. Minor black men now become serial killers in turf wars, but their targets are the same and their resentments are the same. They celebrate the coarse and the common as the "real" qualities of the Negro while hating learning and refinement in black people, which is mocked as "trying to be white." Whatever respect they achieve in the world is commanded by violence and intimidation. Since 1980, street gangs have killed 10,000 people in Los Angeles, which is three times the number of black people lynched *throughout the United States* between 1877 and 1900, the highest tide of racial murder in the history of the nation. Such murderers are surely the *sub-souls* of black folk.

In his own time, DuBois knew well what the serial-killing culture of Southern racism was about and, given his own temperament—which could as easily be that of a nettled aristocrat as a charming and worldly man—he surely had no doubt that his life would not have lasted very long had he been living in the South rather than the North and taking on "the Southern way of life" in his relentless way. Long before anyone of note had ever heard of W.E.B. DuBois, Mark Twain had given us a portrait of the strain of redneck cracker who would have gone up and down the wall and eventually through it and around and around the house and then the county before howling bile at the moon had he ever met such a Negro with that worldly look in his eyes, that cultivated tone in his voice, that self-confident carriage, those elegant clothes. In *Huckleberry Finn,* when Huck's father goes on and on about encountering a well-dressed, sophisticated Negro in a free state, we get a piece of that mind right there in the middle of American literature: bitter, resentful, lazy, and violent—especially when faced with a Negro whose refinement makes his own shortcomings clear.

Washington was not unaware of those men and what they were about, nor was he unwilling to sneak some punches in on them while pretending to be the best customer in the restaurant where they served the best-tasting humble pie in the world. In laying down what Albert Murray calls "antagonistic cooperation" in *South to a Very Old Place* and what that writer has also described as "preparation for aristocratic behavior," the founder of Tuskegee made it obvious that Negroes *could* be made all the better for it if they responded with full will and talent against the limitations imposed by skin tone, *but* that the privileges of color alone guaranteed nothing of quality from those who were not of "an unpopular race." Washington also spoke out for what is now called "meritocracy" in a time when only those considered loons would have proposed that a Negro in the South should get what he or she deserved on a purely unprejudiced basis. His sense of meritocracy presages what Playthell Benjamin writes of Walter Payton in his discussion—is it a tongue-lashing?—of Cornel West and Negro colleges, Howard University in particular. I am quoting this at length because we rarely see any of Washington's thinking or observe how cleverly he put across ideas on which others, even DuBois, played their own variations:

In those days, and later as a young man, I used to try to picture in my imagination the feelings and ambitions of a white boy with absolutely no limit placed upon his aspirations and activities. I used to envy the white boy who had no obstacles placed in the way of his becoming a Congressman, Governor, Bishop, or President by reason of the accident of his birth or race. I used to picture the way that I would act under such circumstances; how I would begin at the bottom and keep rising until I reached the highest round of success. In later years, I confess that I do not envy the white boy as I once did. I have learned that success is to be measured not so much by the position that one has reached in life as by the obstacles which he has overcome while trying to succeed. Looked at from this standpoint, I almost reached the conclusion that often the Negro boy's birth and connection with an unpopular race is an advantage, so far as real life is concerned. With few exceptions, the Negro youth must work harder and must perform his tasks even better than a white youth in order to secure recognition. But out of the hard and unusual struggle through which he is compelled to pass, he gets a strength, a confidence, that one misses whose pathway is comparatively smooth by reason of birth and race. From any point of view, I had rather be what I am, a member of the Negro race, than be able to claim membership with the most favoured of any other race. I have always been made sad when I have heard members of any race claiming rights or privileges, or certain badges of distinction, on the ground simply that they were members of this or that race, regardless of their own individual worth or attainments. I have been made to feel sad for such persons because I am conscious of the fact that mere connection with what is known as a superior race will not permanently carry an individual forward unless he has individual worth, and mere connection with what is regarded as an inferior race will not finally hold an individual back if he possesses intrinsic, individual merit. Every persecuted individual and race should get much consolation out of the great human law, which is universal and eternal, that merit, no matter under what skin found, is, in the long run, recognized and rewarded. This I have said here, not to call attention to myself as an individual, but to the race to which I am proud to belong.

In the wake of such powerful and sly material from Washington, served up to keep his machine going while dispensing with racism as all-powerful and simultaneously giving hope to the fellow members of his "unpopular race," W.E.B. DuBois spoke from another wing of that world. But let us grasp something clearly, which is that Negroes who got anything of significance done were aided and abetted by white people of either paternalistic or liberal inclinations. Booker T. Washington was far from alone. Bluntly, Negroes with either projects in the planning or the functioning stages, as well as Negroes who were creating for themselves positions as intellectuals, were both supported and encouraged by white intellectuals, philanthropists, and those who owned and edited the kinds of high profile magazines that published DuBois, sometimes at his most challenging. As Skip Gates has pointed out in an introduction to a 1989 Bantam Classic edition of this very book, "Between 1897 and 1903 DuBois, starting with an essay printed in *Atlantic Monthly,* became the most widely published black author in the United States. His essays appeared in such prominent publications as the *Independent,* the *Nation,* the *Southern Workman, Harper's Weekly, World's Work,* the *Outlook,* the *Missionary Review,* the *Literary Digest,* the *Annals of the American Academy of Political and Social Science,* and the *Dial,* among other magazines and journals."

After all, in *The Souls of Black Folk,* DuBois himself pointed out that, within the context of Reconstruction, $15 million had been spent and had done much good for the Negro and the nation, and that kind of engagement should have been continued. Where, other than from white people or the federal government, would large amounts of money have come, and where, other than from white people, would the money for the Negro colleges and periodicals and trips abroad to study have come? Yes, there were well-to-do Negroes and a good number of them were committed to do as much as they could for the good old cause of color (which was never a joke in an enduring sense, however much their willingness to make fun of themselves in private has long been an Afro-American tradition, combining gallows wit and satire). The cost of the rope necessary to pull Negroes from the holes into which they had been pushed was well beyond the economic means of black people at that time—not that *any* ethnic group's fate in a democratic society should be determined by the philanthropists within it (and since Negroes to this day maintain a strong position at the bottom rung of philanthropic engagement in comparison to what percentage *any* other ethnic group can count on from their best off, that could never have been any kind of a serious answer). Consequently, any attempt on the part of a Negro to get a better shot for black, brown, beige, and bone people who had gotten such a raw deal for so long meant appealing to white Americans, seeking the better angels of their nature to do battle with the buzzards of their bigotry.

Frederick Douglass knew this well, and had to straighten out his former newspaper partner Martin Delany, both an extraordinary man and a forerunner of contemporary black isolationism and Pan-Africanism. Delany had attacked both Douglass and Harriet Beecher Stowe, about whom we will hear more later:

PITTSBURGH, March 22, 1853. FREDERICK
DOUGLASS, ESQ.: DEAR SIR:—I notice in your
paper of March 4 an article in which you speak of having paid a visit to Mrs. H. E. B. Stowe, for the purpose,
as you say, of consulting her, "as to some method which
should contribute successfully and permanently, in the
improvement and elevation of the free people of color
in the United States." Also, in the number of March
18th, in an article by a writer over the initials of "P. C.
S.," in reference to the same subject, he concludes by
saying, "I await with much interest the suggestions of
Mrs. Stowe in this matter."

Now, I simply wish to say, that we have always fallen
into great errors in efforts of this kind, going to others
than the *intelligent* and *experienced* among *ourselves;* and
in all due respect and deference to Mrs. Stowe, I beg leave
to say, that she *knows nothing about us,* "the Free Colored
people of the United States," neither does any other white
person—and, consequently, can contrive no successful
scheme for our elevation; it must be done by ourselves. I
am aware, that I differ with many in thus expressing
myself, but I cannot help it; though I stand alone, and
offend my best friends, so help me God! in a matter of
such moment and importance, I will express my opinion.
Why, in God's name, don't the leaders among our people
make suggestions, and *consult* the most competent among
their own brethren concerning our elevation? This they do
not do; and I have not known one, whose province it was
to do so, to go ten miles for such a purpose. We shall
never effect anything until this is done.

I accord with the suggestions of H.O. Wagoner for
a National Council or Consultation of our people, pro-

vided *intelligence, maturity* and *experience* in matters among them, could be so gathered together; other than this, would be a mere mockery—like the Convention of 1848, a coming together of rivals, to test their success for the "biggest offices." As God lives, I will never, knowingly, lend my aid to any such work, while our brethren groan in vassalage and bondage, and I and mine under oppression and degradation, such as we now suffer.

I would not give the counsel of one dozen *intelligent colored* freeman of the *right stamp,* for that of all the white and unsuitable colored persons in the land. But something must be done, and that speedily.

The so-called free states, by their acts, are now virtually saying to the South, "you *shall not* emancipate; your blacks *must be slaves;* and should they come North, there is no refuge for them." I shall not be surprised to see, at no distant day, a solemn Convention called by the whites in the North, to deliberate on the propriety of changing the whole policy to that of slave states. This will be the remedy to prevent dissolution; *and it will come, mark that!* anything on the part of the American people to *save* their *Union.* Mark me—the non-slave-holding states *will become slave states.*

Yours for God and Humanity, M. R. DELANY.

REMARKS—That colored men would agree among themselves to do something for the efficient and permanent aid of themselves and their race, "is a consummation devoutly to be wished;" but until they do, it is neither wise nor graceful for them, or for any one of them to throw cold water upon plans and efforts made for that purpose by others. To reject scornfully all aid from our white friends, and to denounce them as unworthy of our confidence, looks high and mighty enough on paper; but unless the back ground is filled up with facts demonstrating our independence and self-sustaining power, of what use is such display of self-consequence? Brother DELANY has worked long and hard, he has written vigorously, and spoken eloquently to colored people—beseeching them, in the name of liberty, and all the dearest interests of humanity, to unite their energies, and to increase their activities in the work of their own elevation; yet where has his voice been heeded? and where is the practical result? Echo answers, where? Is not the field open? Why, then, should any man object to the efforts of Mrs. Stowe, or any one else, who is moved to do anything on our behalf? The assertion that Mrs. Stowe "knows nothing about us," shows that bro. DELANY knows nothing about Mrs. Stowe; for he certainly would not so violate his moral, or common sense if he did. When Brother DELANY will submit any plan for benefitting the colored people, or will candidly criticize any plan already submitted, he will be heard with pleasure. But we expect no plan from him. He has written a book—and we may say that it is, in many respects, an excellent book—on the condition, character and destiny of the colored people; but it leaves us just where it finds us, without chart or compass, and in more doubt and perplexity than before we read it.

Brother Delany is one of our strong men; and we are therefore all the more grieved, that at a moment when all our energies should be united in giving effect to the benevolent designs of our friends, his voice should be uplifted to strike a jarring note, or to awaken a feeling of distrust.

In respect to a national convention, we are for it—and will not only go "ten miles," but a thousand, if need be, to attend it. Away, therefore, with all unworthy flings on that score.—ED.

When discussing those whites who had come South to work at educating Negroes in *Up From Slavery*, Booker T. Washington used his own observations at Hampton Institute to encourage the white reader first to understand the desire and willingness of the Negro to learn, to do for self and family. But he also, by implication, encouraged them to replicate in their own ways what the Northern whites had done during Reconstruction, those who, we can see, continued the work of that greatest of the Quaker abolitionists, Anthony Benezet:

> The great and prevailing idea that seemed to take possession of every one was to prepare himself to lift up the people at his home. No one seemed to think of himself. And the officers and teachers, what a rare set of human beings they were! They worked for the students night and day, in seasons and out of season. They seemed happy only when they were helping the students in some manner. Whenever it is written—and I hope it will be—the part that the Yankee teachers played in the education of the Negroes immediately after the war will make one of the most thrilling parts of the history off this country. The time is not far distant when the whole South will appreciate this service in a way that it has not yet been able to do.

In 1903, Black Willie strung together his own blues to be there at the turn of the century as a black American. He knew what Washington was doing and admired much of it but, from his belly to his brain, he had both moxy and other things going on in his head. Still, he also repeated what Washington wrote just above in the chapter of *The Souls of Black Folk* called "On the Training of Black Men":

> It was not and is not money these seething millions want, but love and sympathy, the pulse of hearts beating with red blood;—a gift which to-day only their own kindred and race can bring to the masses, but which once saintly souls brought to their favored children in the crusade of the sixties, that finest thing in American history, and one of the few times untainted by sordid greed and vainglory. The teachers in these institutions came not to keep Negroes in their place, but to raise them out of the defilement of the places where slavery had wallowed them. The colleges they founded were social settlements; homes where the best of the sons of the freedmen came in close and sympathetic touch with the best traditions of New England. They lived and ate together, studied and worked, hoped and harkened in the dawning light. In actual formal content their curriculum was doubtless old-fashioned, but in educational power it was supreme, for it was the contact of living souls.

Overall, however, for all of its brilliance and for all of the holes it punched in the imposed mask of either the stupid darkie or the darkie made ridiculous by his trying to "get above himself," as supposedly proven in the minstrel's absurdly dressed would-be dandy with a tendency to successive malapropisms, *The Souls of Black Folk* is a messy mix of the lofty and the pedestrian, of clear thinking and heavy fuzz, of lyricism and melodrama. It was as right as it was wrong, and in both its rightness and its wrongness the book of fourteen essays has had considerable influence.

From our hindsight 20-20 perspective, it is easy to see that his thoughts about Africa and the relationship of black Americans to it were absurdly romantic and had some kind of a strange commitment to blood heritage which DuBois went back and forth on throughout his life, rejecting differences as just so much hog slop served to bring out the xenophobic pigs in men but also waxing ineloquently about Ethiopia and so on. Yet I must remind the reader of something mentioned earlier, in the first response: Africans were being sold into America until the Civil War broke out. In fact, the very best growing season and time of profit for the Old South was in 1860, the year that the plantation system wrote its own death warrant in cannon and shot after the election of Abraham Lincoln. So African slaves had not been brought into this country for only eight years when DuBois was born and all of his predecessors had, in one way or another, to deal with Africa. They were actually *stuck* with Africa and had to defend it in some way because one of the justifications for slavery was that nothing of civilized value had ever come out of Africa, that black people, as David Hume asserted, had never been the authors of anything of value, which is to say that they might have existed but that they had no history.

While the central vision of American democracy would make such a fact—true or not—irrelevant had Europeans been the subject, the rules were always different for the Negro. The Negro always had to do something extra. In fact, "extra" should be the Negro's code name in our society. Consequently, though they were Americans and had been born on this soil and were part of a literate minority within the culture at large, those black men who stepped forward and were compelled by their times to reach as far back as they could, eventually landed not in West Africa, of course, but in Egypt, where they could make the case for civilization having been lifted from its very cradle, nursed, and mentored by black people.

As mentioned in the first response, we can even see, in *The White Image in the Black Mind,* that the forerunners of nut cults like the Nation of Islam had done their work by 1840, painting all civilization black and all barbarians white, defining the black man as peaceful and worldly, the white man as violent and tribal. Perhaps the first *Souls of Black Folk* was Robert Benjamin Lewis's 1836 text, *Light and Truth: Collected from the Bible and Ancient and Modern History, Containing the Universal History of the Colored and the Indian Race, from the Creation of the World to the Present Time.* It argued, Mia Bay tells us, "that the Egyptians had descended from the Ethiopians, and that Ethiopians were the children of Ham." However, she informs us that Lewis had more to say than that, and what he said must have been particularly startling for its time: "He maintained that the Garden of Eden was in Ethiopia and that God had created Adam from 'the rich and *black* soil' of the land. Although *Light and Truth* contains no mention of polygenesis, Lewis's account of human origins virtually turned the doctrine of separate creations on its head. Blacks became the first family, and Lewis further insisted that all the early nations were colored: 'Greece, Europe, and NORTH AND SOUTH AMERICA WERE SETTLED BY DESCENDANTS OF EGYPT,' he proclaimed." Old Lewis seems mighty contemporary, a candidate for an Afrocentric appointment and a fantastical forerunner of Martin Bernal, the Jewish Moses of Afrocentrism, whose *Black Athena* now functions as the tablets of the law and an alternative to what those ersatz African academics and Afrocentrists surely consider the golden calf of Eurocentrism. *Lawd, lawd, lawd.* This foreshadowing connection is particularly obvious since old Rob didn't stop there, as Bay informs us: "Recoloring the heroes of the Bible and the ancient world, Lewis maintained that Plato and Julius Caesar were Ethiopians, and that Moses, Solomon, and many other luminaries were men of color. Moreover, in a section entitled 'The Hair on Men's Heads,' he went further still, arguing that biblical descriptions of the hair of both Christ and God himself showed that the Almighty and his Son were colored also."

Such fanatics were taken seriously by neither black people nor whites. As Bay reports, "Martin Delany lambasted Lewis for mirroring the errors of prominent Egyptologist George Gliddon, who 'makes all ancient black men *white*.' 'So this colored man makes all the ancient great white men *black*,' Delany noted in 1852. 'Gliddon's ideal nonsense had found a capital match in the production of Mr. Lewis' "Light and Truth" and both should be sold together.'" But Bay goes on to tell us that Lewis's taking the tar brush to ancient history went through "at least three editions" that were Lewis published himself in four installments, but that, in 1844, a "Committee of Colored Men" published two single-volume editions that considered the book a corrective. "Indeed," concludes Bay, "thanks to Lewis's annual book tours, *Light and Truth* may well have been the most widely circulated of the nineteenth century black publications on ethnology." Perhaps, or almost surely, Lewis is the source of the position held in Afro-American folklore that "proves" Jesus's Negroid identity through the biblical description of his having hair supposedly being like "pure lamb's wool," which is actually a twisting up of Revelation 1:14-15 ("His head and his hairs were white like wool, as white as snow; and his eyes were as flame of fire") in the New Testament.

In the wake of all of those attempts to give an alternate picture of Africa's position in world history and to create belief in a majestic ancestral line, DuBois writes in *The Souls of Black Folk* that, "The shadow of a mighty Negro past flits thorough the tale of Ethiopia the Shadowy and of Egypt the Sphinx." The trouble with "a mighty Negro past" is that it falsely connects black Americans to a part of the African continent from which they did not come and to people who did not then and do not now—and should not—identify with them in any deep sense purely on the basis of skin tone, any more than black Africans, beyond instances of fraudulent public display, tend to identify with each other to any degrees of depth solely on the basis of color and hair texture. Were that not equally true of Europe, even after

Christianity had spread from North Africa to the British Isles and far-
ther North, up into Viking territory, there would not have been such a
bloody imperial history, including Napoleon and Adolph Hitler who,
outside of the context of the Communist mass murderers such as Hold
'Em Joe Stalin, provide us with the worst examples of the side effects of
the rise of the common man, proving that those with not a drop of
supposedly royal blood can wage butchering war with the best of the
highly born, like England's Henry V, whose gruesome invasion of
France foreshadowed the kind of imperial slaughter the uninformed
believe the white man reserved for dark parts of the world. Late in his
life, DuBois admitted that the whole matter of Pan-Africanism had
nothing to do with actual ancestry on his part, which was as much
Dutch as it was African. It was simply a choice that he made out of an
emotional need. In that sense it was an aesthetic choice of the sort
Ralph Ellison defined when saying that while artists cannot choose
their biological parents, they do choose their aesthetic parents, the individuals who guide them into and through the world of art. His having
been so taken by Pan-Africanist Alexander Crummell early in his life
proved that DuBois was not one held back by skin tone prejudice, since
he was clearly of mixed heritage while Crummell looked almost "purely" African. In fact, the sometimes controversial conception of "The
Talented Tenth" derives directly from the thoughts of Crummell is not
at all far out, since DuBois was quite right in saying that all groups are
moved forward, or upward, by the most gifted among them. These are
like the power hitters in baseball, the great pitchers and fielders, the
quarterbacks and defensive linemen in football: those responsible for
leading a team to victory. The big difference in the Talented Tenth
model is that the gifted ones are committed to replicating themselves
in the mass and to removing all obstacles in the interest of fairness from
the paths of the rest. Those who resent the conception as "elitist" seem
not to understand that the democratic improvement on the traditional conception of an elite is founded in the idea spoken of earlier, which

is that it can come from *any* place in society as opposed to a special bloodline or a particular set of privileged families. In fact, those who claim to be opposed to elitism seem to understand little about human nature, since almost anyone met in the world has a superior version of what *he* or *she* likes, from hamburgers to high cuisine, from sandals to running shoes to dressy footwear. They want the best, if the best is what they like. We have to grasp that their best might be our worst. That is to say that even masochists have their individual conceptions of what constitutes a quality beating or whipping. And, in a country as given to sports as ours, I have yet to find fans who focus on players never sent into the game, commending them for the style with which they sit on the bench or wear their warmup jackets or jump up to cheer on the productive members of the team. Sport is *the* world of the elite, the purely objective elite, which might be why we, as Americans, are so hung up on the games played. There are so many stories of people coming from nowhere to the top, regardless *now* of color or sex. Sport is meritocracy in action, the symbol of the democratic dream in practice. What DuBois sought was the preparation of Negroes ready to work hard in college, no matter where they might have come from. At that gloomy time in Afro-American history, DuBois felt that, short of political power and capital, Negroes should not only fight stereotypes in the arena of free speech but they should also, as people like Douglass had, move to redefine the fight as black people always had whenever the opportunity was available. Part of redefining matters was to present an epic view of Negro American life, which is, finally, the greatest contribution of the book. Never before had anyone written so well about the bottom and those shooting for the top as he does in two chapters, first "On the Meaning of Progress," then "On the Training of Black Men." In the first, writing with the intimate melancholy so close in feeling to the blues, we get from him such a clear portrait of the impoverished rural Negroes that he introduced to learning while a student at Fisk, seeing them both at home and at ease as well as over time—as they were when he was young and in his late teens and as they were when he had grown into his thirties. In the other essay, he lays down what must have been a very hot and shocking piece of information. As he says in *The Souls of Black Folk,* "Fifty years ago the ability of Negro students in any appreciable numbers to master a modern college course would have been difficult to prove. To-day it is proved by the fact that four hundred Negroes, many of whom have been reported as brilliant students, have received the bachelor's degree from Harvard, Yale, Oberlin, and seventy other leading colleges." Further, in "On the Wings of Atalanta," DuBois expressed what must have been equally surprising to those who had only known of the Negro through depictions of shiftlessness and trivial concerns, "The function of the university is not simply to teach bread-winning, or to furnish teachers for the public schools or to be a center of polite society; it is, above all, to be the organ of that fine adjustment which forms the secret of civilization." Negroes seeking to be connected to "the secret of civilization"? How absolutely odd!

Yes, that epic vision of a people is key to understanding the book because DuBois felt it necessary to cover all of the bases, so to speak, while introducing to America a kind of Negro American that it was not accustomed to reading at length. Before and during the Civil War, Negroes had been in the middle of the public discourse because they were the central issue. With the fall of Reconstruction and the rise of the redneck, the Negro had to address another set of problems because the trouble was largely localized and no longer seen as one of national concern, even though there was plenty enough discrimination in the North to go around.

Another problem alluded to a few paragraphs earlier was what had happened to the image of the Negro since Harriet Beecher Stowe had written *Uncle Tom's Cabin, or Life Among the Lowly,* and Frederick Douglass had authored his three memoirs and fired up people with his newspaper articles. The humanization of the Negro had gone "on hold," as we would say today; it had stopped. In fact, one could make a case for the Negro being *re-dehumanized* in popular entertainment. Where

Stowe had sought to show just how brutal and evil the plantation system was, the minstrel show that followed the fall of Reconstruction supported the national mood to be wooed by a lie. It depicted slavery as a most happy time for all concerned, white and black alike, with the latter just having the most mighty fine of mighty fine times, strumming de pluck out of the banjo, sanging and dancing, all dey troubles invisible, regardless of the direction into which one looked over yonder. This should have been no surprise to anyone who had lived through the era, since the minstrel shows had removed all of the criticisms and satires of plantation whites that had appeared in the years before the Civil War once it seemed that war was imminent. The shows began attacking abolitionists like Harriet Beecher Stowe. She stood in for the brainless mistresses and masters who had previously been the targets of the routines when minstrelsy had played most roughly with the rudely peculiar institution. For all that she had done, however, neither Stowe nor her work were above the post-Reconstruction fray, as Edmund Wilson reports in *Patriotic Gore,* "By the late (eighteen) seventies, *Uncle Tom's Cabin* was half a minstrel show and half a circus. The live bloodhounds that were supposed to pursue Eliza as she was crossing the ice with her baby—which did not occur in the novel—began to figure in 1879, and were typical of this phase of the play. The original characters were now sometimes doubled: you had two Topsys, two Lawyer Markses, and two Uncle Toms. Topsy sang comic songs, and Uncle Tom was given minstrel interludes, in which he would do a shuffle and a breakdown." So what we have is a reversal across the culture, such a redefining that the themes and characters of the book are so drastically transformed that they work against what they were created to do, which was given humanity to Negroes and draw sympathy from the whites as they became aware of the savage manner in which a tragic set of circumstances were sustained. After all, let us not forget *Uncle Tom's Cabin,* with its enormous sales and all of the discussion that it inspired, turned the nation against slavery and did more to bring on the war than all of the abolition talk and all that the great Douglass had done, which was not only speak so well that he was considered the second greatest orator in the country but so impress William Lloyd Garrison that he took the position in his introduction to Douglass's first book that the author as a man was so impressive that one felt it was quite all right to break the law if it meant helping such a person become free. Watch out now.

Unlike his earlier work, *The Souls of Black Folk* was not meant for a specialized audience in the budding world of the social sciences, nor solely for a gathering of Negro intellectuals. It was meant to introduce America at large to a Negro completely unlike any it had ever had presented in full force since the mighty Douglass had strode the earth. Here was the complete potential of the race poured into one container, or so one assumes the author thought of himself, for DuBois makes it very clear that he believes his talent more than capable of speaking for everyone from the lowliest illiterate to the new class of educated Negroes and professionals whose very existence, along with the Southern institutions where so many Negroes had matriculated since the end of slavery, spoke quite highly of what had come into being over the previous three and a half decades or so. These educated Negroes were truly something new on the American scene—articulate, well-dressed, refined, so proud when they were Southerners and successful that their very presence lit fuses within those who were the spiritual descendants of Huck Finn's father. In riot after riot, those redneck descendants would make it seem that the young Booker T. Washington of the late 1860s was right when he felt upon watching those coal and salt miners go bloody in West Virginia that there was no hope for Negroes "in the entire world."

So, no matter its shortcomings, *The Souls of Black Folk* announced the arrival of the contemplative Negro American. In essence, DuBois, for all of the brilliant black men who had come before him, was essentially an intellectual, not a man of the cloth and not one whose sense of what was to be in the world would result from divine decisions taking place beyond the province of human beings. His education, especially the deep soaking in German thought while studying in Goethe's fatherland, intensified his tendency to stormy contemplation and instilled that German involvement with the romantic ideas about the *folk* that had come into being during the eighteenth century when German nationalism rose up in resentment toward the condescending way the Germans were treated by the French, who had been brought in as cultural missionaries by Frederick the Great. As I implied earlier, it seems to me that those German thoughts, even wrapped in a Pan-African flag, continued to dog DuBois throughout his life, bringing him back and back to race again and again, fogging up his observations with a strange kind of engagement with what might call the *destiny of the blood* or, in street terms, the destiny of the *bloods* (old slang for Negroes). So what we have going on in the mind of this great and, finally, tragic man, is a roller coaster of rhetoric, thought and feeling, a trip that includes both the highs of lyricism and the swift descents into the valleys of myth projected through a sad desire to make more of the Africa from which Negroes came than even those such as his pan-Africanists forerunners like Alexander Crummell, Henry Highland Garnett, James Holly, Henry McNeal Turner, and Martin Delany, had been able to when actually faced with the people themselves. We get a straight assessment of these men in David Levering Lewis's superbly researched and well-written, even witty, DuBois biography, a book that brings forth the man's world with all the nuance and exactitude of an epic novel. (When faced with the contextual degree of detail and human feeling that Lewis is able to give these remarkably varied people—who might be no more than cold sets of statistics and quotes—another charge can be made against the general failure of Negro literature as well as that of America at large. This charge can easily be defended when any characters and contexts in any American novels are compared to the monumnetally epic size of the world through which DuBois passed, engaged himself in, was influenced by and that he influenced in contradictory ways.) Lewis writes of the nineteenth-century pan-African gang that they "all were Victorian imperialists—'Afro-

Saxons'—to whom native Africans were religiously and socially 'primitive' and always sexually scandalous."

These were men who believed in colonizing Africa for its own good, based on what they knew of the icy and unsentimental history of the human species, not innate inferiority. Crummell knew that any people could be brought up from the mud through the fire of imposed education. He was aware of the fact that this was the kind of training, over centuries, that had transformed the illiterate people of the British Isles from the rock-throwing savages in animal skins with blue-painted faces whom Julius Caesar encountered when Rome was colonizing everything that it could and bringing all of its learning along for the trip. Though DuBois would not back such an idea as colonizing for the good of the colonized, he took from it and argues within *The Souls of Black Folk* for a democratic vision in which potential is unpredictable and, like Booker Washington's dictum, neither limited nor guaranteed by color. Along the way, he opens up many of the areas that will be explored by later Afro-American writers. In the truly melodramatic "The Coming of John," DuBois turns away from the essay and provides a piece of fiction intended to take the reader into the inner world of the Negro intellectual. The character who appears is "the refined Afro-American" who, as literary scholar Robert Bone pointed out in *The Negro Novel in America,* became a basic type in black fiction. This character is an aesthetic extension of what Frederick Douglass related in a very famous passage from his first memoir, *The Narrative of the Life of Frederick Douglass, an American Slave, Written by Himself,* a passage that also seems to explain what became the Negro folk expression: "If you want to get a Negro to do something, tell him he better NOT do it." One can easily see how slavemaster Hugh Auld's admonishing his wife, Sophia, for educating Douglass foreshadows the sensibility of "The Coming of John":

> it is unlawful as well as unsafe to teach a slave to read. . . .
> If you give a nigger an inch, he will take an ell. A nigger

should know nothing but to obey his master—to do as he is told. Learning would spoil the best nigger in the world . . . it would forever unfit him to be a slave. He would at once become unmanageable and of no value to his master. As to himself, it could do him no good, but a great deal of harm. It would make him discontented and unhappy.

In his expression of discontent as opposed to the mask of humility Washington wore to protect himself and his enterprise, DuBois reveals a post-Reconstruction sensibility as at home moving from the lowlands to the places where the high-minded congregate and cogitate. This is the DuBois who resonates through the world of Jean Toomer and whose engagement with folk materials surely anticipates, though in different ways, the work of Langston Hughes and Zora Neale Hurston, especially her interpretations of Negro American art styles. Even a writer at such great odds with DuBois as Albert Murray, whose narcissistic sense of his own importance is no less large, can be seen rewriting *The Souls of Black Folk* in his *South to a Very Old Place,* where we get a very different sense of Negro American identity and an unprecedented portrait of Southern black college life as Murray, in quite brilliant and virtuosic prose, recalls his Depression-era days at Tuskegee, Booker T. Washington's creation and command post. Murray describes a favorite teacher's high-minded vision of the inner life and writes: "Morteza Drexel Sprague expected you to proceed in terms of the highest standards of formal scholarship, among other things, not because he wanted you to become a carbon copy of any white man who ever lived, not excepting Shakespeare and even Leonardo da Vinci. But because to him you were the very special vehicle through which contemporary man, and not just contemporary black man even, could inherit the experience and insights of all recorded or decipherable time." In "On the Wings of Atalanta," DuBois had already aimed for the distant star when he wrote, "the function of the university is not simply to teach breadwinning, or to furnish teachers for the public schools, or to be a centre of polite society; it is, above all, to be the organ of that fine adjustment between real life and the growing knowledge of life, an adjustment which forms the secret of civilization." He was, within that volume, already arguing for the contemplative life and raising his voice in opposition to the utilitarian sense of education represented by Booker Washington, of whom DuBois wrote earlier in the chapter "Of Mr. Booker T. Washington and Others": " . . . so thoroughly did he learn the speech and thought of triumphant commercialism, and the ideals of material prosperity, that the picture of a lone black book poring over a French grammar amid the weeds and dirt of a neglected home soon seemed to him the acme of absurdities. One wonders what Socrates and St. Francis of Assisi would say to this." By referring to the Greek philosopher willing to die for his beliefs and the saint of the Catholic church, Du Bois made it clear that he considered himself one who "could inherit the experience and insights of all recorded or decipherable time." This is even true of Ralph Ellison, of whose work the exceptional scholar Robert O'Meally has written in *The Craft of Ralph Ellison,* "In Ellison's fiction, folklore, stylized and transformed by modernist techniques, gives special resonance and power to his language as it frees his characters to fly toward the moon, dive unmarked into the briar patch, or become invisible and sail through the air unseen. Here the vernacular and the symbolist traditions in American literature converge." And who, if not DuBois, foreshadowed with his speaking "from behind the Veil" Ellison's metaphor of invisibility? Who, if not DuBois, provided the point of departure for the conclusion arrived at by Ellison's narrator, which is that, as the older writer says in *The Souls of Black Folk,* "He began to have a dim feeling that, to attain his place in the world, he must be himself, and not another"? This is the same thing that Richard Wright concludes in the full *American Hunger,* itself a source for *Invisible Man!* Who, if not DuBois, by writing elsewhere in that epic contemplation of black souls, "Through history, the powers of single black men flash here and there like falling stars, and die sometimes before the world has rightly gauged their brightness," provided Ellison with a source for his metaphor when the novelist's narrator sees some zoot suit-wearing Negroes on a subway train and wonders if they are culturally parallel to the light from stars long dead?

There are other things as well. As Playthell Benjamin points out in his essay, and as I have said elsewhere ("Who Are We? Where Did We Come From? Where Are We Going?" in the 1995 *The All-American Skin Game),* DuBois was way off base when he spoke of black laborers and craftsmen being insecure about the quality of their work, something Washington had argued for in the supposed "Atlantic Compromise" speech of 1895, responding to the free ride hordes of European immigrants were getting at the expense of already highly qualified black Americans. Beyond that, one wonders how Mr. Benjamin can become so enraged by Gerald Early's discomfort with unrefined Negro behavior when there is little in DuBois that gives one the impression that he was ever one given to celebrating the rude beauty of the Negro at the bottom unless that Negro was on his knees praying or seated and singing in church, or providing what could be reduced to statistical proof of how lowly the life could be due to racism? DuBois could not imagine anything of value coming from "down there," which is why David Levering Lewis criticizes him for the ideas in "Of the Sons of Master and Man" in *The Souls of Black Folk* that support a kind of paternalism quite different from the sort of preparation that Washington promoted, based on skills, ownership of land, and the amassing of finances. In essence, DuBois was a square who never really got it when it came to some things about black Americans. Though he rightly celebrated Negro religious music, this New Englander who learned to appreciate the Negro after going South and studying in Nashville at Fisk University, never got the point when it came to a new vision of aesthetic achievement such as the one that arrived when Negroes invented ragtime in the 1890s. The very same quality in *The Souls of Black Folk* for which so many black people praised DuBois, is at the core of ragtime, an instrumental recognition of Negro refinement and sophistication in rhythm and tune. Ragtime is the theme music of the New Negro and gave America its first fully urban music, its praise song of the city, of freedom and high style of the sort seen in the cakewalk, which swept this nation and Europe. As a lover of German opera, DuBois could probably hear the American version of Germanic intensity available in Negro religious music, both its melancholy and transcendent lyricism as well as its sheer power, something that whites recognized at the Christian gatherings when Negroes, after the whites had gone to bed, sang throughout the night during the Great Awakening of the eighteenth century. What Buddy Bolden was doing way down yonder in New Orleans musically paralleled the overarching achievement of *The Souls of Black Folk,* and might well be seen to exceed it, given that, as the first man of jazz, Bolden pulled open the door to a new sense of allusion, reconfiguration, transformation, and improvisation that, as many have by now pointed out, brought the democratic proposition into music, given that the art is about the balance between the individual and the mass, with improvisation, invention on the moment and within the context of a mobile environment, the action that brings all of it together. Here I'm talking about an aesthetic achievement, not the sweep of issues that DuBois put on the intellectual and cultural menu.

It is nearly impossible to imagine DuBois getting much out of an encounter with con man, pool shark, sharp shooter, hustler, and jazz composer Jelly Roll Morton (who wore diamonds in his teeth and sometimes carried a concealed battery attachment that provided the power for a pair of lights attached to his shoes, which shook up night life gatherings when he turned them on). Having provided background music for the erotic wrestling matches of New Orleans whorehouses, and having seen many come and many go, Morton would probably have seen the New England scholar as no more than a snooty sucker. Given that David Levering Lewis reports that DuBois was not happy at the end of World War I when he found in France that James Reese Europe and his army musicians had introduced Paris to jazz, and since he never makes mention of jazz, we can assume that he would probably have dismissed Louis Armstrong as an eye-rolling minstrel with a trumpet and a most unpleasing voice that failed to meet any standards of skill above the gutter. He never got it.

DuBois even seemed to have missed his most complete musical counterpart when it come to documenting the souls of black folk, Duke Ellington. We can be sure that the greatest of all jazz musicians was well aware of DuBois, having performed at benefit fundraisers for the NAACP since the late twenties. Including the romantic ideas about Africa, Ellington was involved in orchestrating and harmonzing "Negro feeling in rhythm and tune," which is how he defined jazz. Forty years later at Carnegie Hall, Ellington was surely after just what DuBois was seeking to do in 1903. Through the medium of music, he was present-ing the epic range of Negro America as he understood it. Yet it might not have done DuBois any good had he been there and heard Ellington's 40-minute work, "Black, Brown, and Beige," which was his "tone par-allel to the American Negro," his own aesthetic tale of the Negro, from slavery through freedom, from the rural to the urban, from the cabin in the woods to the Sugar Hill Penthouse. DuBois most probably would not have gotten it.

But he wasn't your classical square since DuBois was something of a dancer in his youth and, given his looks, his commanding presence, his eloquence, fire, and learning, was also a ladies' man. Both David Levering Lewis and Brent Edwards have taken him down in terms of contemporary feminist standards that have nothing to do with human interaction. What exactly did such writers expect sophisticated Negro women to do other than feel attracted to a man like DuBois who seemed to wear the radiance of the race—its pride, its wonder, and its possibility—like a crown? Were they no more than dupes, victims of a supposed "womanizer"? I think not. DuBois observed that his wife did not like sex but we have no doubt that he himself enjoyed the intimate company of women. As one woman told me in response to the boudoir details of the DuBois story, "A fine black intellectual like him at the turn of the twentieth century—the *premiere* black intellectual, and with a big dick, too? Give me a break, honey. He *had* to have women all over him." It is also highly possible, as yet another woman said to me, that "DuBois was probably influenced in his thinking by those women. These were *very* sophisticated women. They read books. They thought *thoughts*. He *did* advance on the woman question over the years, didn't he? And that could be the result of those secret meetings before *and* after they went to bed. You can't rule out all of that talking and listening and we know there was *plenty* of that, because that's what intellectuals love to do, which is talk and listen, especially when there is someone interesting to talk *with* and listen *to*." That makes Himalayan sense, particularly since romance, even the illicit kind, cannot sustain itself on purely sensual terms. How the other person talks and what that person has to say, has lived, knows, fantasizes about, makes the object of wit and humor, are all part of romance, and I am sure that both DuBois and his peccadillo partners enjoyed those aspects over time as much as they did the exchanges of touch, flesh, and rhythm. After all, as Negro legend has it, even the great Booker T. was, as they are so crudely described today, "a poonsman." In the folklore of black America one often heard that the Great Accommodator—known to his friends as "Big Red"—could so well get boudoir accomodations ready, turning back the covers, that he died from a caning received after being caught in bed with the wife of a white patron. As one older wag and phi beta kappa keyed Negro said to me when I was in my late teens, twirling the key on his watch chain and smiling, "Old Booker T. did not just say "uplift the race," he also said, 'Lift up them goddam white thighs, *baby*.'" All I can say of such matters in the private lives of the high holy men of Afro-American history is what I wrote elsewhere and consider watchwords, "You got to watch that Negro. He'll upset you."

IV: THE LEGACY OF DuBOIS

The Civil Rights Movement began to lose its center as Black Power rose and the lesser side of DuBois's thinking, coupled with the hostility that he felt toward whites and that periodically overcame him, was given redefinition. The wack vision of address that caused him to leave the NAACP in the middle 1930s when he proposed that Negroes cease trying to integrate into American society and segregate themselves in order to build up their own resources was at the core of the thinking that led to whites being thrown out of SNCC and a politics of racial animus replacing one that called for America living up to its own credos. In order to grasp how strange and out of touch DuBois was at the time, one only has to consider the fact that the legal genius Charles Hamilton Houston, the architect of the strategy that eventually snapped the back of Jim Crow law in the Supreme Court was then making a move within the NAACP Legal Defense Fund. As Roy Wilkins reports in *Standing Fast,* "There was Dr. DuBois, the most uncompromising intellectual leader of the race, retreating to the philosophy of Booker T. Washington, the very philosophy Dr. DuBois and the N.A.A.C.P. had fought so hard in the early days of the association." Wilkins cites the response of William H. Hastie, "a young lawyer who later joined the N.A.A.C.P. legal team and ultimately became a federal judge." Hastie, whom Wilkins describes as "the angriest critic" of the many who wrote letters to the organization, wrote:

> For fifty years, prejudiced white men and abject, boot-licking, gut-lacking, knee-bending, favor-seeking Negroes have been insulting our intelligence with a tale that goes like this: "Segregation is not an evil. Negroes are better off by themselves. They can get

equal treatment and be happy, too, if they live and move and have their being off by themselves, except, of course, as they are needed by the white community to do the heavy and dirty work."

Hastie went on to write:

> In theory there can be segregation without discrimina-tion, segregation without unequal treatment. Buy any Negro who uses this theoretical possibility as a justifica-tion for segregation is either dumb, mentally dishonest, or else he has, like Esau, chosen a mess of potage.

As Wilkins continued, "Hastie's words were even harsher than the criticism Dr. DuBois had leveled at Booker T. Washington thirty years earlier—but I found it hard to disagree with him."

The Black Power Movement and the attendant Black Arts Movement chose the potage of ethnic narcissism, segregation and racial animus, Pan African romance, and, eventually, an even more romantic idea of color-coded Marxist-Leninism thinking pigged up in a poke called Third World Revolution. It all replicated DuBois's fall from rea-son and grace, a fall that was not always clear because DuBois was too complex a man to pin down when his reports from Germany during the thirties made it so obvious that the treatment of Jews was even worse than that of Negroes in America. DuBois, unlike Paul Robeson, was not something of a dupe when it came to Russia; he knew what was going on and, as David Levering Lewis says, "Oh, DuBois knew what had happened; he was not shocked like Robeson, who believed in the Soviet side of the story. In the case of DuBois, I would say that he prob-ably believed that the 20 million murdered by Stalin only squared the millions who had died under racist and capitalist exploitation and colo-nialism the world over." Yet if we look at things in context, it may well have initially been much harder for either man to accept as gospel American definitions of Russians and their politics, given the unrelenting level of xenophobic slander Negro Americans suffered through. That is: if they have lied so viciously about us, and we are right here in front of them, why should we accept their version of people 10,000 miles away? Still, I would especially put the dunce cap of dupe on Robeson, of whom we get an eyewitness portrait from the Czech novelist and jazz musician Josef Skvorecky in his preface to *The Bass Saxophone,* which details "the censors of a new dictatorship," the Russian Communists following World War II:

> In place of Kenton, they pushed Paul Robeson at us, and how we hated that black apostle who sang, of his own free will, at open-air concerts in Prague at a time when they were raising the Socialist leader Milada Horakova to the gallows, the only woman ever to be executed for political reasons in Czechoslovakia by Czechs, and at a time when great Czech poets (some ten years later to be "rehabilitated" without exception) were pining away in jails. Well, maybe it was wrong to hold it against Paul Robeson. No doubt he was acting in good faith, convinced that he was fighting for a good cause. But they kept holding him up to us as an exemplary "progressive jazzman," and we hated him.

When we come to DuBois, we are looking at something far more monstrous, it seems to me, but something that he shares with all of those who would look the other way and hold their noses when either confronted with the murders of totalitarian or the great stench of the corpses rotting in mass graves dug in Russia, Asia, and Africa. In an especially profound summing up of the bear suits intellectuals have been willing to wear, Tony Judt wrote in the November 4, 2002 issue of *The New Republic:*

Western intellectual enthusiasm for Communism peaked not in the time of "goulash communism" or "socialism with a human face," but rather at the moments of the regime's worst cruelties: 1935-1939 and 1944-1956. Writers and professors and teachers and trade unionists admired and loved Stalin not in spite of his faults, but because of them. It was when he was murdering people on an industrial scale, when the show trials were displaying Communism at its most theatrically macabre, that men and women beyond Stalin's grasp were most seduced by the man and his cult. Likewise the cult of Mao in the West reached its zenith . . . just as— and just because—Mao was torturing writers, artists, and teachers.

For men and women in search of a Cause, Judt believes, there is a seductive character to a Great Social Experiment doing evil in the name of ultimate good.

One begins to question both his motives and his sanity when one reads DuBois's absurd celebration of Stalin in 1953:

Joseph Stalin was a great man; few other men of the 20th century approach his stature. He was simple, calm, and courageous. He seldom lost his poise; pondered his problems slowly, made his decisions clearly and firmly; never yielded to ostentation nor coyly refrained from holding his rightful place with dignity. He was the son of a serf, but stood calmly before the great without hesitation or nerves. But also—and this was the highest proof of his greatness—he knew the common man, felt his problems, followed his fate.

In that very piece, every aspect of Tony Judt's argument is made clear. DuBois has chosen a Cause and he has proven that "there is something diabolically seductive about great evil performed in the name of ultimate good," which might be why we can observe that he has made an all too separate peace with the "suffering of others" unto to death during Stalin's watch. In those words we can see all of the super left fantasies—the common man who rises to power and knows what he is doing; who is not intimidated by those either higher born than he or who represent older regimes, generations of power supposedly superior through deeper conceptions of life and richer understandings of history; who sustains his ease while remaining "simple, calm, and courageous." That a man as superior as DuBois could make himself a political Oedipus and pluck his eyes out rather than look upon the world with the care that he had brought to his best moments is a signal human truth of our age, providing us with another example of exactly what the Nazis proved, which is the most important thing that we may ever learn about our species, which is that no amount of learning or scholarship or great predecessors guarantees that civilization will forever be chosen over self-righteous tribal xenophobia or the reigns of terror that promise to right an uneven and unfair world.

What DuBois lacked is common to those overcome by the far left and its great, naive ideal, its vision of life in which everything is explained by class and exploitation, reducing all things of importance to the relationship of human life to goods and services, a materialist vision that fails to take into consideration either the tragic components of our lives or the mysterious appetites that drive us as well as the endless compromises that make social existence what it is. There is also the vulnerability that certain kinds of intellectuals have to "men of action." When writing of Jefferson Davis in 1890, DuBois had admonishing reservations about "the strong man" but, like so many of the kind whom Tony Judt identified, he finds that figure acceptable once he mounts a death machine bent on proletarian revolution, out of which will come the worker's paradise, the new man, and the dictatorship of the proletariat as represented by the totalitarian central committees descended from those men such as Robespierre who sat with sanguinary confidence on the Committee for Public Safety.

But DuBois was not just a writer or a teacher or one in support of trade unionism. He was also more than a member of that endless army of hostile academic nerds who do most of their asserting by browbeating students or trying to become the heads of college committees or departments. He was not another of those immasculine men who, like the physical trifle that was Nietzsche, can seem to endow brute force with a kind of magic, the spirit of the masses become the revolutionary bull that will not step lightly in the china shop. DuBois did, however, harbor inside his soul a vast bitterness and a great rage, the combination of which allowed for the fantasies of a world revolution that would make the last first, the lowest the most high, the least respected the revered. When he was able to separate the black struggle from any European context and begin to dream of third world revolution or, better, the liberation of the Negro and the fall of colonialism, DuBois may have been happiest, trusting more the possibility that dark people would rise together than any coalition with white Americans or Europeans. To that end, he had led Pan-African conferences in Europe and had spoken out against colonialism for decades before helping the NAACP maneuver itself into a position that might make it possible to influence the wording of the Charter of the United Nations.

Perhaps the greatest appeal of revolutionary variations on Marxism is the pretense of conflating history and science, of bringing together the story of the species and the objective analysis of the intellectual force that began to rise in the eighteenth century and that so dominates, for good as well as for bad, the nature of our world. One thing, of course, that science sustains is a battle against disease made ever more effective by the clarity of the objective analysis in the laboratory. To the Marxist the sentimentalities of culture are set aside in favor of a supposedly objective analysis that explains the origin of social disease—exploitation for profit—and fills up the pipe with dreams of a classless society in which the ruling class becomes the masses. So far, that has worked nowhere that we know of, though we should be well aware of the aforementioned facts in which the scientific method has flexed itself by removing millions upon millions of germs essential to the social disease of exploitation for profit. I would imagine that when DuBois, after all of his research and all of his traveling, looked hard at the world by which he was surrounded, bit the bullet of that bullshit science and was able to mix it with his antipathy toward whites, who had so often failed not only black people but white people and America and civilization itself. Mammon was their god and they had worshipped it at the expense of everyone on the earth. With the component of racism added, they had driven him nearly mad, primarily, it seems to me, because DuBois was much more sensitive than we might want to think, especially in face of how tough and unrelenting he had been in his fight for Negro rights and his vision of international non-white rebellion. That sensitivity was at the center of his tragedy. It won out over his reason as the ongoing and ruthless unfairness of those in power pushed itself into his consciousness. That is why he was celebrated during the sixties as much for his bitterness as for his greatness. He fit the bill of those who had been worn down by the violent recalcitrance of the South, which remained in rebellion against democracy and hid or supported those who would shoot down men in their driveways, Northern white women driving civil rights workers, and blow up little girls on Sunday mornings in church. They were shell-shocked and so was he.

One can, with some surprise, discover in Mia Bay that even the boundlessly bad poetry of the Black Arts Movement, headed up by LeRoi Jones—a man far more confused and pernicious than *anyone* in DuBois's era—is foreshadowed by the New Englander:

> And conquerors of unarmed men;
> Shameless breeders of bastards,
> Drunk with the greed of gold,

Bating their blood-stained hooks,
With cant for the souls of the simple;
Bearing the white man's burden
Of liquor and lust and lies....
I hate them, Oh!
I hate them, well...

It is obvious in looking back that what should have become no more than the twaddle of a cult that had no national or international significance, sustains itself. In one way, Pan-Africanism begat "identity politics" and, through the influence of Black Power, all of the self-segregation along the lines of color, sex, and sexual preference that keep us pretentiously Balkanized. And, quite surely, there are still many of those who pretend that they are Africans "lost" in America, or that others are "dead monkeys," as they were once described in the Nation of Islam, meaning black people who do not know who they are, having denied their heritage is one of African aristocracy.

As lost subjects go, however, there is something more than impressive to a majestic degree about what American Negroes actually added up to and what they came to mean to the world at large. Through what has been called "the crucible of slavery," arrived something perhaps as extraordinary as anything else in the history of humankind: full validation of the democratic ideal that it does not matter where one comes from, whether by blood or place. That very fact is at odds with all of the heavy breathing about African identity, as if knowing an African language or one's African cousins or adhering to African customs has done anything of special importance for Africans themselves. Africans followed their traditions into supporting the slave trade and were knocked down, one by one, as the Europeans colonized the continent after having the infamous Berlin Conference in 1885, where the map of Africa came as close as cartography ever does to replicating the meat map of a cow on the wall of a butcher shop. No amount of African identity put a stop to any of that. So the idea that set flowing purple tears as black people were told that they would do better in the United States if they "knew who they were" was garbage with a capital "G."

Here is that proof: From one of those tragic ironies that contain both periodic victories and harrowing sorrow, arose the most remarkably influential black people on the face of the earth, an ever greater black, brown, beige, and bone force in the worlds of intellectual engagement, politics, science, medicine, the arts, entertainment, the military, technology, and sports. They were not to be held back forever by the enormous limitations of their African heritage or the previous condition of slavery or the racist definitions, laws, exclusions, and physical threats that lifted a mocking middle finger at American ideals. Within a grotesquely flawed democratic context, their minds were remade so differently from their African forebears that they would remake their nation not for the worse but for the better. In the process, they would make it clear to all but the most stubborn bigots that what one looked like or where one came from meant nothing in the arena of potential. Beyond purifying the ideals of the Enlightenment, that proof of the accuracy of the democratic credo is the greatest ongoing achievement of black Americans.

Was it worth the price? It's too late to say anything reasonable about that—though it is never too late to *be* unreasonable. What great thing in the history of the species has ever really been worth what it costs those who brought if off, who were killed in the process or crippled or blinded or deafened—those whose corpses rise higher than the tallest skyscrapers and whose tales make injustice a very, very weak word?

There is a tragedy fundamental to human life and that tragedy plays itself out differently depending upon exactly where it takes place. That is why the high-mindedness and the unfairness of the conflicted story of the United States has to be looked at very closely and with no fear of comparison to other societies either born during the Industrial Revolution or sometime after the revolutionary totalitarian butchery of the twentieth century. As far as all of that goes, we can compare what black Americans have given the world to all that has come from West Africa itself and from the descendants of those others brought into the Western Hemisphere as slaves and see how those blood-encrusted chips fall.

Clear as the summer sun. That Negro American impact on the world grew even beyond the borders of America in more ways than the cultural influences we have seen since ragtime and the Fisk Jubilee Singers went abroad in the 1890s.

At one point, a fairly contemporary event that popped open the eyes of the world illustrated another aspect of Negro American power in evolution. It was largely the result of Negro American influence that built from and came to include black students organizing divestment conferences on American universities, to black American reporters pushing the story of an undemocratic regime from the back of their papers to the front, black Americans raising millions of dollars for legal defense in that country, black American mayors refusing do business with companies financially involved with the regime, and the coalition between the Congressional Black Caucus and the Republicans led by John Danforth that passed the sanctions against South Africa over Ronald Reagan's veto at the height of his popularity. Due as much to those actions as anything else, including local demonstrations and military defeats in Angola, the apartheid South African regime had to back down and release Nelson Mandela from prison.

We all saw that happen but, black American sentimentality about Africa—sort of a seeking out of a pan-African paternalism—meant that when Mandela himself arrived in America and traveled the length of the country, he was greeted as though he was a savior of those who had been so instrumental in saving *him* from the death of a martyr behind prison bars! As the old saying goes, "They didn't know their own strength." They had not only made the DuBoisian choice to impose an African identity upon themselves, they had also sought out both a paradise lost and a patriarch whom they could worship at the expense of perceiving their own actual relationship to him. It takes quite an imagination to bring something of that sort off and continue the rhetoric of the impotence of black Americans "lost" in this nation when the whole enterprise should have been quite instructive about exactly what Negroes need to incrementally put out in order to bring about monumental change. The Nelson Mandela affair should be the be the model for how Negro American efforts should address our present dilemmas in a time when what we most need is the rebuilding of the public school system from sea to shining sea, for those graduating illiterates and near-illiterates are not much better off than those slaves thrust out into the world of freedom after the Civil War, for they are doomed to the lower rungs of society.

Further, the burden of anarchy and murderous crime sustained by street gangs and drugs dealers needs to be lifted through the creation of partnerships between police departments and the community that focus on criminals with and without badges, since the bad cop is liberated to use excessive force when there is alienating hostility between the people and the police, just as the criminal benefits in large measure from that very same hostility. Moreover, to remove the onus of black imprisonment for so many drug-related crimes, our nation needs to stand up as it did when the wages of Prohibition became obvious and legalize drugs, which would destroy the multi-billion dollar business, put the product in the willing hands of our pharmaceutical companies, which would provide the nation with much tax revenue, enough, by the way, to work ever harder at drug use prevention and the creation as well as the maintenance of the highest quality rehabilitation programs. Those who think these things impossible should look at how long the Afro-American struggle in the interest of black South Africans took and begin to realize, as Playthell Benjamin said, "Charity begins at home." It would be wonderful to see that same level of engagment put out in the interest of Negro Americans, since black people are probably the only group in the history of the world who have not fully recognized that one should straighten up conditions where one resides before becoming ardently international. Though one could say that low level of interest in the ongoing problem of slavery in Africa does not seem to spark the same degree of concern, since the white man has been out of the trade for over one hundred and fifty years, putting the facts of culpability in the laps of black Africans and Arabs (whose racism toward black Africans as well as the tribal racism of black Africans toward each other—both of which make the slave trade still possible—were never addressed at the infamous Durban Conference on Racism, which is why the abolitionist organization SOS Slaves Mauritania did not sign the preliminary papers or the final papers). Apparently, it is still as easy to put one's thumbs in one's eyes when confronting internal Third World racism as it was to go blind when confronted with Comrades Stalin, Mao, and Pol Pot. The Oedipus approach to political vision maintains itself.

In conclusion, I would say that the greatness and the tragedy of W.E.B. DuBois is the result of how often his brilliance was counterstated by romantic or poorly reasoned ideas. In fact, had he not been so wary of social events with whites he did not know and had he accepted the invitation to spend an afternoon with Henry James, something astounding might well have appeared in the fiction of James and, therefore, in American and European fiction. Had James been sufficiently taken by DuBois, and it is hard to imagine him *not* being taken, and had the novelist gotten details of his childhood, his college years, and his career and begun to correspond with him, that psychologically oriented writer so fascinated by the ironic quicksand into which so many lives sink, might well have decided to create another kind of character at odds with the nature of the world, a favorite theme. This time the character would be a cultivated Negro from humble beginnings who had gone on to be educated in Europe and in the best American universities, found himself in education and politics, waging war against those mediocre and sub-mediocre people who were considered better than this superior man solely due to the accident of color. No American character in the history of our fiction has come close to being as complex as DuBois: so given to swinging from one end of the spectrum to the other; so widely experienced; so graceful and so rageful; so insightful and so square (he even married his daughter off to Countee Cullen, one of the sweetest homosexuals in the history of homosexual sweetness); so given to ethnic epiphany (hearing the Negro music at Fisk, hearing Alexander Crummell speak); so much of a high-minded, prudish, midnight creeping sweetback; so ready to organize conferences, edit magazines, lecture around the country; so willing to burn the midnight oil in the library and to do house-to-house sociological research among the lowly or travel to Europe and report back on what was happening during World War I and, later, just before World War II. Since the death of this estimable intellectual sharpshooter and loose cannon, it is only in the dense brilliance of Leon Forrest's flawed masterpiece, *Divine Days,* with its astounding vision of the high-minded, the middle range, and the lows of Afro-American life, do we get anything that we might say is in the neighborhood of paralleling the sweep and complexity of DuBois's sensibility. William Edward Burghardt DuBois was surely a man of epic proportions and more of a tragic figure than he is recognized as, for he encompasses all of the best and the worst of Afro-American thinking, which makes him much like a character out of the mythic universe in which the hero embodies both the antidote and the poison, or out of the kind of music-dramas that Richard Wagner wrote. We were both lucky and damned to have had him rise up in this land and strike a mighty kitchen match across the grill of the American night then use that match to set afire a veil that has yet to be fully burned off, for what he wrote in *The Souls of Black Folk* is as true about the tragic condition of the species now as it was then:

> And herein lies the tragedy of the age: not that men are poor,—all men know something of poverty; not that men are wicked,—who is good? not that men are ignorant,— what is Truth? Nay, but that men know so little of men.